The Case for Fanfiction

The Case for Fanfiction

Exploring the Pleasures and Practices of a Maligned Craft

ASHLEY J. BARNER

McFarland & Company, Inc., Publishers
Jefferson, North Carolina

LIBRARY OF CONGRESS CATALOGUING-IN-PUBLICATION DATA

Names: Barner, Ashley J., 1986– author.
Title: The case for fanfiction : exploring the pleasures and practices of a maligned craft / Ashley J. Barner.
Other titles: Case for fan fiction : exploring the pleasures and practices of a maligned craft
Description: Jefferson, N.C. : McFarland & Company, Inc., Publishers, 2017. | Includes bibliographical references and index.
Identifiers: LCCN 2017029607 | ISBN 9781476668772 (softcover : acid free paper) ∞
Subjects: LCSH: Fan fiction—History and criticism. | Fan fiction—Authorship
Classification: LCC PN3377.5.F33 B37 2017 | DDC 809.3—dc23
LC record available at https://lccn.loc.gov/2017029607

BRITISH LIBRARY CATALOGUING DATA ARE AVAILABLE

ISBN (print) 978-1-4766-6877-2
ISBN (ebook) 978-1-4766-3103-5

© 2017 Ashley J. Barner. All rights reserved

No part of this book may be reproduced or transmitted in any form or by any means, electronic or mechanical, including photocopying or recording, or by any information storage and retrieval system, without permission in writing from the publisher.

Front cover image © 2017 iStock

Printed in the United States of America

McFarland & Company, Inc., Publishers
 Box 611, Jefferson, North Carolina 28640
 www.mcfarlandpub.com

To all the great friends, online and IRL,
who have squeed with me over our favorite fandoms

Acknowledgments

I would like to express my sincere gratitude to Dr. Marsha L. Dutton for all the time she spent working directly with me to revise my dissertation—the original version of this book—in preparation for my defense, and for encouraging me to send it to publishers. Without her, this book would never have seen the light of day. I would also like to thank the rest of my dissertation committee—Dr. Thomas Dancer, Dr. Robert Miklitsch, and Dr. Katherine Jellison—for the way they challenged and expanded my thinking.

My sincere thanks also goes to Dr. Matthew Kinservik and Dr. Linda Zionkowski for the way they encouraged me to write about what interested me, and the time they invested in helping me to do so.

Finally, I thank my family and friends for all their encouragement and support, and all the fans whose work has inspired me.

Table of Contents

Acknowledgments	vii
Introduction	1
1. "Nouseled" in Books	7
2. Getting Above Themselves	35
3. Story Sue-icide	58
4. Scope for Discontent	85
5. Please Don't Kill the Author	97
6. Follow the Money	123
7. Damaging the Brand	145
8. Schrödinger's Legolas	161
Conclusions	181
Glossary	185
Chapter Notes	191
Works Cited	193
Index	205

Introduction

On a popular culture website, writer Shana Mlawki makes what she calls an "embarrassing admission" about a personal habit, one that she still engages in. "But only sometimes!" she quickly adds. "Once or twice a year—at most, I swear!—I indulge in what I admit is a very guilty pleasure."

What bad habit could possibly require so much apology? Is she taking illegal drugs? Binge eating? Frequenting strip clubs?

No, the bad habit Mlawki is admitting to is a habit of a very different kind: she reads fanfiction.

Fanfiction is a genre in which fans write new stories about other writers' characters, from Mr. Spock and Elizabeth Bennet to Robin Hood and Odysseus. This sounds innocuous enough: what makes it a guilty pleasure? In fact, how did the enjoyment of any genre, short of enthusiastically affirmative readings of works like *Mein Kampf* or *Lolita*, come to be so tinged with guilt? Why do fanfiction readers like Mlawki feel the need to defend themselves from attack by assuring their audience how rarely they partake of a genre they enjoy?

This book examines why reading fanfiction is considered such a guilty pleasure. Yes, fanfiction is mostly written by amateur writers, without the benefit of professional editors. It might be full of spelling errors and grammatical mistakes, but that's not enough of a reason for writers like journalist Ewan Morrison to observe, "For many the rise of fanfic is 'the end of the world.' Fanfic is seen as the lowest point we've reached in the history of culture—it's crass, sycophantic, celebrity-obsessed, naïve, badly written, derivative, consumerist, unoriginal—anti-original." Where is all this vitriol coming from? The answer is complicated, involving an entire network of cultural assumptions about reading, age, gender, literary quality, intellectual property, originality, and profit, and this book attempts to explain how these elements connect to produce negative reactions to fanfiction. It also examines what the effects of these negative reactions are on fanfiction as a genre.

Chapter 1, "'Nouseled' in Books," offers a description of a practice that I call absorbed reading, in which the reader feels that he or she has entered into the world of the book. Because absorbed reading gives characters a seeming reality, this reading/viewing technique can lead to the creation of fanfiction and even makes fanfiction possible in the first place. Absorbed reading is a very old practice, and while readers often attribute many beneficial effects to it, there is also a long history of criticisms connected with it. For at least five hundred years, critics have feared the effects of absorbed reading on supposedly mentally vulnerable readers such as young people and women. These criticisms are still alive and well today, and not only target the young and female but emotionally invested readers and readers of genres that are considered to be of poor literary quality. Fans and creators of fanfiction frequently fall into all of these categories, so fans' reading and the fanfiction they produce comes under fire for their connection with absorbed reading.

One prominent area where criticisms of absorbed reading collide with fanfiction is in the case of Mary Sues. Chapter 2, "Getting Above Themselves," explains how this complicated fanfiction character type, associated with idealization and self-insertion into the text, actually functions as a metaphor for absorbed reading. Mary Sue characters are inserted into fictional worlds as placeholders for the absorbed readers/writers, allowing them to imaginatively experience the setting, form reciprocal relationships with fictional characters, become heroes, and affect the plot of the story directly. The term "Mary Sue," though it could be applied to characters across many genres, arose from the fan community and is particularly associated with fanfiction. The hatred that fans often pour out on Mary Sue characters derives from the concept of *bovarysme*: the fear that less powerful members of society, such as women and young people, will learn from fiction to view their lives as myth and themselves as fictional heroes. This idea of *bovarysme* is sexist: while the practice is condemned in female characters like Mary Sues, it is traditionally expected from male characters, and may be connected to the lack of important, fully realized female characters in modern and traditional media.

Chapter 3, "Story Sue-icide," demonstrates the effect criticisms of *bovarysme* have on fanfictions. The chapter analyzes two fanfictions with Mary Sue premises that attempt to distance themselves from the *bovaryste* idea of the Mary Sue. "Don't Panic!," a *Lord of the Rings* fanfiction by Boz4pm, immediately sets Mary Sues and their connection with pleasure reading and changes to the canon[1] in opposition to realism. In order to counter the Mary Sue stereotype, the fanfiction puts the female main character through an emotional hell and forbids her from altering the story of *The Lord of the Rings*. In doing so, the fanfiction accidentally negates its own concept of pleasure reading as an escape from reality and calls into question the very changes to the canon that are the basis of fanfiction.

Likewise, the fanfiction miniseries *Lost in Austen* is torn between gently mocking Austen fans, who are the main audience of the series, and celebrating their escapist reading of romance novels. This series sets itself up to discuss both historical and modern ideas of how such escapist reading could ruin women's lives by giving them a false idea of their own importance and raising their standards for men to impossibly high levels. The series attempts to praise such absorbed reading for leading women to pursue true happiness in life, but cannot seem to break free of society's negative stereotypes about women's self-indulgent reading of romances. *Lost in Austen* and "Don't Panic!" sabotage their own projects by their failure to fully reject negative stereotypes of Mary Sues.

As such criticism of Mary Sues within fanfictions imply, the genre of fanfiction itself is constructed as much from critical reading as from absorbed reading. Chapter 4, "Scope for Discontent," establishes that these two reading techniques, so often contrasted, are clearly not mutually exclusive, and gives us a clearer understanding of how both criticism and absorption actually function for fans in their construction of fanfiction. Fanfiction often comes as much from dissatisfaction with the canon as it does from love of the canon. Many fanfictions are written specifically to "fix" perceived flaws in the story cycles in which they participate. They also include greater representation for women, racial minorities, LGBTQ people, etc. This concept of representation—allowing more people to "see themselves" in more diverse casts—is closely linked to the ideas of absorbed reading and *bovarysme*: it allows more diverse audiences to imagine themselves as heroes.

Chapter 5, "Please Don't Kill the Author," looks at other ways fans use their critical reading: to police tastes within fandom itself. Fanfiction is frequently criticized by non-fans, and one way that fans deal with this is to displace such criticisms onto other fans so as to escape them for themselves. This is a common expression of internalized discrimination occurring among members of the same cultural group, and it can lead to fan-on-fan bullying. One example of such bullying appears in the Protectors of the Plot Continuum series. Even though the community of fan writers who participate in this shared metafictional universe condemns *ad hominem* attacks on other fan writers, because of the close association of Mary Sue authors with Sues, PPC stories frequently target the creators of Mary Sues rather than the Mary Sue characters themselves.

Another problem such fan criticism of fanfiction encounters is a lack of objective standards of literary quality. This is demonstrated by the *Lord of the Rings* fanfiction "The Official Fanfiction University of Middle-earth." While this fanfiction ostensibly teaches fan writers to improve their work, it also undermines its own strictures by depicting its "students" as continuously ignoring them. If fanfiction is written primarily for pleasure, and pleasure is idiosyncratic, then there can be no objective basis for criticism. The PPC, however, does find a way out of this bind by basing its criticism on the absorbed reading experience itself. The PPC criticizes fanfictions for creating disruptions to the absorbed reading experience, thus creating a seemingly objective standard of quality for fanfictions.

Chapter 6, "Follow the Money," moves away from the subjects of reading and literary quality to discuss another aspect of fanfiction's reputation as a guilty pleasure: its complicated relationship with copyright law and profit. Fanfiction's reputation for being potentially illicit is a major reason critics consider it a *guilty* pleasure. But modern internet fanfiction is the inheritor of a millennia-old tradition of derivative literature, a tradition formed by the practice of absorbed reading and listening. Only after the advent of modern copyright law in the early eighteenth century did originality come to be considered a hallmark of great literature. Copyright law and regulations based on intellectual property right were instituted to protect authors' profits.

It is no wonder, then, that fanfiction suffers a poor reputation in this system, not only as a derivative genre, but because most fanfictions legally cannot make money for fan writers. Fanfiction's lack of monetary value leads to a perceived lack of *any* value. Unless it is a tie-in or written about a canon that is out of copyright, fanfictions must generally cease to be fanfictions before they can legally be published for profit. Meanwhile, the authors of those fanfictions that can make money often draw a line between their own writings and amateur fans' very similar works, contrasting professional and amateur fanfiction based on professional fanfiction's ability to create profits. Attempts to monetize amateur fanfiction have often failed because fanfiction, as a free offering within a community of fans, offers an alternative to profit-based publication.

In the absence of case law to create precedent, the legality of amateur fanfiction remains a gray area. However, fan writers who write for enjoyment rather than profit are unlikely to be sued by canon authors, both because there are too many of them and because members of fandom constitute any canon's biggest fanbase. As a matter of fact, fanfiction can actually function as free advertising for a canon work. And as fanfiction becomes more widely written and accepted by the culture, professional authors are beginning to better understand the genre and change their minds about fanfiction's legitimacy and legality.

Chapter 7, "Damaging the Brand," looks at a related concern about professional fanfictions: how adaptations may affect the reputation of a canon work, and therefore its profits. The chapter focuses particularly on the BBC's television series *Sherlock*. When another television network, CBS, began working on a similar series updating Sherlock Holmes, the creators of *Sherlock* worried that it might harm their own profits by "damaging the brand." The first two seasons of *Sherlock* itself figure concerns about its own effects on the reputation of the canon. For example, in this series Holmes' downfall comes about not simply because of his nemesis' desire to get him out of the way, but because he has become famous and the public has begun to believe lies about him. Holmes' downfall in *Sherlock* is directly tied to his public reputation, strongly informed by information gleaned from his brother Mycroft. As Mycroft is played by series creator Mark Gatiss, this character can also functions as a symbol for the show itself and what it tells the public about Holmes. Ultimately, while fanfiction may be criticized for its ability to affect the public's concept of a character or canon, it is professional fanfictions and adaptations which, though considered far more legitimate, have the greatest ability to reach the public and affect their opinions.

Finally, Chapter 8, "Shrodinger's Legolas," combines the discussions of intellectual property and absorbed reading in an examination of how fanfiction's appropriation of canon characters is figured, both by canon authors and by fanfictions themselves. Professional authors often speak of fans' appropriation of their characters as the theft of an object or the kidnapping of a child. However, some fanfictions offer alternative images of fan appropriation, based on fans' absorbed reading. Angela Vaughan's

"Salt in the Wound" suggests that fanfictions can be more true to the characters than the originating canon is, and that given the chance, some characters might prefer the treatment they receive at the hands of fan writers. In Theresa Green's "Owner's Manuals," characters are mass-produced androids that can be legally manipulated by fan owners. Carrie Rivard, in the epilogue of "Mary-Sue Mockfest," depicts canon characters as actors who appear voluntarily in fans' fictions. Finally, fandom uses terms like "bookverse" and "movieverse" that remind us that even different parts of the canon can contradict one another. Similarly, "head-canon" implies that every absorbed reader will have a slightly different mental image of the characters and events in the text. As soon as a story is read by more than one person it becomes manifold. In the same way, multiple versions of events and characters can exist simultaneously in fanfictions, based on but not negating the canon. These alternative views of fanfiction and its acts of appropriation are far more positive than the views our culture has often expressed about the genre. I hope that this chapter will give us all a new way to think about the project of fanfiction and its interactions with canon.

This book reveals the subtle and subtly disturbing ways our culture talks about fanfiction and other embattled genres. The way our culture discusses such literature has become so natural for us that we do not realize all the assumptions we accept when we make fun of teenage fans of *Twilight* or mutter that this book or that television show is just a guilty pleasure. When we understand these assumptions about fanfiction and other genres we can consider them clearly—and combat them directly rather than repeating them. We can thereby combat the shaming of fans, both external and internalized, and the misogyny, classism, and other unjust assumptions that informs it.

Fanfiction is not the "lowest point in the history of culture," but rather part of an ancient tradition of renewing and rethinking narratives: a fascinating, exuberant, enjoyable, shareable genre through which fans can both communally celebrate and question the stories that constitute our culture.

1

"Nouseled" in Books

Much of the negative reputation of fanfiction, the reputation that makes fans call their reading a guilty pleasure and makes critics call it the end of the world, actually comes from how our culture conceptualizes reading, especially the reading habits of women and young people. Part of the degrading of fanfiction is related to our culture's reactions to a practice I call *absorbed reading*. Fanfiction has a very close relationship with this reading practice, which for centuries has been unjustly characterized in our culture as inferior or even psychologically dangerous. This chapter explicates fanfiction's connection with absorbed reading and our culture's long history of criticizing the absorbed reading of women and young people.

Absorbed Reading Defined

Absorbed reading does not just mean that readers are so absorbed by the text that they are deaf to all that is happening around them—though this can be a side effect of such reading. It is more than that: absorbed readers feel like they have been absorbed *into* the text. These readers mentally construct a picture of the characters and settings they are reading about, using their imaginations to watch and listen to the narrated action, recreating the characters' sensations and emotions in themselves—as if they were watching a film or even taking part in a play. Absorbed readers find themselves inside the world of the text, transported to foreign lands and foreign eras and embodied in many different fictional characters. Absorbed readers are, in a sense, entering into the book.

To many of those who read fiction for pleasure, this practice may seem the natural and obvious way to read. It is so natural and obvious that fantasies about reading are often based on it. One example is Jasper Fforde's *Thursday Next* series, in which some characters can read so absorbedly that they can actually physically enter the story and interact with those inside it. Likewise, the *Inkheart* books by Cornelia Funke and the film adaptation of the same name follow a family who can read out loud so feelingly that the characters emerge from the book into the real world. Absorbed reading is very familiar to pleasure readers, and may seem to be the most obvious way to read.

However, there are many other approaches to reading fiction. Literary academics, for instance, are often trained to perform a kind of critical reading that is in some ways almost the antithesis of absorbed reading. In "Reading Like a Woman," scholar Anne G. Berggren describes her habits of absorbed reading and then states, "When I entered a doctoral program in English and education at age fifty-two, I noticed immediately that my lifelong reading practices—personal, accepting, emotional, addictive—contrasted sharply with the critical, cognitive approaches to novels that my more recently trained fellow students employed.... Apparently, instead of reading like a scholar, I was reading like a woman" (167). Berggren sees the academy as rejecting absorbed reading in terms of gender: you should read like a scholar (and, by implication, a man), not like a woman (and, by implication, an uneducated person). For many years, almost all scholars and highly educated people were men. Higher thought was masculine, while the uneducated and women were believed to approach texts more through feeling than critical thought. What is seen as masculine, critical, scholarly reading was constructed as a rejection of supposedly feminine, uncritical, uneducated, and highly emotional reading. Critical reading—scholarly reading—is frequently gendered as masculine, and involves a metaphorical emotional distance between the reader and the text.

Critical methods of reading, Berggren observes, "involve setting oneself apart from the reading, regarding the novel as 'text,' and analyzing it from the outside rather than living in it as a participant" (171). What is called "resistant reading," for instance, would be a form of critical rather than absorbed reading, in which one interrogates the text, testing all its assertions and regarding its conclusions with some suspicion. Reading techniques such as close reading that focus on structure and language—the surface of the text rather than the emotional experience of it—would also tend to be critical rather than absorbed. Critical reading could be described as thinking (and to a lesser extent, feeling) *about* the text—not thinking and feeling *with* the text, as in absorbed reading. If absorbed reading is reading from inside the book, then critical reading is reading from a distance.

Another scholar, Janice Radway, agrees that as a scholar she stopped practicing absorbed reading. In *A Feeling for Books*, Radway tries to reconcile the pleasure she felt at the new, critical reading practices she was taught in graduate school with the sense of loss she experienced when she realized she had stopped reading absorbedly. She observes, "The standard practice in English education [seems] to dictate disapproval of this sort of readerly absorption in supposedly bad books.... Clearly, I had been asked by that professional training to identify against myself, my family, and my past in order to construct myself as an intellectual" (121). Radway sees the rejection of absorbed reading, not in terms of gender, but in terms of class and taste hierarchies: you should read like a scholar, a person of high-class taste, not like a "middle-brow" reader with middle-class tastes. But both she and Berggren observe that absorbed reading is considered inferior to the critical reading they were asked to do as scholars.

A Gateway to Fanfiction

Fanfiction comes directly from the absorbed way that fans read or view the canon—the work on which the fanfiction is based. When absorbed readers read a book or watch a film, they feel themselves such a part of the fictional world that the characters take on a certain reality and become almost as real to them as actual people. In fact, fans may feel that they know the fictional characters better than they know the real people in their lives. These absorbed readers use their imaginations to bring fictional people to life.

Absorbed reading seems to give the characters an existence of their own, independent from the books and movies in which they appear. For instance, Berggren writes, "It becomes clear to me that while others in [my graduate class] are deconstructing the novel as artifact, I'm believing in it as historical and personal truth. To me, [the fictional heroine] is as real as a current neighbor or a friend from my past" (167). Fan scholar Henry Jenkins has also observed this form of reading in fans: "Fans seemingly blur the boundaries between fact and fiction, speaking of characters as if they had an existence apart from their textual manifestations, entering into the realm of the fiction as if it were a tangible place they can inhabit and explore" (*Textual Poachers* 18). It is this way of thinking of the character as having an existence separate from and larger than the narrative that makes fanfiction possible. Readers who feel this way about characters in narratives can imagine a past or future for those characters, or even an alternative version of the events in the canon plot.

Once fictional people seem to have this real, individual, and larger existence, they are available to make stories out of. In *The Democratic Genre*, Sheenagh Pugh demonstrates how fans take canon characters and create new tales for them. She describes playing Legos with her children, using the Robin Hood figures to act out Robin Hood stories they had read or watched. Then they began to invent new episodes: Pugh writes,

> Sometimes we explored aspects the canonical stories didn't touch on.... Now and then, we departed from the canon altogether to produce a "what if." What we were doing, in essence, was writing fan fiction.... We had a canon of stories invented by others, but we wanted more, sometimes because the existing stories did not satisfy us in some way, sometimes because there are simply never enough stories and we did not want them to come to an end [9].

Absorbed reading or viewing of Robin Hood stories brought the characters to life in the imaginations of Pugh and her children, so they in turn made more stories, more adventures, for those imaginary people to experience. Absorbed reading is therefore the source of fanfiction: it lends a reality to fictional characters and makes them available for new writers to play with.

Fanfiction's close relationship to absorbed reading has increased its likelihood of being seen as an inferior and even psychologically dangerous genre. Western culture has often been wary of absorbed reading and its effects on readers, particularly young, female readers: there is an underlying fear that such absorbed readers can't tell the difference between fiction and reality and will therefore allow the two to bleed into one another in dangerous ways. Sometimes this fear is couched in terms of concern for the reader; sometimes it is couched in mockery. Genres that are associated with absorbed reading (or absorbed viewing, as in television and film) come in for their share of this disgust and mockery: "escapist" science fiction, Harlequin romance novels, "pulp fiction," popular film and television, soap operas, etc. These genres invite absorbed reading/viewing, so some critics may warn parents to limit their children's exposure to them or make fun of people who are too obviously enjoying these "guilty pleasures." Because fanfiction is a product of absorbed reading, the stereotypes associated with this reading practice are often the stereotypes of fans and the fiction they produce and consume.

Praise for Absorbed Reading

While we will discuss many negative cultural assumptions about absorbed reading, its reputation isn't entirely bad, partly because so many people confuse absorbed reading with any reading of fiction. Because absorbed reading seems to many people the natural and obvious way to read, books and reading are often praised for effects that are actually specifically the results of absorbed reading. Former United Kingdom Children's Laureate Julia Donaldson describes absorbed reading in a poem that celebrates reading:

> I opened a book and in I strode.
> Now nobody can find me.
> I've left my chair, my house, my road,
> My town and my world behind me.
>
> I'm wearing the cloak, I've slipped on the ring,
> I've swallowed the magic potion.
> I've fought with a dragon, dined with a king
> And dived in a bottomless ocean.
>
> I opened a book and made some friends.
> I shared their tears and laughter
> And followed their road with its bumps and bends
> To the happily ever after.
>
> I finished my book and out I came.
> The cloak can no longer hide me.
> My chair and my house are just the same,
> But I have a book inside me.

This poem describes the experience of absorbed reading and the aspects of it that are often praised. In the first stanza, Donaldson describes how the absorbed reading of books provides readers with an escape from their everyday existence. Readers often describe absorbed reading in terms of escaping into the story or feeling transported into the text. The same educational benefits that people often attribute to physical travel are sometimes attributed to the imaginative travel experienced through absorbed reading. *BookBub* ran an article by writer Ashley Hamilton called "17 Secrets Only Book Lovers Are in On," which included quotations like "Reading is a discount ticket to everywhere" from Mary Schmich. Additionally, those who praise absorbed reading often attribute to this imaginative escape an inspirational benefit: Hamilton adds, "Reading is dreaming with eyes open." Leaving the mundane world behind and entering the world of the book is sometimes referred to as escapism. Supporters of absorbed reading may praise the pleasures of this escapism: Hamilton's article includes the quotation "A book a day keeps reality away."

The second stanza of Donaldson's poem emphasizes how absorbed readers enter the action of the book as well, feeling as if they are protagonist, enacting his or her adventures: "I'm wearing the cloak, I've slipped on the ring, / I've swallowed the magic potion." Because the experiences, feelings, and thoughts of the main character are so closely described, the readers can imagine that they *are* the main character, experiencing that character's adventures. As in the comparison of absorbed reading to travel, readers often consider this participation in the action of books to be educational and inspirational. A popular slogan that has been passed around various social media emphasizes this point: "I am a reader. Not because I have no life.... But because I choose to have many." This statement pushes back against some of the criticisms of the escapism described in the first stanza of Donaldson's poem: the image insists that escapism in books is not a useless, time-wasting activity that carries one away from one's own life, but rather an activity that enhances that life by allowing the reader to experience the lives of other people.

Donaldson's third stanza describes how characters in books can also become surrogate friends and role models to the absorbed reader: "I opened a book and made some friends. / I shared their tears and laughter." In this stanza, Donaldson describes characters, not as vessels for her own imaginative adventures, but as people whom she feels she has come to know and journey alongside. J. K. Rowling, among other commentators, has praised this imaginative experience of fictional characters as real people for the way it provides role models to readers: "The advantage of a fictional hero or heroine is that you can know them better than you can know a living hero, many of whom you would never meet. You can have a very intense relationship with fictional characters because they are in your own head" (qtd. in "Barnes and Noble"). A popular meme among fans on *Tumblr* emphasizes the superiority of fictional friends to real ones: often superimposed over pictures of favorite fictional characters, the meme reads, "You say they're only characters / You say they're not real / But where were you / When I needed to grow? / Where were you / When I needed to believe? / Where were you / When I was dying? / Who saved my life? / Because it wasn't you. / They're more than fiction. They were there for me even if they weren't real. They were there when you weren't. They're more than you think they are" (Behindtheplottwist). The fictional friends produced by absorbed reading provide an ever-present support that real friends cannot.

Finally, Donaldson asserts that absorbed reading absorbs not only the reader into the text, but also the text into the reader. The lessons and experiences of the book stay with the readers because of their strong imaginative involvement: "I have a book inside me." A book can have a strong and long-lasting effect on the absorbed reader. An often-reblogged statement from Suzanne Collins, author of the *Hunger Games* novels, describes this effect:

> You know what's sad about reading books? It's that you fall in love with the characters. They grow on you. And as you read, you start to feel what they feel—all of them—you become them. And when you're done, you're never the same. Sure you're still you, you look the same, talk in the same manner, but something in you has changed. Something in the way you think, the way you choose, sometimes, even the things you say may differ. When you've recovered from that state it's just ... quite sad [qtd. in atomos].

Donaldson and these others readers agree that absorbed reading comes with a number of benefits: imaginative travel, education, escapism, friendship, role models, and personal change. They also seem to assume that most fiction reading is absorbed reading. Here, absorbed reading is clearly a fun and even beneficial and educational activity. This is how many absorbed readers regard their reading habits—but these opinions are far from universal.

Dangerous Reading

While some people praise absorbed reading, others regard it with suspicion. For centuries, critics have expressed fears about absorbed reading's effects. Believing that some readers, like young people and women, are particularly emotionally and mentally vulnerable, these critics have worried that absorbed reading might lead them into delusional thinking. While it seems natural to worry that very young children might believe that fiction depicts life as it is, or even to make sure that possibly naïve adolescent readers be able to distinguish unrealistic elements in stories from realistic ones, the focus on adolescent or adult women readers and not adolescent or adult male readers is clearly sexist.

In her overview of criticisms of the practice that I am calling absorbed reading, scholar Anne G. Berggren calls it "reading like a woman" because she has noticed that this absorbed reading is more often attributed to women than to men. Berggren notes that criticisms of women's absorbed reading as a supposedly inferior and even dangerous practice date from at least the sixteenth century, "by which time," she explains, "women readers were sufficiently numerous to influence the writing and publishing of books" (168). She quotes *The Woman Reader: 1837–1914*, in which scholar Kate Flint gives numerous examples of the stereotypes of women's reading from the sixteenth century to the twentieth, stereotypes that clearly apply to the practice of absorbed, rather than critical, reading. Flint explains why women were a particular focus of such fears about the effects of reading: "It was often put forward that [the female reader], as woman, was peculiarly susceptible to emotionally provocative material" (22). Flint quotes an unnamed critic who stated in "Moral and Political Tendency of Modern Novels" in 1842 that "the great bulk of novel readers are females; and to them such impressions (as are conveyed through fiction) are peculiarly mischievous: for … they are naturally more sensitive, more impressable, than the other sex" (Flint 12). Women were believed to be more emotional than men, and therefore more easily influenced by the emotions they experienced through absorbed reading.

English critics, believing in women's emotional susceptibility, expressed fears that women readers would become emotionally involved in sexual scenes they read in books, which would both harm their sexual purity and make them wish to recreate such scenes in their own lives. Particularly because of the supposed emotional susceptibility of the female absorbed reader, these critics believed that such sexual scenes would have a corrupting effect. Edward Hake wrote in 1574 that the female fiction reader "is so nouseled in amorous bookes, vaine stories and fonde trifeling fancies, that shee smelleth of naughtinesse even all hir lyfe after" (qtd. in Flint 23). In *Shamela*, Henry Fielding's 1741 response to Samuel Richardson's *Pamela*, Fielding expresses concerns for the mental purity of well-bred young women who absorbedly read some of the provocative scenes of the novel: "I cannot agree that my

Daughter should entertain herself with some of his Pictures; which I do not expect to be contemplated without Emotion, unless by one of my Age and Temper, who can see the Girl lie on her Back, with one Arm round Mrs. *Jewkes* and the other round the Squire, naked in Bed, with his Hand on her Breasts, *&c.* with as much Indifference as I read any other Page in the whole Novel" (Fielding 7). Although Fielding's speaker is indicating, tongue-in-cheek, that any reader would be affected by such sexual scenes, he is also putting specific emphasis on young women as vulnerable readers: because young women were considered particularly susceptible to the emotional effects of absorbed reading, they were thought to be equally susceptible to sexually exciting material, which might incite them to pursue illicit outlets for their desires.

Critics have also worried that female absorbed readers of fiction would model their behavior on that of fictional characters. *Pamela* tells the story of a servant girl who marries her master; in *Shamela* Fielding warns that "the Instruction which it conveys to Servant-Maids, is, I think, very plainly this, To look out for their Masters as sharp as they can. The Consequences of which will be ... that if the Master is not a Fool, they will be debauched by him; and if he is a Fool, they will marry him. Neither of which, I apprehend, my good Friend, we desire should be the Case of our Sons" (6). In this commentary, Fielding indicates that female readers won't be able to tell the difference between behavior that is acceptable or likely in fiction and acceptable or likely in real life.

Such criticisms of women's absorbed reading could encompass all manner of terrible outcomes for these readers: indeed, in *Women's Reading in Britain, 1750-1835*, Jacqueline Pearson writes that in this period, "it seems there was hardly any crime, sin or personal catastrophe that injudicious reading was not held to cause directly or indirectly—from murder, suicide, rape, and violent revolution, through prostitution, adultery and divorce, to pride, vanity, and slapdash housewifery" (7). Criticism of women's absorbed reading was clearly functioning as a tool to keep women "in their place": to control their behavior and compel them to perform the role that society had assigned them.

We can also see this aspect of social control in discussions of young readers in general. Critics do not only fear the absorbed reading of women: they also categorize young readers, who have not yet had much experience of the world, as vulnerable. Fielding warns of the negative effects absorbed reading of sexual scenes may have on young men: "There are many lascivious Images in [*Pamela*], very improper to be laid before the Youth of either Sex." Further, he fears that young men may also try to follow the example of fictional characters; he expresses the hope that his parody "will make young Gentlemen wary how they take the most fatal Step both to themselves and Families, by youthful, hasty and improper Matches" (52). It was not only women that this patriarchal society wished to retain control over, but the young. Adult men, who were most likely to have a voice as critics, feared that exposure to new and revolutionary ideas of acceptable behavior could influence both adult women and minors of both sexes, making them less manageable by their husbands and fathers.

One very clear statement of how novels could upend adult male social control appears in George Colman the Elder's 1760 farce *Polly Honeycombe*. The titular character is a marriageable young woman whose mind has been led astray by novel-reading. While her father wishes her to marry the rich young man Ledger, Polly instead falls in love with a poor attorney's clerk, a fellow novel-reader named Scribble. When her father tries to control Polly's communication and movements by locking her in her room, Polly follows the novelistic example of heroines like Richardson's Pamela and writes to Scribble with pen, ink, and paper she has hidden away in her clothes. In the end, she and Scribble publicly pledge themselves to marry, thus checkmating her father, who exclaims, "You're an impudent slut—You're undone—[!]" In this play, novel-reading is shown to lead directly to sexual impropriety in women.

Though the farce mocks the ineffective father who is unable to control his daughter's sexuality and thus his family's socioeconomic standing, it depicts Polly herself in an even worse light. Praising novel-reading in the epilogue, Polly paints a picture of a world gone mad through women's wild, reading-infected sexuality:

> Tho' Parents tell us [daughters], that our genius lies
> In mending linen and in making pies,
> I set such formal precepts at defiance
> That preach up prudence, neatness, and compliance:
> Leap those old bounds, and boldly set the pattern,
> To be a Wit, Philosopher, and Slattern—
> O! did all Maids, and Wives, my spirit feel,
> We'd make this topsy-turvy world to reel:
> Let us to arms!—Our Fathers, Husbands, dare!
> NOVELS will teach us all the Art of War:
> Our Tongues will serve for Trumpet and for Drum;
> I'll be your Leader—General HONEYCOMBE!

> Too long has human nature gone astray,
> Daughters should govern, Parents should obey;
> Man shou'd submit, the moment that he weds,
> And hearts of oak shou'd yield to wiser heads:
> I see you smile bold Britons!—But 'tis true—
> Beat YOU the French; –But let your Wives beat You.—

The message clearly is that when women read too many novels, they learn the cunning (untempered by patriarchal wisdom) to defy their parents' control over them. And once they have learned this "Art of War," they will then have the freedom and power to overturn all patriarchal hierarchies, so that children will rule their parents and wives their husbands. Women will be able to speak and act as they wish. It is difficult for us, in the twenty-first century, to understand how topsy-turvy and horrifying was the thought of a society in which women were soldiers and the acknowledged heads of households. It was so extreme as to be farcical, and yet the playwright warns amused audience members that their very masculinity and "rightful" control over their wives was in danger when they allowed them to read novels. Novel reading, Coleman implies, leads directly to men being dominated by their wives and daughters.

One of the reasons critics like Fielding and Coleman feared the absorbed reading of women and young people was because they believed that such naïve audiences would absorb unrealistic expectations of their romantic partners or of love from the romances they read, mistaking the fictional incidents and emotions for reality; Flint observes that romances were believed to "instil false expectations, 'insinuate themselves into their unwary readers'" (24). She writes that, particularly after the creation of circulating libraries, when popular fiction was more widely available to women, "one encounters the familiar fear that young women will be corrupted by what they read, and, becoming preoccupied with the importance of romance, will seek perpetually for excitement" (24). If they could not find that excitement within marriage, it was feared, they might look elsewhere.

Besides exciting in themselves potentially harmful feelings and aspirations, critics have worried that absorbed readers would also pick up other behaviors from fiction, following the example of characters from the books they have read. Behavior that is wise or acceptable in fiction is not necessarily wise or acceptable in real life, and some commentators have feared that absorbed female readers will not be able to tell the difference. Critics also worried that absorbed female readers would neglect their proper duties, literally reading pot-boilers while the pots boiled over. They believed this intense reading of fiction to be useless and non-educative, good only for wasting time and taking women away from their household duties.

These critics assert that uncritical absorbed readers, particularly the young and female, might accept, believe, and enact what they read in books, even when it was dangerous to their happiness or morally questionable. As the example of *Polly Honeycombe* indicates, this opinion does not just appear in dry tomes complaining about women or young people and their reading: it also appears in fiction. One well-known example is Jane Austen's *Northanger Abbey*, published in 1817. When Austen originally wrote this book, ca. 1798–99, novels were a genre with little cultural prestige, and were particularly associated with absorbed women readers. On one hand, Austen argues against the harsh judgment of novels and novel-readers: she is, after all, a novelist who must defend her craft. On the other hand, the plot of *Northanger Abbey* seems to accept the negative stereotypes of absorbed female novel-readers as true: Austen cannot seem to completely reject them. This is a common theme when people push back against the negative stereotypes of absorbed reading: the assumptions those stereotypes are based on are so deeply ingrained in our culture that many people have difficulty looking beyond them.

Austen initially defends novels from their detractors:

> I will not adopt that ungenerous and impolitic custom so common with novel-writers, of degrading by their contemptuous censure the very performances, to the number of which they are themselves adding—joining with their greatest enemies in bestowing the harshest epithets on such works, scarcely ever permitting them to be read by their own heroine, who, if she accidentally take up a novel, is sure to turn over its insipid pages with disgust.... Let us not desert one another; we are an injured body.

Novels were attacked because they were believed to be harmful and useless to female readers, who would learn terrible lessons from the romances they read. Austen complains that, in order to make their own work seem superior and more acceptable, many novelists criticized one another's work, and even refused to depict their own heroines reading such works.

However, Austen then subtly goes on to do the same thing as these critics in subsequent chapters. Her heroine, Catherine Morland, has a deep interest in Gothic novels, and her absorbed reading of them leads her to believe that real life works like a novel: she makes a fool of herself in front of Mr. Tilney, the man she loves, by baselessly accusing his father of murdering his late wife. Mr. Tilney tells her that such things may happen frequently in Gothic novels but do not happen nearly so much in nineteenth-century England. Austen claims to be defending novels, so often believed to mislead the young female reader, and then immediately warns the young female reader against the absorbed reading of them. She tries to distance her own novel from these criticisms by implying that it is the even more culturally devalued Gothic novels that pose the real danger to naïve female readers, because they are more unrealistic than hers. In order to defend her own novels, she attacks others': precisely the behavior she argued against.

As a matter of fact, Austen herself was an absorbed reader—or at least, an absorbed writer, who imagined her characters as having an almost real existence, more detailed than merely the facts she put on the page. She would have claimed that the difference between herself and Catherine Morland was that she, Austen, knew the difference between fiction and reality, though one might be forgiven for raising a doubtful eyebrow at some of her letters. In one, written to her sister Cassandra on May 24, 1813, Austen describes seeing an exhibition of paintings with her brother Henry on the twenty-first:

> I was very well pleased, particularly (pray tell Fanny) with a small portrait of Mrs. Bingley [Austen's own character, Jane Bennet Bingley], excessively like her.... Mrs. Bingley's is exactly herself—size, shaped face, features, and sweetness; there never was a greater likeness. She is dressed in a white gown, with green ornaments, which convinces me of what I had always supposed, that green was a favourite colour with her. I dare say Mrs. D. [Elizabeth Bennet Darcy, Jane's sister] will be in yellow ["Letter 61"].

Though Austen certainly knew the difference between the characters she put on the page and the real world she interacted with—as do all but the youngest or most mentally ill readers—she still spoke of Jane and Elizabeth Bennet as if they were real people with tastes, etc., that were not expressed on the page and not even entirely known to the author herself. Austen was an absorbed consumer of fiction, just like Catherine, and her depiction of Catherine as not knowing the difference between fiction and reality therefore seems especially unfair. Austen's writing also clearly incited absorbed reading in others—as revealed in an article by scholar Lance Bertelsen, in which he attempts to establish which portrait was the one of Jane Bennet, so that fans could know what she "really" looked like.

This pattern of fans claiming to defend other fans and really doing so by attacking them extends to some feminists as well, especially when they are discussing absorbed reading. Since absorbed reading has historically been labeled feminine, one would think that at least feminists would have defended it and fought back against the negative stereotypes of women that inform these criticisms. Instead, as Berggren points out, feminists have frequently depicted women's absorbed reading as naïve, sentimental, and useless. Instead of defending absorbed reading, they have recommended that women employ more critical reading—that is, those reading practices that are generally considered more masculine and rational and less feminine and emotional—in order to advance the position of women. Flint notes that in *A Vindication of the Rights of Woman* (1792) the early feminist Mary Wollstonecraft "criticizes sentimental fiction for encouraging 'a romantic twist of the mind,' a false view of human nature, and for teaching women to articulate 'the language of passion in affected tones,' placing more reliance on their sensations than on their reason. The best way to correct a fondness for novels, she believes, 'is to ridicule them'" (Flint 25).

Same Old Story

Most of the criticisms quoted above seem terribly out-of-date to modern readers. It may therefore come as a shock that many of the same arguments against women's absorbed reading are still extant and powerful, used by many modern critics as a matter of course. Take, for example, the reactions of popular culture to the bestselling *Twilight* novels by Stephenie Meyer. Some commenters, like earlier critics who believed that romance novels would ruin women for marriage by filling them with false expectations, are concerned that female *Twilight* fans will never be satisfied in real-life relationships because they will come to want an idealized boyfriend like *Twilight*'s Edward Cullen. One such modern critic, posting on a feminist blog, writes, "A common complaint I've heard from the female fans of *Twilight* is that Edward ruined men for them. He's the perfect man; the boyfriend they desperately want. Nobody is as 'good' as him. I've heard married women say in all seriousness that they'd leave their husbands for Edward Cullen" (Emily [The Slut]). Of course the fact that Edward Cullen is not a real person and that these women know this calls the "seriousness" of their statements into question.

These modern absorbed women readers are also depicted as being somehow sexually corrupted because of their interest in fictional characters. For instance, critics frequently depict older women who like the *Twilight* series, sometimes called "Twimoms," as pedophiles. Like critics of the eighteenth century, these people characterize women who are too emotionally involved in romance novels and films as oversexed and even sexually perverse: a pie graph by Lukipela titled "People That Should Have to Register as Sex Offenders" shows two equal sections labeled "Actual Sex Offenders" and "*Twilight* Moms." As in eighteenth-century criticisms we've seen, the underlying fear and disgust here is of female sexuality.

Critics frequently characterize middle-aged women who are fans of *Twilight* as neglectful wives and mothers, like eighteenth-century novel readers who should be spending their time on their domestic duties rather than reading: "The *Times* found women who have nearly lost their marriages by neglecting their husbands in favor of 'Twilight' fan sites, blogs, and message boards," one *Yahoo* article claims (qtd. in Lylestyles). Likewise, the most popular definition of "Twimom" on *Urban Dictionary* reads,

> A group of "adults" who have children and/or are married, who are overly obsessed fans of the overrated "Twilight" book series. They usually spend their time, neglecting their children, ie—forgetting to feed them.
> "Hey, that kid looks pretty down, underfed and neglected."
> "Oh. His mother must be a twimom" [Twimomsdiaf].

The anger and hatred that underlies such descriptions is clear from the screenname of this contributor, "twimomsdiaf," which stands for "Twimoms, die in a fire."

Some articles on *Twilight* really read like eighteenth- or nineteenth-century complaints about women's absorbed novel reading. One, "The *Twilight* Obsession and Its Effect on Marriages" by Laura M. Brotherson, runs the entire gamut of historical fears about women's reading: Brotherson worries that *Twilight* "paints an unrealistic picture of what love and relationships are all about" and that it wastes time "that could be better spent ... [on] one's spouse and family, or other worthwhile endeavors." Brotherson complains that *Twilight* creates "pretty impossible expectations for a real-life husband (or boyfriend—for the young women also obsessed with *Twilight*) to meet." She asserts, "An overabundance of chick flicks or other romance novels can have the same effect." Brotherson compares a wife's obsession with the *Twilight* novels, which contain no sex scenes, to a husband's obsession with pornography. Furthermore, she suggests that women will get the psychological excitement of sex from these books and then not want to have sex with their husbands. Apparently, novel-reading both oversexes women and paradoxically endangers their husbands' source of sexual gratification.

While women and teenage girls tend to be the most obvious modern targets of criticisms of absorbed reading, young men are sometimes targeted as well. One example of an exaggeratedly negative depiction of young men's absorbed media consumption appears in the 1982 Tom Hanks film *Mazes and Monsters*. Hanks' character, Robbie Wheeling, is a college student who likes to play the RPG (role-playing game) Mazes and Monsters, clearly based on the popular RPG *Dungeons & Dragons*. After a psychotic break, Wheeling comes to believe that he is the fictional character he plays in the game and tries to jump off of one of the Twin Towers in the belief that he will magically be able to fly.

Clearly, this depiction of young men's absorbed play in RPGs is similar to stereotypes about young women's absorbed reading: it reveals the belief that these absorbed consumers will eventually be unable to tell the difference between reality and fiction and thereby ruin—or end— their lives. Journalist Adam Rosenberg historicizes these stereotypes about RPGs:

> Mazes and Monsters reflects the strange moment in pop culture when polite society viewed role-playing games like *Dungeons & Dragons* as a corruptive influence on younger minds. Many thought that immersing yourself in the fantasy fiction of an RPG could lead to flirtations with Satanism, occult worship—and, in turn, criminal behavior. Look, it was a weird time. No one demonizes anybody for their entertainment preferences anymore, right? Right? Sigh.

While the furor over RPGs has somewhat died down, some critics still believe that young men's absorbed consumption of video games will have a similar effect, leading players to physically enact the violence they imaginatively participate in while playing. The many studies done on whether video games actually have this effect have been famously contradictory and inconclusive, as have studies on whether young men's consumption of music from artists like Marilyn Manson leads them into violent and mentally unhinged behavior. *New York Times* journalist Clyde Haberman notes in his article, "When *Dungeons & Dragons* Set off a Moral Panic," "Although researchers detect short-term increases in aggressive behavior by some habitual gamers, they say the long-range impact is harder to discern." Furthermore, Haberman points out, as video games have risen in popularity, rates of youth violence have declined sharply.

Fortunately for young men, most of these negative stereotypes seem to be changing. Cheryl Eddy, a writer for the science fiction site *Io9*, agrees with Rosenberg that the 1980s, when *Mazes and Monsters* was made, saw a "Satanic Panic" which targeted "heavy metal songs (and the subliminal and backwards messages supposedly contained therein) and album art, horror movies, and fantasy games like *Dungeons & Dragons*." Luckily, this panic has now mostly died out. At the same time, video games are now becoming so mainstream—and so frequently played by adults—that many journalists are now proclaiming that playing video games can be beneficial. Unfortunately, these instances of mainstreaming and acceptance have been slower to affect women than men because they are the mainstreaming of certain masculine-coded media, not of absorbed consumption as a whole, which is still widely considered feminine and dangerous. Teenage boys can once more enjoy video games and RPGs without being considered potential criminals, but women who enjoy *Twilight* are still depicted as potential sex offenders.

Stereotypes and Sexism

The validity of critics' fears about the effects of absorbed reading are questionable at best. Social scientists have conducted many studies on the subject, and the results have been decidedly mixed: there is little proof that absorbed reading really does affect behavior. But because these beliefs about the intense consumption of fiction—and the cultural and gendered fears on which those beliefs rest—are so deeply embedded in our culture, it can be easy for us to defend them, to say that these critics are right about some of their fears for women readers.

What really stands out about these fears, however, is their sexism. If absorbed reading were really a threat, it would be dangerous no matter who was doing it. However, we clearly do not talk about men's absorbed reading the same way we talk about women's absorbed reading. In *The True Story of the Novel* (1996), Margaret Anne Doody points out this sexism: "Outside the academy, the reader is still a bit of a problem—the female more than the male. We produce anxious books on women's reading of cheap paperback formulaic love-stories. Nobody studies male reading in that way" (281). Critics might worry that women who watch too many "chick flicks"—that is, romance films—could develop unrealistic expectations of the world. But what about men who watch a lot of action movies—movies in which, frequently, the hero not only saves the world but gets the girl? No one seems to be complaining about these films and the lesson they may be teaching men: that they deserve to be accepted by women they find attractive. It is female readers and viewers and the media made specifically for women that are most frequently attacked.

These attacks on feminine-gendered media and women's absorbed consumption are sometimes presented in terms of concern. In discussions of *Twilight*, for instance, many critics worry that the relationship between the main characters Bella and Edward is an abusive one and that young women who enjoy the novels will see abusive behavior as acceptable and even romantic in their real-life relationships. In a scholarly article on *Twilight*, Anna Silver writes,

> Claims such as these reveal the concern that many critics and readers feel about the books' tremendous popularity and the messages that they impart to girls about romance and women's roles in sexual relationships. Do the books promote retrograde ideas about female submission to male authority? Are the books particularly troubling in the genre of young adult (YA) literature, whose readers might not yet have developed the *critical apparatus* of the adult reader? [Silver, italics mine].

While this fear that our media consumption can reinforce cultural assumptions may in fact be valid, if it is not balanced by criticisms of young men's reading of "masculine" literature that reinforces the same message, or if it is based on the belief that young women are somehow more vulnerable to these messages than young men, the criticism is still sexist. It is less about protecting all readers from harmful messages, and more about attacking young and female readers and the media they enjoy.

Indeed, the cultural disdain for young women as media consumers is so strong that simply by liking something, teenage girls have the power to make it seem less prestigious, artistic, and valuable to the rest of the culture. Journalist Laura Moss discusses this phenomenon in her article "Why Must We Hate the Things Teen Girls Love?"

> "For many people, the fact that teenage girls like something—whether that something is Taylor Swift or One Direction or 'Twilight'—is a reason to write it off completely," said YA author and blogger Kerry Winfrey.
>
> Winfrey was a teen herself when she learned that simply by liking something, she had the ability to make it uncool.... "Because once teenage girls start liking something, it's over."

Just by virtue of being young women, teenage girls can smirch or even destroy the reputation of the media they enjoy.

Media that is written specifically for teenage girls tends to be relegated to the bottom of the pile in terms of quality, often as a knee-jerk reaction merely to the perceived gendering of the media. Moss quotes Melissa Rosenberg, the screenwriter of the *Twilight* movies and her statements to Women and Hollywood on the gendered double standards in fantasy films: "We've seen more than our fair share of bad action movies, bad movies geared toward men or 13-year-old boys. And you know, the reviews are like 'OK that was crappy, but a fun ride.' But no one says 'Oh my god. If you go to see this movie you're a complete xxxxing idiot.' And that's the tone. That is the tone with which people attack 'Twilight.'" Just the fact that it was made for teenage girls rather than teenage boys means that such media and its fans are much more strongly castigated.

Part of the problem is that the enthusiasm with which teen girls respond to their favorite media is seen as aberrant, annoying, and stupid. These "rabid fangirls" supposedly let their emotions run away with them and respond to media "hysterically." Moss observes that even the term "hysteria" derives from sexist attitudes in psychology from the nineteenth and early twentieth centuries, which assumed that women overreacted emotionally because of their sexual organs. She quotes feminist activist Bailey Poland, who argues that while critics seem to assume that teen girls are not in control of their excitement—sexual or emotional—these media consumers "deliberately use excitement and passion as the foundation for community-building and empathetic development."

Female media creators unfortunately receive their share of this dismissive attitude toward the quality of girls' media, frequently ignored by the public and by award nomination committees while men are celebrated. Moss quotes Kelly Jensen, who observes, "We know why it is that men like John Green write Love Stories and women like Sarah Dessen write Romances. It's not the quality. It's the way the system is built that makes women the outsiders in the category of fiction they made." Criticisms of absorbed reading, though they can occasionally target men as well as women, are based on sexist concepts of women and their media consumption and therefore, unsurprisingly, are much more commonly directed toward women than men.

Furthermore, if the issue were really one of concern about what vulnerable absorbed readers were learning from books, then children, not teenage girls, would the group most discussed in criticisms of absorbed reading. After all, children would be the most likely to confuse fiction with reality or to have their views of the adult world formed by fiction rather than direct observation. They often read fairy tales, magical stories, and books about anthropomorphic animals, so their reading material would seem to be the most divorced from reality. However, what we find is that absorbed reading and its effects on children are often idealized. We actually encourage children to immerse themselves in fiction and pretend to be knights and princesses. It's no coincidence that Julia Donaldson, who wrote such a beautiful, poetic celebration of absorbed reading, was a *Children's* Poet Laureate. It is when women begin to reach sexual maturity, in their teenage years, that their absorbed reading, especially of fantastic and feminine genres, is suddenly seen as a threat and a disgrace. It is therefore also difficult to escape the conclusion that criticizing absorbed reading and genres like romance is partly about controlling women by controlling their sexuality. Our culture's continued reliance on the tropes of the eighteenth-century novel-reading woman indicates that many of these fears of women's independent sexuality are still in force.

Genre Problems

There are three major criteria which determine how strongly any instance of absorbed reading is likely to be censured by critics. As already noted, the first criterion is who is doing the reading, with women and the young receiving the harshest criticism. The level of criticism is also based on what is being read, and the emotional intensity of the absorbed reading experience. These three criteria all interact so closely that it is often difficult to separate them.

In terms of which texts are most criticized for their effects on absorbed readers, as noted above, it is the stereotypically feminine genres that most often get the short end of the stick. Sentimental novels, Gothic novels, romance novels, "chick flicks," *Twilight*'s supernatural romance: all of these are specifically aimed at female readers and considered to be feminine genres. They are also considered popular, rather than literary, books and films, and are written specifically for absorbed audiences rather than critical ones. Because of this, they are considered to be lower quality literature, and such literature is often depicted as more of a danger to absorbed audiences.

In *Textual Poachers* (1992), Henry Jenkins' seminal work on fandom, Jenkins explains this connection between the supposed quality of a book and the fears critics express for its absorbed readers:

> "Bad taste" is not simply undesirable; it is unacceptable. Debates about aesthetic choices or interpretive practices … often draw upon social or psychological categories as a source of justification. Materials viewed as undesirable within a particular aesthetic are often accused of harmful social effects or negative influences upon their consumers. Aesthetic preferences are imposed through legislation and public pressure; for example, in the cause of protecting children from the "corrupting" influence of undesired cultural materials. Those who enjoy such texts are seen as intellectually debased, psychologically suspect, or emotionally immature [16–17].

Media that is considered "bad" aesthetically is also often believed to be bad for you, or morally bad in and of itself. I can attest from my own experience that discussions of aesthetic relativism—the belief that there is no universal standard of good art or literature, but that all such judgments are based on personal opinion and social construction—often give way to charges of moral relativism. Morals and aesthetics are so closely linked in our society that if you say that no art or literature is aesthetically good or bad in and of itself, many people come to think that you are saying that there is also no universal moral truth.

It is not coincidental that the popular genre fiction that is most obviously written for absorbed readers—the supposedly most "intellectually debased, psychologically suspect, or emotionally immature" consumers—is the least likely to be considered high quality media. "High-brow" literary novels are often written to create an emotional distance between the characters and the reader: it is common for such works to star anti-heroes or repellent protagonists (like Humbert Humbert, the pedophiliac main character of Nabokov's *Lolita*) in order to discourage absorption. Such works also frequently emphasize and encourage the intellectual contemplation of characters' actions and motivations. This kind of literature tends to appeal to and inspire critical reading: thinking and feeling *about* the text and characters rather than thinking and feeling *with* them.

In contrast, popular literature texts in genres like romance are often meant to be experienced rather than analyzed: they invite absorbed rather than critical reading, and this often reflects negatively on them and their supposed literary merit. Among the popular fiction that receives this criticism, genres like popular romance that are considered feminine or likely to appeal the most to female absorbed readers are often the most strongly censured for their potential effects on said readers. Critics are more likely to speak disparagingly of the supposedly feminine genre of Harlequin romance novels than of the supposedly more masculine spy capers. Within the hierarchy of literary quality, highbrow literature for more critical reading is at the top, popular literature for absorbed reading is down below, and popular literature for absorbed women readers is down near the bottom, being compared to genres that are considered morally suspect in their subject matter, such as pornography.

It is not only popular and "feminine" genres that are most strongly criticized, but also "unrealistic" or "escapist" genres. In an article defending escapist fiction, journalist Sana Hussein notes that in Western culture, science fiction and fantasy are genres without much cultural prestige. Likewise, in "Fantasy, Reading, and Escapism," Jo Walton describes how her tastes for certain genres are received differently than her taste for reading in general:

> I love reading. If I say this, people generally look at me with approval. Reading is a culturally approved practice, it improves my mind and widens my cultural capital. But if I admit what I read—more fiction than non fiction, more genre books than classics, fantasy, science fiction, romance, military fiction, historical fiction, mysteries and YA [young adult literature]—then I lose that approval and have to start justifying my choices.

The problem is that many of these popular genres are considered unrealistic and therefore less valuable than nonfiction or literary fiction.

In *The True Story of the Novel*, Margaret Anne Doody explains the rise in anxiety about the novel in the eighteenth century as partly caused by a rise in female interest in the genre: more and more women were both writing and reading novels in that century, and critics could no longer assume that their readers had both a man's education and a man's good sense and good taste. The novel therefore came to be seen as dangerous to the civic order, in that it might spread improperly vetted ideas to improperly prepared readers. In order to "tame" novels, critics began to demand that they be "realistic." They were no longer to be written about extraordinary heroes and heroines, kings, giants, and dragons, but about the more probable events of everyday life. That way, novels could present moral lessons to underdeveloped (female and lower-class) readers.

Unfortunately, this move toward realism in fiction necessarily shunted all "unrealistic" genres into the realm of the aesthetically, and therefore morally, unacceptable. These unacceptable genres came to include the old knights-and-dragons Romances; novels set in foreign, especially exotic, climes and cultures; the often supernatural and always fantastical and emotional gothic novels; and historical novels. Even today, genres like fantasy and science fiction that carry readers away from life as we know it are some of the most strongly censured genres. As they do not depict life as it is, some critics warn, genres like fantasy may give unwary absorbed readers a dangerously incorrect view of the world. John Rogers responds to and resists this cultural association of fantasy literature with the negative effects of absorbed reading and escapism when he writes, "There are two novels that can change a bookish fourteen-year old's life: *The Lord of the Rings* and *Atlas Shrugged*. One is a childish fantasy that often engenders a lifelong obsession with its unbelievable heroes, leading to an emotionally stunted, socially crippled adulthood, unable to deal with the real world. The other, of course, involves orcs."

Being Into It

The intensity of the reader's absorbed experience also affects how much critics condemn this reading practice. Simply enjoying *Twilight* would not be enough for a middle-aged woman to be considered a "Twimom": she must be more intensely absorbed in the text than that. In other words, she must be a passionate fan.

The often derogatory term "fangirl" is defined almost entirely by the level of intensity the female fan is exhibiting. *Urban Dictionary* offers a number of definitions of the term that highlight intensity of obsession: "A female who has overstepped the line between healthy fandom and indecent obsession" (monkey). "A female fan, obsessed with something (or someone) to a frightening or sickening degree. *Fangirl: OMG!!!!! i luv {insert celebrity's name} to!!!!!!!!! hes got a hot ass! ive spent teh last 6 munths planin our weding!!*" (Stephemu). "Female of approximately 12–17 years old, (though this can vary) who are obsessed by some sort of celebrity/group/band. Contrary to popular belief, fangirls are not always to be confused with stalkers.... However then there are the dangerous fangirls, the kind that hound said celebrity/group/band.... Fangirls very often give a bad name for true, normal fans" (wibbleformebibble). The more emotionally intense the fan's interest, the more she is criticized.

It is interesting to note that female fans' intensity is more likely to be described in negative terms—*indecent, frightening, sickening, dangerous*—than male fans' intensity. The term "fanboy," also derogatory and linked to level of obsession, is generally defined on *Urban Dictionary* using much more neutral terms: "A passionate fan of various elements of geek culture … who lets his passion override social graces" (Horn). "A person who is completely loyal to a game or company reguardless [sic] of if they suck or not" (Sega Slayer). "An extreme fan or follower of a particular medium or concept.... Known for a complete lack of objectivity in relation to their preferred focus" (Lig Na Baste). Greater intensity and passion leads to greater criticism and the use of derogatory terms across the board, but women's passion is also censured far more than men's.

The sexism and unfairness of negative stereotypes of passionate absorbed readers, passionate fans, is clear when it is compared to the general perception of another kind of fan: sports fans. Media fandom is not as different from sports fandom as we sometimes think: both kinds of fans may get very excited, shout and scream about their favorite "characters," pay a large amount of money to get together and celebrate their shared passion, and even dress in strange ways to attend these gatherings. In fact, one much-reblogged (and difficult to source) *Tumblr* post from the weekend of the Super Bowl in 2016 read, "Apparently there's an important episode of football on this weekend." Someone responded, "Yes, the football fandom is going nuts. Lots of cosplaying going on. Tickets to the con are outrageous, though" (qtd. in Barner, "Apparently There's"). Sports fans also become deeply emotionally invested in their teams in much the same way that media fans do: they often refer to their team as "we," as if they were actually players themselves, and they consider their sports affiliations to be major parts of their own and even their families' identities: "I'm a fifth-generation Yankees fan!"

Despite the similarities in behavior, level of passion, and obsession with a "storyline" that isn't part of "real life," media fans are more often *othered*, discussed as an aberrant subculture, than sports fans, who are accepted as perfectly normal. In fact, it is expected that everyone know something of the rules of the most popular sports and the names and cities of the most famous teams. *Tumblr* user Linzeestyle points out, "Sport fandom is so ingrained in our culture that major events are treated like holidays (my gym closes for the Super Bowl)—and can you imagine being laughed at for admitting you didn't know the difference between

Supernatural and *The X Files* the way you might if you admit you don't know the rules of football vs baseball, or basketball?" (qtd. in Barner, "Do You Ever Think"). Despite similar levels of passion and excitement in their fans, our culture is very accepting of the sports fandom and even expects non-fans to know something about it, but marginalizes media fandom. This is partly because sports fandom is considered to be masculine but media fandom is considered to be feminine and is more closely associated with absorbed reading/viewing.

Fans: Ticking Boxes

These three criteria of the most stringently criticized media consumers particularly impact fans, who fulfill each of the criteria for the most stringently censured readers: they are often young and female, they become deeply emotionally and imaginatively involved in their favorite works, and these works frequently have little cultural prestige. Consequently, the worst stereotypes of absorbed readers are also the worst stereotypes of fans. While some of this criticism of absorbed reading is voiced as concern for the well-being of fans, a great deal of it also appears in the form of ridicule.

Fans fulfill the first criterion for supposedly at-risk absorbed readers: they are frequently young and female. In an article on the stereotype that "Most Fanfic Writers Are Girls," *TV Tropes* draws on statistics to indicate that this characterization is probably true: "Studies of early *Star Trek* fanfiction showed as many as 90% of authors were female in the 1970s." Establishing how many fans involved in fanfiction are female is a tricky proposition; a study of age, sex, and country of *FanFiction.Net* users concluded that only 10 percent of users identified their sex in their profiles. Of those 10 percent, 78 percent self-identified as female (Sendlor). In a 2013 survey by Centrumlumina on *Tumblr* (a blogging website popular among fans) of users of the popular fanfiction site *Archive of Our Own* (AO3), 80 percent of the 10,005 voluntary respondents self-identified as "female"—in fact, more respondents identified as "genderqueer" (6 percent) than as "male" (4 percent) (Centrumlumina, "Gender"). Whatever the actual numbers are, it is clear that women are at least a sizeable majority in the part of fandom that creates and consumes fanfiction.

Centrumlumina's survey also indicates that many fans involved in the creation and consumption of fanfiction on *Archive of Our Own* are young. The largest group, 23 percent, self-identified as being between the ages of 19 and 21. Twenty percent were between 22 and 24, 19 percent between 25 and 29, and 16 percent between 16 and 18. The average age of respondents was 25 ("Age"). FFN Research's study indicates that users of *FanFiction.Net* are younger than users of *AO3*: 80 percent of those users who revealed their age were between 13 and 17 years old (FFN Research "Fan Fiction Demographics"). Incidentally, partly because of the younger average age of *FanFiction.Net*'s users, the website has gained a reputation among some fans for hosting worse fanfiction than *Archive Of Our Own*: one writer on *Urban Dictionary* notes, "After banning all adult content, ff.net became known for an absurd ratio of incredibly bad and juvenile fanfiction" (Treehouseman).

Critics also consider fans to be an at-risk population for absorbed reading because of the quality of media they consume and write about. Henry Jenkins observes in *Textual Poachers* that one of the stereotypes of fans is that they "place inappropriate importance on devalued cultural material" (10). Fans write and consume fanfiction based not only on books, but on the less culturally valued media of films, television shows, cartoons, anime, and video games. Jenkins points out that critics "who have a vested interest" in maintaining the old standards of taste feel threatened by the ways fans see new value in these media:

> The fans' transgression of bourgeois taste and disruption of dominant cultural hierarchies insures that their preferences are seen as abnormal and threatening by those who have a vested interest in the maintenance of those standards.... Fan culture muddies [taste] boundaries, treating popular texts as if they merited the same degree of attention and appreciation as canonical texts. Reading practices (close scrutiny, elaborate exegesis, repeated and prolonged rereading, etc.) acceptable in confronting a work of "serious merit" seem perversely misapplied to the more "disposable" texts of mass culture [*Textual Poachers* 17].

Fandom is not only closely connected to devalued media like television, but to devalued literary genres like science fiction. Fanfiction has an old and deep connection with science fiction: Joan Marie Verba explains, "Science fiction (sf) fans formed clubs as early as the 1920s, and published science fiction fanzines (amateur fan magazines) since the 1930s. Therefore, it was natural for the science fiction fans who went to the World Science Fiction Convention in Cleveland in 1966 and who saw the pilot of *Star Trek*, which Gene Roddenberry had brought to the convention, to put out a fanzine devoted to that program" (1). The fanzine *Spockanalia*, published in September of 1967 at the beginning of the television show's second season, contained the first collection of stories based on someone else's characters and formed by a community of media fans: the first works of this new genre of fanzine/internet fanfiction.

Fandom has been particularly connected with science fiction and fantasy ever since. Centrumlumina's survey of *AO3* users asked respondents, "Do you regularly read and/or produce works for any of the following popular fandoms?" Fans were permitted to indicate multiple fandoms they were a part of. While the most popular fandom among respondents was the television show *Sherlock* (41 percent), almost all the rest of the twenty top fandoms were in the science-fiction/fantasy genre: Marvel films, *Teen Wolf* (TV), *Supernatural* (TV), *Harry Potter*, and *Merlin* (TV) filled the next five spots ("Popular Fandoms"). Likewise, as of 27 October 2015, the most commonly represented fandoms on *FanFiction.Net* were almost all science-fiction/fantasy: the top five were *Harry Potter*, *Naruto*, *Twilight*, *InuYasha*, and *Hetalia: Axis Powers* ("*FanFiction.Net*"). Three of these are also anime: because western culture often associates cartoons with children, fans of anime may also be seen as particularly immature.

Fans are not only frequently young, female, and readers of devalued cultural material, but they also perform a particularly intense form of absorbed reading, with deep emotional attachment to characters. The fan would seem to be the obsessed, absorbed reader *par excellence*. He or she is absorbed imaginatively into the world of the text, comes to care personally for fictional characters, and writes about them as if they had an actual existence. One anonymous *Tumblr* user asks another fan, "Will it ever stop? Will I ever stop falling in love with fictional characters? I'm 30 and married, for God's sake!" Anunexpectedhotdwarf replies with a gif of Aragorn in *Return of the King*: "A day may come when we will stop falling in love with fictional characters, *but it is not this day!*" (Anunexpectedhotdwarf). *Tumblr* user Mandalorianed, whose real name is Dora, posts about how deeply she feels the emotions of the characters in the television show *Criminal Minds*, a result of her intense absorbed consumption: "'hey dora how bad is your second hand embarrassment for fictional characters?' well, spencer reid was about to embarrass himself in front of a bunch of college students and i literally had to pause the episode and walk it off." Likewise, Forablueeyedmiracle writes, "Fandom is knowing that, across the globe, hundreds of other people are screaming 'NO FUCK YOU' at their televisions and curling up on the floor and crying at exactly the same moment as you are." These fans are all engaged in an especially intense form of absorbed reading or viewing of fictional texts.

Fans unite the characteristics of the supposedly most vulnerable and transgressive absorbed readers: they are often young and female; consume culturally devalued materials like science fiction, fantasy, anime, video games, young adult novels, television shows, and popular film and literature; and they consume them in especially intense and absorbed ways. Because fanfiction has its source in absorbed reading, critics often associate fans and their work with that reading practice's reputation for delusion, social isolation, sexual perversion, etc. Absorbed reading is therefore both the source of fanfiction and the source of fanfiction's harshest criticisms.

2

Getting Above Themselves

Many years ago, when much of internet fandom was interacting on *LiveJournal*, I ran across an *LJ* icon of a green loop of ribbon on a black background. It read, "Friends don't let friends write Mary Sues." At the time, as a newcomer to fandom, I thought this was funny and clever. Now I think the sentiment the icon expressed, that fans should discourage their fellow fans from writing Mary Sue characters, was rather sad. What is even sadder is how many fans follow this advice, not realizing how they are reinforcing the sexist concepts of absorbed reading that discriminate against them as fans.

Mary Sues are a kind of fanfiction character ubiquitous in fanfiction and yet very unpopular with fans: though Mary Sue characters are everywhere in fandom, criticisms of them are everywhere, as well. The inherent sexism of criticisms of Mary Sues is beginning to be better understood than it was when I first entered fandom in the early 2000s, and the term is beginning to be reclaimed: one of the most popular female-focused science fiction websites is titled *The Mary Sue*. But the sexism in criticisms of Mary Sues goes even deeper than is generally known by fans, and is closely connected with the negative stereotypes surrounding absorbed reading. Because Mary Sues are so prevalent in fanfiction, and because they are the result of the absorbed reading that is so much a part of the genre, the condemnation of these characters is an important component of the condemnation of fanfiction itself.

What Is a Mary Sue?

What is a Mary Sue? It's a difficult question: many fans will say that they can identify a Mary Sue character when they see one, but they have a hard time coming up with a foolproof definition. The *TV Tropes* article on the subject agrees: "Mary Sue is a derogatory term primarily used in Fan Fic circles to describe a particular type of character. This much everyone can agree on. What that character type is, exactly, differs wildly from circle to circle, and often from person to person." Fans tend to identify two major traits as signifying a Mary Sue: the character's idealization, and her role as an author avatar.

Fan definitions often emphasize a Mary Sue's unrealistic perfection: the first definition of *Mary Sue* on *Urban Dictionary* begins, "A female fanfiction character who is so perfect as to be annoying" (nscangal). Another definition, by monkmunk, agrees: "A female character ... that is annoyingly perfect. Often unique in some implausible way, any problems they face are typically intended to make them seem tragic or emotionally deep, rather than complex or flawed." *Fanlore*'s article on Mary Sue also emphasizes this idealization: "A character may be judged Mary Sue if she is competent in too many areas, is physically attractive, and/or is viewed as admirable by other sympathetic characters" ("Mary Sue" *Fanlore*). However, given the number of idealized characters in the history of literature, an overly perfect character does not seem like enough of a reason to castigate authors for writing such characters.

However, the *Fanlore* article on Mary Sue also emphasizes that it is the character's position as an author avatar that incites criticism: "Mary Sue is often denigrated specifically because she's assumed to be a 'self-insert,' author avatar or alter ego. In fan fiction it is considered extremely gauche and immature for authors to create characters based on themselves. By extension, any original female character, when written by a female, might be seen as a self-insert" ("Mary Sue" *Fanlore*). The common wisdom goes that a fan loves a story and its characters so much that she wants to be part of the story, to interact with her beloved characters. She therefore creates a fictionalized, idealized version of herself and puts it into the story.

Mary Sue's Origin Story

The term *Mary Sue* comes from "A Trekkie's Tale": a *Star Trek* fanfiction written in 1974 by Paula Smith and published in the fanzine *Menagerie*. It is a parody mocking the trope of the perfect female original character, which was already widespread in fanfiction. In an interview with Cynthia W. Walker for *Transformative Works and Cultures*, Paula

Smith explains the pattern that she noticed in early Star Trek fanfiction that led her to write "A Trekkie's Tale":

> It all goes back to the early 1970s.... I bought every zine I could lay my hands on.... I read everything. Some of it was pretty good. Some of it was extremely good. But an awful lot of it was just plain awful.
> As Theodore Sturgeon said, 90 percent of everything is crap. The amazing thing was, the crap had so much of a pattern.... You could see that every *Trek* zine at the time had a main story about this adolescent girl who is the youngest yeoman or lieutenant or captain ever in Starfleet. She makes her way onto the Enterprise and the entire crew falls in love with her. They then have adventures, but the remarkable thing was that all the adventures circled around this character. Everybody else in the universe bowed down in front of her. Also, she usually had some unique physical identifier—odd-colored eyes or hair—or else she was half-Vulcan. The stories read like they were written about half an hour before the zine was printed; they were generally not very good [qtd. in Walker].

Smith's "A Trekkie's Tale" delineates the characteristics of what came to be known in fandom as the Mary Sue. She is young and surprisingly accomplished: she reflects in the opening lines, "Here I am, the youngest lieutenant in the fleet—only fifteen and a half years old" (qtd. in Bacon-Smith 94–96). She, like Spock, is half-Vulcan, and easily wins the admiration of canon characters like Spock and Captain Kirk. Mary Sue, her popularity among the most beloved characters established, participates in the canon characters' adventures, joining in a landing party and saving her comrades: "Captain Kirk, Mr. Spock, Dr. McCoy and Mr. Scott beamed down with Lt. Mary Sue to Rigel XXXVII. They were attacked by green androids and thrown into prison.... She sprung the lock with her hairpin and they all got away back to the ship." Mary Sue is clearly highly competent: on their return to the ship she takes command while the other officers are incapacitated, and is awarded "the Nobel Peace Prize, the Vulcan Order of Gallantry and the Tralfamadorian Order of Good Guyhood" for her excellent leadership. In the end she dies and is mourned by all the canon characters.

Smith's parody resonated with fans who had also noticed this trend of idealized female characters in fanfiction. Original characters like the one Smith describes here—young, perfect, attractive, admirable to canon characters, heroic—soon became known in fandom as Mary Sues. Female characters with these characteristics show up in many genres, but the fact that the name for them arose in the fanfiction community as an embodiment of everything that was wrong with "bad fanfics" indicates how closely Mary Sues—and by extension, their condemnation—

are associated with the genre of fanfiction as a whole and contribute to its questionable reputation.

Mary Sue as Metaphor for Absorbed Reading

This pattern of idealized young female characters in fanfiction who draw the entire narrative to themselves is not limited to the *Star Trek* fandom of the '70s. Such characters are still frequently written in the internet fanfiction of many different fandoms. In 1992 Camille Bacon-Smith wrote in *Enterprising Fiction*, "most fans will readily admit to having written at least one Mary Sue story.... Usually it is the first story a fan writes, often before she knows about the literature or its forms" (97). This is still considered to be true by fans today: *Fanlore*'s article on Mary Sues mentions, "it is not uncommon for an author's very first pieces of writing to contain Mary Sues" ("Mary Sue" *Fanlore*). Many fans write such characters until they are taught by the fandom that Mary Sues are considered unacceptable.

The ubiquity of Mary Sue stories originates in the fact that they are themselves a metaphor for the act of absorbed reading: they act as vehicles for writers—and readers—to imaginatively enter the story and participate in it. The absorbed reader feels like she is "striding into the book," so she creates a Mary Sue character, a representation of herself, and writes that character into that text. Mary Sues result when the absorbed reader makes her reading experience visible in her fanfiction. The self-inserted character can inhabit the setting alongside the canon characters, experiencing the action as an imaginative placeholder for the fan reader/writer, becoming friends with the other characters, or even becoming romantically entangled with them. She can interact more directly with the characters and the plot than even the absorbed reader can on her own: the Mary Sue can have a two-way relationship with other characters, can experience the setting and the emotions of the plot for herself, and can participate in the plot directly, even changing events. She thus becomes a vessel, not only for the fan writer to experience the canon, but also for readers of the fanfiction to become absorbed into. Mary Sues provide a character for absorbed readers to inhabit.

The metaphorical relationship between Mary Sues and absorbed reading is even more obvious in a popular Mary Sue variant: the modern fan who is transported into the world of the source material. Unlike Smith's

Mary Sue, who is a native of the world of *Star Trek*, these Mary Sues travel from reality into the fictional setting: a Narnia fan might find herself in Narnia, a *Lord of the Rings* fan could be sucked through her TV into Middle-earth, a Trekker might suddenly appear on the bridge of the USS Enterprise, centuries in the future. Such characters are often identified as Mary Sues even without being obviously perfect: the movement of the fan into the fictional world within the story mirrors the way the fan or Mary Sue author puts herself into the canon story through absorbed reading. This self-insertion of the female fan is the essence of Mary Sue.

It is true that not all self-inserts would be considered Mary Sues, and that not all Mary Sues are necessarily self-inserted characters. Nonetheless, the underlying belief that Mary Sues are author avatars is a large part of the animus against them, and the opportunities such characters present for readers to become absorbed into them and experience their adventures alongside the canon characters is part of Mary Sue's perpetual, if embattled, popularity.

Mary Sue in Action: "Changing History"

The Mary Sue story "Changing History: Choices" by fogisbeautiful provides an example of how absorbed reading is figured in the Mary Sue character. Like the absorbed reader, who feels as though she has entered the text of the story through her intense emotional and imaginative engagement, the Mary Sue in this piece, Melody (Mel) Bernston, magically enters Tolkien's Middle-earth and becomes part of the story of *The Fellowship of the Ring*.

Melody is a Tolkien fan who just wants "to be in a place where she could just be her crazy, *Lord of the Rings* obsessed, [sic] self, with no one around to judge" (Chapter 1). A fan who wishes to escape from her everyday life into a book, Mel goes to a local park to be alone. Like an absorbed reader entering into the fictional world of the book, Melody is then transported into Tolkien's Middle-earth by a magical ring, meets the character Boromir, and travels with him to Rivendell.

Mary Sues like Melody get to experience the setting of the novel in the same way the absorbed reader does, but even more intimately. The description of Melody's first actual sight of this place she has only read about is full of emotion. When they first reach Rivendell, Boromir shows it to her with the words,

"Look, my lady.... The place of tales, both yours and mine."

They stood upon a ridge looking down into a quiet little valley, white buildings half hidden in the forest, blending perfectly into the surroundings. As Mel watched, tiny lights began to blink on throughout the valley, flaring up and lighting the darkness that descended on the place, like tiny stars come to earth.

"Rivendell ..." she whispered, feeling a hush fall over her, an almost reverent awe [Chapter 1].

Just like absorbed readers, who feel that they know the fictional characters they read about personally, Mary Sues often become friends with characters from the canon. They do what absorbed readers long to do: they interact directly with the characters, responding to them physically and emotionally. Mary Sues get to be in real relationships with these fictional people. While the absorbed reader feels as though she knows the characters she reads about, the relationship is only one way: *they* don't know *her*. But Mary Sues like Melody gets to spend time with characters and establish two-way relationships with them. She and Legolas soon become friends and Melody recognizes this new two-way relationship between them: "Sometime in the last few weeks, Legolas had transformed, so slowly that she hadn't even realized it was happening until this moment. He was no longer a character in a book, a prince in a fairy tale. Now, when she looked at him, she just saw her friend. They really were friends now" (Chapter 9).

Melody's relationships with the characters are not limited to friendship: over the course of the fanfiction, she and Boromir fall in love with one another. Melody recognizes her own love for Boromir first, and believes it to be unrequited. This one-way relationship once again mirrors the position of the absorbed reader who is attracted to a fictional character: "*He doesn't love me.* Those were words that, until now, she hadn't even dared to think. But now cold reality settled in the pit of her stomach. She loved him.... And the hard truth of it made her feel hollow and very lost.... What good was it to come to this place, only to fall in love with the one man that she knew wouldn't live to love her back? What crazy, twisted reality had Yavanna dropped her in?" (Chapter 27). However, as in the case with Legolas, Boromir eventually returns Melody's affections—though not until one of the sequels. The Mary Sue character gets what the absorbed reader longs for: a two-way relationship with the characters she knows so well and has developed so much affection for.

Along with interacting with the characters, Mary Sues also get to participate directly in the action of the story. Julie Donaldson's poem describes the absorbed reader feeling as if she were the one having the hero's adventures, through an imaginative absorption into the character. However, Mary Sues like Melody have the opportunity to engage in the action *in propia persona*, and to the fan author who has written the Mary Sue as a self-inserted character, this is one step closer to participating in the action herself. Creating a female character for imaginative absorption may be particularly useful for female readers when, as in *The Fellowship of the Ring*, almost all of the characters who participate directly in the action are male. It may be difficult for female readers to feel absorbed into these male characters. "Changing History" is a "tenth-walker" fic, a term used by the *Lord of the Rings* fandom to describe works in which an original character joins the nine members of the Fellowship of the Ring on their quest to destroy the One Ring: Melody, as a tenth walker, gets to participate in the Fellowship's adventures.

As the Mary Sue has now become one of the heroes, she is herself transformed into a heroic character. Just as many of the members of the Fellowship have special talents and abilities, Melody discovers her own magical power, one that comes with a special destiny. The magical ring that brought her to Middle-earth turns out to be the "Yavannacor": a ring of great power that allows Melody to talk to plants, particularly trees. Like other characters in Tolkien's story, Melody has a special destiny: a rhododendron tells her,

> [The goddess] Yavanna took this ring and sent it far away, across land and sea, and spoke that it would only be found by one who could honor the bond between all children, be they of earth, or stone, or light. This one she would name as her own and would call upon her only at great need.... The one who wears the Yavannacor carries a great burden.... Her work is not complete until all of Yavanna's children have been brought to the light [Chapter 6].

Frodo's destiny is to destroy the One Ring; Melody's is to fulfill Yavanna's prophecy.

Finally, the Mary Sue figure functions to create actual changes to the plot. Melody, now a heroic figure like her comrades, does not merely participate in the action but actually changes the story by her presence. The absorbed reader may wish she could save the heroes of the fictions she consumes: a Mary Sue actually can. As the prophecy about the Yavannacor and the title "Changing History" indicate, Melody's role is to change Tolkien's narrative. In the original canon, Boromir is killed at the end of *The Fellowship of the Ring*. In "Changing History," Melody realizes that she can save him. Galadriel sees hope for things to turn out differently. The element that has the power to change the outcome of the story is the original element the fanfiction writer has included: the Mary Sue character. Melody asks Galadriel, "'I can save him?' Galadriel turned back to her, and then hesitantly reached out and took her hand, her blue eyes piercing. '*Only* you can save him,' she said" (Chapter 28). Mary Sue is an element from outside the story that can dive in and change the course of the narrative.

Melody uses the power of the Yavannacor to save Boromir: when she is hurrying to do so, the trees guide her along the best and fastest path. She stops Boromir from being corrupted by the One Ring and fights by his side when they are attacked by the monstrous Uruk-Hai, who kill Boromir in the original novel. Fogisbeautiful implies that it is Melody's actions, the catalyst for the changes to Tolkien's narrative in this fanfiction, which lead to a new outcome and Boromir's survival in this fight.

What Is She, That All the Fans So Hate Her?

So what is so wrong with Mary Sues? If they are author avatars, why is that a bad thing? Some fans argue that Mary Sues are only bad because they are the creation of immature writers, who overidealize their heroines to an unrealistic degree and do not offer them real challenges to overcome over the course of the story. However, while this may be true of some Mary Sues, it hardly explains the vitriol directed toward these characters in general. After all, all beginning writers have to learn to craft good characters. This doesn't explain phenomena like entire *LiveJournal* blogs that have been dedicated to mocking Mary Sues. *The Mary Sue Report* advertises, "If it's a Mary Sue, drag it here and put a stake through its black heart before it breeds" ("Profile," *Bastion of Questionable Sanity*). One person comments on a fic entitled "Who IS She?": "I'll also tell you who she [the Mary Sue] is: a bitch who should be choked. Where's Wayne Brady when you need him?" (bryanthechosen1). Some of these blogs criticize the Mary Sue line by line. One fan critic quotes a Mary Sue story: "She had no plan, no family, and no motivation to live on. What else was there to live for?" The critic then replies, "Nothing—kill yourself" (musashden). If Mary Sues are only bad because they're the result of juvenile and undeveloped writing skills, these vicious remarks certainly aren't justified. Clearly there is something else going on here. What is it about these characters that enrages people?

The *Fanlore* article on Mary Sues expresses one of the most common reasons fan critics see this kind of character as undesirable: a Mary Sue often becomes the new heroine of the narrative. "Someone at *TvTropes* observed that 'Mary Sue' is actually the *reaction* that fans may have to a work that 'is unduly favoring a character by changing other characters or the environment in inappropriate ways'" ("Mary Sue" *Fanlore*). The article calls such Mary Sues "Attention Hogs" or "Warpers": "The focus of reader and character attention is unduly placed on the guest star rather than on the leads.... The primary defining characteristic of these stories is that the 'canon characters and plot warp around her to fit the author's wish fulfillment,' allowing the Mary Sue to make the decisions and take the actions normally taken by others" ("Mary Sue" *Fanlore*). These criticisms of Mary Sue for usurping the position of hero from the canon characters ultimately derive partly from fans' love for and desire to see more narratives about their favorite canon characters, not other people's self-insertions.

However, the larger reason Mary Sues are so hated is because of their relationship with absorbed reading. Critics have frequently expressed fears that absorbed readers, especially women, may develop *bovarysme*. *Bovarysme*, as defined by Chris Baldick in *The Concise Oxford Dictionary of Literary Terms*, is

> a disposition towards escapist day dreaming in which one imagines oneself as a heroine or hero of a romance and refuses to acknowledge everyday realities. This condition (a later version of Don Quixote's madness) can be found in fictional characters before Emma Bovary, the protagonist of Gustave Flaubert's novel *Madame Bovary* (1857), gave it her name: for example, Catherine Morland in Jane Austen's *Northanger Abbey* (1818) makes similar confusions between fiction and reality. Novelists have often exposed *bovarysme* to ironic analysis, thus warning against the delusive enchantments of the romance tradition [29].

As Baldick makes obvious, the fear of people developing delusions of heroic grandeur is often linked to absorbed reading: some critics fear that too intense an absorption into texts may cause the boundaries between text and real life to break down, and that these absorbed readers will come to view their lives as novelistic romances or adventures and themselves as heroes or heroines. These absorbed readers, often female like Emma Bovary or Catherine Morland, may then unwisely enact the behaviors they have read about in fiction.

In *The True Story of the Novel*, Margaret Ann Doody describes this common fear that absorbed novel readers would see themselves as fictional heroines in their own lives. The criticisms she describes partly derive from a desire to keep certain absorbed readers in their place, socially:

> It was always to be feared that the novel allowed both young men and young women too much scope for protest and discontent. That is, it is inconvenient to society for young persons or the poor to feel their individual life as myth. Such discontent was hastily labeled idle self-indulgence. *Bovarysme* is the result of much novel reading, as Moliere had foreseen. The proliferation of conduct books in the eighteenth century bears witness to social fears that females, influenced by the pernicious novel, might get above themselves, take themselves too seriously [280].

Fears of *bovarysme* result not only from a belief that absorbed readers, especially mentally and emotionally vulnerable ones, may read devalued cultural materials too imaginatively and may then enact the dangerous lessons of these materials in their real lives. *Bovarysme* takes this a step farther: it is the fear that such fluidity between fiction and reality may make such readers see themselves as heroes and heroines, may give them a self-esteem and feeling of power that they do not have in the everyday social structure. The idealized self-insertion of the Mary Sue is not only a metaphor for the act of absorbed reading: she is a metaphor for *bovarysme*. Female fan writers insert fictional, idealized versions of themselves into texts and turn themselves into fictional heroines. They are therefore reconceptualizing themselves as heroic, an act that is frequently described by critics as self-indulgent. A Mary Sue is both an indicator that the fan writer has read the text with intense imaginative absorption, and an opportunity for other fans to inhabit the character imaginatively through their own reading of the fanfiction. Mary Sues are therefore a site of female absorbed readers enabling other female absorbed readers to reinvent themselves as fictional heroines. She is a vector for *bovarysme*.

Fan critics take the idealization of Mary Sue characters to be warning signs of female fans' self-indulgent approach to the text, of their imaginative reinvention of themselves as heroines. Aesi's example of the usage of *Mary Sue* on *Urban Dictionary* figures the writing of a Mary Sue as an act of unpresentable self-indulgence: "That fic was ridiculous. I could overlook the atrocious grammar, but not such an obvious and annoying Mary Sue. What's the point of releasing a story to the unsuspecting public if it's only written for the masturbation of the author's ego?"

Likewise, Valis2 points out in an essay the role of transgressive wish-fulfillment in the condemnation of Mary Sues, which she contrasts with the form of self-insertion that occurs in the writing of any fictional character whatsoever. This "regular self-insertion," she asserts, "happens all the time in all writing, because you need some little bit of yourself to put in the clay to make it come to life." However, she believes that problems arise from "wish-fulfillment self-insertion." Valis2 claims that "wish-fulfillment is usually only satisfying to the one making the wish. To everyone else, it can be annoying because the character has so many unusual qualities and, more upsettingly, she warps the story until everything and everyone references her in some way." Not only does the Mary Sue change the canon characters that are beloved by the reader, but she aggrandizes herself in the process: she displays the female author's ego through the process of absorbed reading, which may allow this ego to bleed over from fantasy to fiction to real life. Those who are sensitive to this process of *bovarysme* may then find the character off-putting.

In the essay "Shameless Setteis[1] and Mary Sues" a fan named Jeanne talks about the phenomenon of *bovarysme*, though not under that name, and its connection to Mary Sues and their condemnation by modern western culture. Jeanne describes the "head stories" she always told herself at night before falling asleep: "I've been making up stories and acting them out in my head for as long as I can remember, which takes me at least back to age five. The settei at that point was that I was one of three red-haired identical triplets ... and our mother was the Queen of the Universe. Five years later I was one of a dozen girls living in a big old house with no adults in sight and a horse for each of us." In these stories, Jeanne and her female imaginary friends were important characters with interesting and heroic lives. This daydreaming both displays a *bovarysme* that allows Jeanne to see herself as a fictional heroine, and mirrors the imaginative play that Sheenagh Pugh describes as the first step in creating fanfiction. In fact, one *Tumblr* user, ilovecatz44, posts that she has also created such "head stories" as a brainstorming for fanfiction creation: "Does anyone else just lay in bed for an hour or so before they fall asleep and generate their own fanfictions? And they are super elaborate and you just sit and go through it and wasting precious sleeping time." (Reminding us that the creation of fanfiction is very similar to the creation of any kind of fiction, user naomideplume responds, "Careful that's how I wrote my first novel.")

However, Jeanne recognized from a young age that these head stories are not acceptable in public because they are too self-indulgent:

> Of course I always knew enough to keep these stories to myself. I figured other people told themselves *normal* stories, about dating neat guys and winning debating tournaments.... Out in the light of day head stories look embarrassingly childish and self-indulgent. Besides, they're just too personal. There's a high and unrestrained id content contained in them, as in one's more disturbing dreams, and like certain bathroom functions they're nothing a civilized person talks about in public. So I didn't talk about them.

Jeanne had been socialized to consider such *bovarysme* shameful: too self-indulgent, too personal, too embarrassing to be shared. Part of the reason for this may be that Jeanne was a girl: if she had been a boy, she would have found plenty of these "self-indulgent daydreams" widely shared and celebrated in books, film, and television.

Eventually Jeanne did find published stories that echoed the feminine *bovarysme* of her personal daydreams, but she did not find these stories in modern western literature. They were in Japanese *manga*, or comic books. Though such self-indulgent fictions were not acceptable to the western culture she was familiar with, they were accepted and enjoyed in Japanese culture: "There everyone was, having the same fantasies as me and putting them in print as if they were the most normal Cherry Ames[2] stuff in the world. Queen of the Universe? Check out Meiteru's Mom from *Galaxy Express 999*. Schoolgirl affairs and cabals? Swing on by *O-nii-sama e*."

What Jeanne concludes from this difference between modern western and Japanese literature is that the taboo against *bovarysme* is culturally dependent, not universal. In fact, she points out that the *bovarysme* and personal daydream content of literature has become less and less acceptable in western culture since the nineteenth century, and even in the last few decades:

> Our "young adult" books would never dare be so openly, innocently, and dangerously self-indulgent [as Japanese anime and manga].... It wasn't always thus in the west, which is why you've got oodles of homoerotic subtext in Huckleberry Finn and Classic Trek, and wallows of masochism in Elsie Dinsmore. Not any more.... Anderson's Little Match Girl got to die of cold in the street, Bronte's Jane Eyre got to be abused by her horrible family, you the reader got to cry your eyes out. Does anyone do that any more over here?

The sentimental literature that allowed absorbed readers of the nineteenth century to have strong emotional, "self-indulgent" absorbed experiences has now, Jeanne asserts, been pushed out of most of western literature: except fanfiction.

It is interesting that Jeanne describes masochistic fantasies as self-indulgent in the same way power fantasies are. This again applies to Mary Sues. Some Mary Sues are the result of power fantasies, but others are written as figures of pity rather than of admiration. Nscangal's definition of *Mary Sue* on *Urban Dictionary* identifies a number of types of Mary Sues, including "Warrior!Sues," "Mage!Sues," and "Punk!Sues." However, the list also includes "Victim!Sues" and "Misfit!Sues": "This includes all Sues who are supposedly geeks, nerds, misfits, etc. Usually, the Misfit!Sue doesn't start out as inhumanly beautiful, but winds up getting a makeover and finding out she had the potential to be a guy-magnet (or girl-magnet, depending on the genre) all along." Warrior!Sues and Mage!Sues could be called power fantasies. However, a number of others—Victim!Sues in particular—are tragic figures. Nonetheless, in all these cases the Mary Sue draws attention to herself in some way: she garners either the admiration of the canon characters, or their affection and care. While the Victim!Sue is physically weak, she does have emotional power over her romantic interest, and she is the center of his—and the reader's—attention. The tragic past of the Warrior!Sue makes her an object of the reader's and other characters' interest and sympathy; the Punk!Sue obtains sympathy for her "angst" and possibly redresses the situations that led to it; the Misfit!Sue starts out average and has all her wishes come true as she "becomes a star." In all of these cases, the Mary Sue character is the center of attention, whether that attention be of a sympathetic or admiring nature. Yet all of these different kinds of attention-seeking in the characters are seen as self-indulgent for the writer.

But whether power fantasy or masochism, Jeanne celebrates the self-indulgence in fanfiction: "I take heart from the apparently undying figure of the Mary Sue…. All-competent or all-wise, spunky ensign or serene survivor of hideous happenings, we still got 'em, and everyone in the story loves them unreservedly. And more power to them, say I." Mary Sues allow for a female *bovarysme* is that is widely condemned in modern western culture.

The Sexism of Bovarysme

One might expect the condemnation of *bovarysme* to be unisex: after all, Don Quixote, the original *bovaryste*, was a man, and was gently mocked by Cervantes' narrative. However, as Doody's discussion of *bovarysme* points out, these accusations of self-indulgence are often aimed at readers whom the culture has a particular reason to want to disempower. This is the reason that the term "Mary Sue" is applied primarily to female characters: it is part of a deep sexism in the criticisms of absorbed reading, which sees women's *bovarysme* as inconvenient to those who benefit from the patriarchal status quo.

A little critical thinking about the way fans discuss Mary Sues brings this sexism to the forefront: female characters are often condemned as Mary Sues for exhibiting characteristics that are taken as a matter of course in male characters. *TVTropes*' article "So You Want To: Avoid Writing a Mary Sue" especially censures the self-indulgence of Mary Sue authors in the section "Falling in Love (You, Not the Sue)." The article asserts that the problem with Mary Sues is that they steal the show, that "Mary Sues are fundamentally about authorial favoritism." It compares such favoritism to loving one of your children more than the others. The author concludes, "Writing good stories means giving everyone in the story their due attention and development." The problem is that this statement isn't actually true. Authors of original fiction always give their protagonists more time in the spotlight, more careful development, than other characters. However, while some fans may identify idealized main characters in canon as "Canon Sues," many of them are not censured as harshly as the Mary Sues in fanfiction. One of the reasons for this is the gender of Mary Sues versus the most common Canon Sues. Most fanfiction Mary Sues are female, and many of the most obvious Canon Sues are actually "Canon *Stus*": they are male.

Bacon-Smith compares the reception of Canon Stus to fanfiction Mary Sues, seeing the difference in their reception as an indicator of misogyny: "Other fans have noted that James Kirk is himself a Mary Sue, because he represents similarly exaggerated characteristics of strength, intelligence, charm, and adventurousness. They note that the soubriquet 'Mary Sue' may be a self-imposed sexism—she can't do that, she's a girl" (97).

One prominent example of a much-hated Gary-Stu/Marty-Stu (male Mary Sue) only serves to emphasize the power dynamics, if not the sexism, involved in the condemnation of *bovarysme*. One of the most vocally hated characters in *Star Trek: The Next Generation* is Wesley Crusher, a teenager whose brilliance leads Picard to make him an Ensign and allow him to serve on the Bridge. In a fan discussion on the website

Quora about Wesley's intense unpopularity, many of the commenters agree that he was specifically included to be a vessel for young men's absorbed viewing and *bovarysme*: "he was intended to be the character kids would relate to and want to be like" ("Why Does Everyone Hate").

The reason he was so hated seems to be that he was considered too brilliant for such a young character, and that viewers therefore often found him annoyingly unrealistic. Craig Weiland writes, "The *Enterprise* may be home to families, but that doesn't mean the bridge must serve as a day care" ("Why Does Everyone Hate"). It seems to have been generally, if vaguely, felt that, as a teenager, he was "getting above himself" by inhabiting this special position. Viviane Valvezan, in the same conversation, writes,

> He was a "snot-nosed kid" constantly one upping adults and being right all the time. I don't think it's people my age that dislike Wesley so much as older fans. As a kid who was exactly the same age as him during first run episodes, I felt more connected to what was happening on the show because there was someone I could (roughly) identify with interacting with my favorite characters and being a part of space exploration ["Why Does Everyone Hate"].

Wesley was hated, particularly by many older fans of *TNG*, because he was inverting the power dynamics of age. When comparing the criticisms of Wesley Crusher to the criticisms of Mary Sues, one cannot help concluding that our society feels that overachieving teenagers who show up adults and women who show up men are equally annoying.

Ladyloveandjustice on *Tumblr* has written a popular short essay on Mary Sues that points out the misogynist application of the term Mary Sue primarily to female characters:

> So, there's this girl. She's tragically orphaned and richer than anyone on the planet. Every guy she meets falls in love with her, but in between torrid romances she rejects them all because she is dedicated to what is Pure and Good. She has genius level intellect, Olympic-athelete [sic] level athletic ability and incredible good looks. She is consumed by terrible angst, but this only makes guys want her more. She has no superhuman abilities, yet she is more competent than her superhuman friends and defeats superhumans with ease. She has unshakably loyal friends and allies, despite the fact she treats them pretty badly. They fear and respect her, and defer to her orders. Everyone is obsessed with her[;] even her enemies are attracted to her. She can plan ahead for anything and she's generally right with any conclusion she makes. People who defy her are inevitably wrong.
> God, what a Mary Sue.
> I just described Batman.

The characteristics that are so widely condemned in Mary Sues are taken as a matter of course in male superheroes.

Likewise, a graphic that was frequently shared on *Facebook* shortly after *Star Wars Episode VII* hit the screens, with its revolutionary female hero Rey, contrasts how this idealized female character has been received by some members of the fandom with how similarly idealized male characters have been received:

> Luke was a crack shot and an awesome pilot and rescued a princess and became a powerful Jedi and *destroyed the Death Star with his eyes closed.* Han was a crack shot and an awesome pilot and a great mechanic and was multilingual and flew the coolest spaceship and *a princess fell in love with him.* Anakin was a crack shot and an awesome pilot and a great mechanic and married a queen and survived being hacked to pieces and became *the most feared Sith in the galaxy.* But sure let's talk about how Rey is a Mary Sue I guess [qtd. in Barner, "Found on *Facebook*"].

Male idealized characters that are available for male absorbed identification—Superman, Captain Kirk, John Carter, Hector and Achilles, King Arthur, Robin Hood—often go unidentified as Gary Stus. Consequently, they also go unstigmatized. It is female idealized characters who are usually seen as transgressive, especially in the particularly intensely absorptive genre of fanfiction. Western culture thereby encourages a sort of *bovarysme* in male absorbed readers, for whom critics have expressed less concern than the supposedly more impressionable and less rational and critical female absorbed readers. At the same time, critics strongly discourage *bovarysme* in women, attacking the Mary Sue character because she is such a strong metaphor for this *bovarysme*. Love of a male idealized character like King Arthur or Batman is acceptable—after all, look at how many awards and nominations the 1989 film *Batman* nabbed![3]—but love of a female idealized character like *Twilight*'s Bella Swan or the myriad Mary Sues of fanfiction is condemned.

It has to be said that while many fans have joined in the condemnation of Mary Sues, that is not to say that the misogyny of the term's application has been totally lost on the fan community. The sexist application of the term Mary Sue only to female characters has been a source of conflict in fandom from the beginning. Bacon-Smith notes that "in her 1980 commentary that accompanied the reprint of 'A Trekkie's Tale,'" Paula Smith found it necessary to explain that "her intent was never 'to put down all stories about aspiring females'" (qtd. in Bacon-Smith 96). Nonetheless, Edith Cantor writes, "in terms of their impact on those they affect those words [Mary Sue] have got to rank right up there with the Selective Service Act" (qtd. in Bacon-Smith 96).

Fans sometimes do inveigh against the sexism involved in criticizing Mary Sues: the second most popular definition of *Mary Sue* on *Urban Dictionary* reads,

> A sexist term used to enforce the misogynistic ideals that female characters/authors shouldn't be allowed to fantasize or write anything along the lines of wish fulfillment. Its misogynistic qualities are exemplified in many ways, most notably being the fact that it's not a term dominated by the male counterpart despite existing in a patriarchal society, as well as the fact that the male counterpart is largely undecided upon in name and also undefined (see urban dictionary's Gary Stu entry which has no definition but to say "A Male Mary Sue," and the Marty-Stu entry which involves the "Mary Sue" definition to define it) [Urmamason].

Fans are increasingly recognizing the use of "Mary Sue" as a derogatory term to be a form of sexism within fandom.

Inverting Roles

The strong taste taboos against women's *bovarysme*, their seeing themselves as fictional heroines, may be partly because of the stereotypical connection of absorbed reading with women. Women, the thinking seems to go, are particularly given to absorbed reading and, because of their supposedly emotional natures, are more vulnerable to the dangers of that reading practice than are the more intellectual and critical male readers. Of course, another explanation for the focus on female Mary Sues rather than male Gary Stus could be that our culture values selflessness, caring, and humility in women, and still sees women's desire to personally excel as particularly self-centered and ungenerous, while men are expected to strive for excellence, success, and notoriety in their careers. Men are encouraged to be heroes and to make the most of their accomplishments; women are encouraged to encourage men. And while this misogynist critical focus on female heroes is problematic in any genre, it is particularly disturbing that the term itself arose from fanfiction, as fanfiction is predominantly written and consumed by women. The castigation of Mary Sues in fanfiction too often represents women discouraging other women from seeing themselves as potential heroines. In the criticism of *bovarysme*, our culture criticizes women for acting with the self-empowerment expected of men.

We can see this sexist social control over women and their *bovarysme* operating in George Eliot's 1883 essay "Silly Novels by Lady Novelists." Eliot describes the heroines of these novels in terms of their idealism, which makes them sound much like modern Mary Sues: "Her eyes and her wit are both dazzling; her nose and her morals are alike free from any tendency to irregularity; she has a superb *contralto* and a superb intellect; she is perfectly well dressed and perfectly religious; she dances like a sylph, and reads the Bible in the original tongues.... She is the ideal woman in feelings, faculties, and flounces" (178–79).

Eliot indicates that the female creators of these characters are showing off by writing such idealized heroines. She frequently describes the writers as being represented by their characters: for example, while mocking the excessive erudition of these heroines, Eliot observes, "Greek and Hebrew are mere play to a heroine; Sanscrit is no more than *a b c* to her; and she can talk with perfect correctness in any language, except English. She is a polking polyglot, a Creuzer in crinoline.... There can be no difficulty in conceiving the depth of the heroine's erudition when that of the authoress is so evident" (181–82).

Like Valis2, Eliot describes in critical terms how these authors' idealized heroines take over the spotlight, relegating male characters to mere supporters: "The men play a very subordinate part by her side. You are consoled now and then by a hint that they have [business] affairs, which keeps you in mind that the working-day business of the world is somehow being carried on, but ostensibly the final cause of their existence is that they may accompany the heroine on her 'starring' expedition through life."

Interesting to consider in this particular criticism is the fact that female characters frequently play this negligible and supporting role to male characters in western literature, but it is rare that anyone calls such texts "silly novels by male novelists." The frequency with which texts contain women only as supporting characters for their male counterparts is indicated by the Bechdel Test for films. This test, originally suggested by cartoonist Allison Bechdel in 1985, contains three criteria by which one can tell if a film allocates "a bare minimum of depth" to its female characters (Hickey). The film must have (1) at least two named female characters who (2) speak to one another (3) about something other than a man.

Walt Hickey, writer for *FiveThirtyEightLife*, did a study in which he tested a large number of films to see if they passed the Bechdel test and whether that affected their box office earnings. Hickey observes, "You'd be hard pressed to think of a single film that doesn't have a scene where two men have a conversation that isn't about a woman. Plots need to advance, after all. But it's remarkable how many iconic films disastrously fail the Bechdel test.... In a larger sample of 1,794 movies released from 1970 to 2013, we found that only half had at least one scene in which women talked to each other about something other than a man." Eliot and fan critics criticize female characters for taking the spotlight away from male (canon) characters because they take this as a sign of these female characters—and therefore their self-inserting, absorbed female authors—getting above themselves. In fact, these female characters are being condemned merely for inverting the gender dynamics western culture is used to seeing in fictional narratives.

An example of this gender role inversion can be seen in the 2016 remake of *Ghostbusters*. Unlike the original 1984 film, in which all four ghostbusters were men, the 2016 remake features four female ghostbusters. The only male "hero" is their gorgeous but dimwitted secretary Kevin, whose only real role in the film besides eye-candy and comic relief is to be possessed by the villain—and then saved by the heroines. The gender inversion involved in this was puzzling to some viewers because it is so uncommon to see women in all the heroic roles and a man being rescued. One *Tumblr* user, Mae, described a conversation with a young man at the theater after the film:

> We were both enthusiastic about the film and its quality, but suddenly he stopped and frowned.
> "I'm just not sure about Kevin," he said in confusion. "He's kind of pointless, isn't he? Why did they need a character like that? I've never seen anything like it before…"
> I gaped at him briefly. "Haven't you ever heard about the Dumb Blonde Trope?"
> He wrinkled his nose. "Yeah, but isn't that typically for…" His eyes got wide, and he looked at me in absolute terror. "Oh."
> "Oh" is right, buddy [Mae].

Movie-goers are so used to seeing men as heroes and women as supporting characters that when the gender dynamics are inverted, they may be puzzled, like this young man, or even angered, like George Eliot was.

The complaints against narratives like those Eliot castigates that put women in the spotlight may also be related to a phenomenon in which women are perceived as talking more than men when they are actually having an equal say. Sady Doyle points out in her article "The 'Feminized Society' Myth" that many of us are more used to seeing and hearing men than women, which may lead people to overestimate the number or talkativeness of women in any given group. For instance, she quotes Geena

Davis of the Institute for Gender in Media, who points out that if only seventeen percent of any group is made of up women, "the men in the group think it's 50–50.... And if there's 33 percent women, the men perceive that as there being more women in the room than men."

Doyle also states that multiple studies have shown this overestimation of women's presence and power in a number of situations:

> In one study on gender parity in the workforce, ... it was found that men "consistently perceive more gender parity" in their workplaces than women do. For example, when asked whether their workplaces recruited the same number of men and women, 72 percent of male managers answered "yes." Only 42 percent of female managers agreed. And, while there's a persistent stereotype that women are the more talkative gender, women actually tend to talk less than men in classroom discussions, professional contexts and even romantic relationships; one study found that a mixed-gender group needed to be between 60 and 80 percent female before women and men occupied equal time in the conversation.... "[In] seminars and debates, when women and men are deliberately given an equal amount of the highly valued talking time, there is often a perception that [women] are getting more than their fair share."

Because readers and film audiences are used to seeing men taking starring roles, they may be reacting more strongly when women take those same roles. And because these audiences are more used to seeing men take more attention, and more of the script, for themselves, female protagonists may be perceived as taking far too much attention and dialogue when the tables are turned.

A final part of the anger, particularly of men, at the appearance of women as the main characters in formerly male-centric franchises like *Ghostbusters* and *Star Wars*, is the way that this focus on women relegates men to the background. *Tumblr* user princessamericachavez discusses this phenomenon in her essay post "On *Star Wars*, Representation and Straight White Males":

> Left without lead characters to identify with, minorities ... had to desperately search for themselves in background characters. A big part of the fandom consists of women, people of color, queer or with disabilities, latching on to the few characters they could find representation in. They get attached to this [sic] characters, love them like part of their own family and friends, because they provide something that is so rare to them in mass media: a voice.
> One can only imagine what it is like to be a straight white male. To go to the movies, enjoy the story fully, and then leave without the necessity to form any kind of emotional attachment to the characters. Why would they? They will find themselves perfectly represented all over again in the next movie they decide to watch, whichever it might be, and the next one, and the next one. Representation to them is not a luxury, it's a given right.

Seeing this, it's no wonder how confused and scared straight white males are, now that they can't find themselves leading the charge of the new *Star Wars* franchise. Two movies in a row they've had to sit on that theater and face the minority's reality, facing a situation that is so unlike anything their psyche is used to they react like wounded animals, with a primal fear of being erased from a narrative they are sure to own.

The backlash against women's *bovarysme*, as demonstrated in narratives that focus on heroic women rather than heroic men, is partly the result of men finding their world turned upside-down, and themselves placed in the position that minority fans have so long held. It is a reaction of fear and anger to an unexpected loss of privilege. Hatred of female protagonists, of Mary Sues, is the result of fears about changes to the male-dominated gender hierarchy.

Eliot, like many other feminists before and after her, argues against the idealized female characters created by female writers by claiming that they set back the goal of female education by making men believe that women are incapable of truly serious thought. Eliot prefers, instead, that a woman "of true culture, whose mind had absorbed her knowledge instead of being absorbed by it" should present her ideas in debate with men with more humility, enacting the more feminine role of comforting her male interlocutors emotionally: "She does not write books to confound philosophers, perhaps because she is able to write books that delight them. In conversation she is the least formidable of women, because she understands you, without wanting to make you aware that you *can't* understand her. She does not give you information, which is the raw material of culture—she gives you sympathy, which is its subtlest essence." In short, Eliot believes that the female novelists who write the novels she inveighs against have gotten above themselves and above their proper social role of comforting and delighting men, and she would prefer a woman who "does not make [her education] a pedestal from which she flatters herself that she commands a complete view of men and things, but makes it a point of observation from which to form a right estimate of herself." Eliot condemns these novels for their *bovarysme*: the way they cause women to "get above themselves."

The accepted status of Gary Stus and the underrepresentation of Mary Sues in modern media can also be seen in discussions of the 2015 film *Jupiter Ascending*, which is akin to Jeanne's "head stories" and is therefore associated with women's *bovarysme*. Teresa Jusino writes, "We ... loved that incredibly bad movie way too much, and with good reason.

It was all of our fan-fics brought to life." *Tumblr* user Sashayed points out that the care that was taken to cater to women's tastes and women's *bovarysme* in this film is sadly rare in comparison to the care taken to cater to men's tastes in many others: "'Is this how straight dudes feel at the movies all the time????' I hissed at daeontherun SEVERAL times during this movie. 'Like someone carefully noted down your early pubescent fantasies and then threw 100 MILLION DOLLARS at them?'" Mary Sue stories like *Jupiter Rising* are criticized for doing for women what literature has historically always done for men.

Concern or Control?

Criticisms of *bovarysme* are clearly not about protecting absorbed readers from the folly of confusing fiction with reality. Just as in the question of absorbed reading, which is encouraged in young children and discouraged in teenage or adult women, *bovarysme* is encouraged and idealized in children, who would supposedly be the most mentally vulnerable readers. One prominent example appears in *A Little Princess* by Frances Hodgson Burnett. In this famous children's novel, the young Sara Crewe, who loses her father and her fortune and is forced to become a servant for a cruel mistress, fuels her imagination with her reading and pretends that she is a prisoner in the Bastille or a princess in disguise. This *bovarysme* is lauded by the book, not only for the way it helps Sara bear her terrible situation, but for the way it influences her behavior, urging her to be kind and generous to the less fortunate, like a princess would. The book therefore encourages *bovarysme* in young girls, the same *bovarysme* they are criticized for as they age.

Even here, however, the concern with the genres Sara takes as her guides is apparent. In Hodgson Burnett's original serial, "Sara Crewe: or, What Happened at Miss Minchin's," Sara reads everything she can get her hands on: not only philosophy and history, but "feminine" popular literature.

> She liked romances and history and poetry; she would read anything. There was a sentimental housemaid in the establishment who bought the weekly penny papers, and subscribed to a circulating library, from which she got greasy volumes containing stories of marquises and dukes who invariably fell in love with orange-girls and gypsies and servant-maids, and made them the proud brides of coronets; and Sara often did parts of this maid's work so that she might earn the privilege of reading these romantic histories [101].

Though the valorization of Sara's reading, imagining, and *bovarysme* remains in the later novel, this reference to cheap, sentimental, and romantic literature has been excised. A little girl can pretend to be a princess from a ("masculine") history book because it will make her decorous, calm, noble, generous, and docile. But she cannot pretend to be an attractive young woman from the lower classes who has the gall to marry a nobleman, as described in supposedly lower-class, feminine genres of literature. Even at this young age, Sara's *bovarysme* must come from genres that will encourage her to play her properly assigned social and gender role.

Likewise, while *bovarysme* is encouraged in young children—and in Sara is seen as a sign of her maturity, intelligence, resilience, and creativity—it is discouraged in teenagers and adults as immature, reality-denying, and a sign of lack of resilience or intelligence. Sara Crewe, a little girl who quietly pretends to be a victimized but noble princess, is discovered by her father's friend and returned to a life of luxury. If this character were a teenager or an adult woman instead of a child, this story of riches to rags to riches would probably be labeled one of those same "greasy volumes" that were condemned for teaching women to expect an extraordinary life. While the culture encourages *bovarysme* explicitly in children and implicitly in adult men, it quashes it ruthlessly in teenage girls and in adult women.

Complaints about Mary Sues as self-indulgent, as a marker of *bovarysme*, and as a sign of female writers' overinflated egos are sexist and are based on an unspoken cultural code that allows and even encourages men to engage in absorbed reading and to create and become absorbed in unrealistically heroic male characters, but condemns women for doing the same. This code is reinforced by the large number of narratives on paper, television, and film that revolve around male heroes, and the comparatively small number that revolve around female heroes. When such fictional heroines do appear, the narratives that depict them are often strongly censured by the culture or automatically relegated to a position in the less prestigious popular fiction genres, like romance and fanfiction. Fanfiction is filled with Mary Sues, with the results of female fans' *bovarysme*, and the genre's reputation suffers from the condemnation of this female literary empowerment. Fans' criticisms of one another's Mary Sue characters on these grounds indicate that they have internalized misogynist criticisms of fanfiction rather than combating them head-on. In other words, friends *should* let friends write Mary Sues.

3

Story Sue-icide

Fanfiction is closely associated with, and even based on, absorbed reading. Therefore, fanfiction as a genre, and Mary Sue stories in particular, suffer from negative stereotypes about absorbed reading and readers. Fanfiction writers frequently attempt to distance themselves from Mary Sue stories in order to avoid these stereotypes. However, this often leaves them in a self-contradictory position: embracing absorbed, escapist reading in the creation of fanfiction itself and eschewing it in its association with Mary Sue characters. Boz4pm's "Don't Panic!" and the BBC miniseries *Lost in Austen* both find themselves in this self-contradictory position.

"Don't Panic!" tries to distance itself from Mary Sue stories by depicting their opposing characteristics—realism, unhappiness, powerlessness—in the main character Penny, but ends by creating a story that some would find too unhappy and unrealistic and that its own main character wouldn't find enjoyable. Likewise, *Lost in Austen* depicts a fan whose absorbed, escapist reading lands her in trouble: between celebrating and mocking escapist reading, the miniseries is ultimately unable to answer whether absorbed, escapist reading is beneficial or dangerous, or even whether its own main character finds her happy ending.

"Don't Panic!"

When fanfiction readers and writers unquestioningly accept the host of negative stereotypes under which absorbed reading and Mary Sues suffer, they frequently find themselves in self-contradictory positions, questioning their own project of creating fanfiction in the first place and whether their work can be pleasurable and still be of a culturally acceptable literary quality. Fanfictions can end up promoting pleasure and escapism in reading while still questioning the basis of that pleasure. One such fanfiction series consists of "Don't Panic!" and its sequel "Okay, NOW Panic!" by Boz4pm.

These fanfictions are in the *Lord of the Rings* fandom and deal with the problem of Mary Sues as self-indulgent self-inserts. The works try to distance themselves from the charges of self-indulgence and Mary-Sueism through an emphasis on realism and the main character's suffering. However, by relating suffering with realism and changes to the canon with unrealizable fantasy, this fanfiction ultimately becomes self-defeating in its attempt to be both realistic and enjoyably escapist.

"Don't Panic!" begins with an average English 23-year-old Tolkien fan named Penny Baker waking up in an unknown wilderness, alone and in her pajamas. She encounters a strange man who speaks no English and dresses like a medieval reenactor. Eventually, Penny comes to realize that she has traveled back some six thousand years to Tolkien's fictional Middle-earth, and is being escorted to the elven realm of Rivendell by the ranger Halbarad.

Penny has a dreadful time adjusting to Middle-earth's medieval culture and to the fictional people, like elves, that she meets there. She struggles particularly with the fact that she knows what will happen to many of the people she meets: the main characters of Tolkien's *Lord of the Rings*. "Don't Panic!" follows Penny's journey to Rivendell and her struggle to adjust to her new life—particularly when her friend Halbarad goes off to war, since Penny knows from the books that he will be killed in battle. The sequel, "Okay, NOW Panic!," picks up after the war, as Penny travels with the elves through Middle-earth to Gondor. There she meets Halbarad's surviving sons, Halladan and Arvain. She discovers that Halladan is suffering from posttraumatic stress caused by his experiences in battle, and she helps him to cope as he helps her to mourn the loss of her family back in her own time. Eventually the two fall in love and marry.

Realism vs. Mary Sues

These fanfictions were written in response to a post by Viv on the *Open Scrolls Archive*:

> Stuck (Really) in Middle-earth—We've read them before: 21st c. gal is zatted back to Middle-earth. But what would it really be like for a modern person to find herself

(or himself) in Middle-earth? Fic should tackle such issues as getting lost, not having appropriate survival skills, craving Twinkies and other processed-food treats, having no air conditioning, being surprised by the plumbing (or lack of it) situation, experiencing uncomfortable allergies to dragon scales, etc. The intrepid time-traveller could also answer, once and for all, those niggling questions (do elves wear underwear?) and set the record straight [qtd. in "Don't Panic!" Ch 1].

The prompt does not mention Mary Sues directly. However, as discussed earlier, the very trope of a girl being "zatted" back to Middle-earth is clearly perceived as being a Mary Sue plotline. Both on *Stories of Arda* and on *FanFiction.Net*, Boz4pm feels the need to specify in the description of the fic that it is "NOT a Mary-Sue."

Unlike *FanFiction.Net*, *Stories of Arda* is a privately run fansite that has to approve fanfics for quality and content before they are posted: guidelines warn that the site does not accept slash or femslash, real person fic, crossovers, Mystery Science Theater-style story commenting, "general silliness," male pregnancy fics, stories with too many writing errors, plotless fics, or parodies ("Guidelines for Authors"). The guidelines also specifically disallow "modern character insertion—modern day people fall into Middle-earth" and "Mary-Sue's [sic]." The guidelines warn, "OFC's [Original Female Characters], even in romances with canon characters, are not automatically Mary-Sue's [sic]. But if she joins the Fellowship or requires you to seriously violate canon, steals lines from canon characters or changes the course of the story ... she is more than likely a Mary Sue. No Mary Sue parodies either, please."

Because of these strict rules, "Don't Panic!" is prefaced on this site with a notice that the story was posted at the request of the site owner. The first chapter includes this message in the author's notes:

> Note from Nilmandra, site owner: "I invited Boz to post her stor[ies] 'Don't Panic!' and 'Okay, NOW Panic,' which were written in response to a challenge for what might really have happened had a modern day person fallen into Middle-earth. This is the quintessential story for me of the problems such a person would face, and perhaps how Middle-earth would have seen her. Those familiar with our guidelines will know we do not accept this genre of story—I made this exception and asked her to post. Please note that the site guidelines have not changed for existing authors or new submissions" [qtd. in Chapter 1, *Stories of Arda*].

All these interactions with the site guidelines indicate that "modern person in Middle-earth" stories are held to be closely related to Mary Sues, and consequently seen as a sign of lack of realism and poor writing, to be avoided. Nonetheless, this particular fanfiction was still considered worthy of being posted on *Stories of Arda*. In fact, Nilmandra seems to be implying that Penny is an anti–Sue, thus demonstrating to fans what would realistically happen to a modern person in Middle-earth. The implication is that Mary Sue stories are overly idealized in many ways, not just in the characteristics of the heroine: they are seen as self-indulgently unrealistic. "Don't Panic!" is meant to "set the record straight" by bringing realism to this fanfiction premise.

Boz4pm also specifically states that avoiding writing a Mary Sue is one of her goals in the story. In the author's notes in chapter 17 on *FanFiction.Net*, Boz4pm replies to reviewers' questions about whether or not Penny will be joining the Fellowship during her sojourn in Middle-earth:

> I wanted to add that Penny won't join the Fellowship not simply, or even primarily, because that would make her Sue-ish. If I could think of a genuine reason why she WOULD go with them then she would because, frankly, it would be interesting to see it all through her eyes. But there is no earthly reason why she would. Yes, it would make a good story but the whole point of this fic was *realism*.... Sorry, guys. *smiles apologetically* It's realism first with anti–Mary-Sue a very close second. Or at least that's what I am trying to achieve. Hope I am getting somewhere near both [Chapter 17, *FanFiction.Net*].

The two concepts of unrealism and Mary Sues are so closely related that Boz4pm seems to have taken the challenge for "realism" as also including the challenge not to write a Mary Sue.

Having been set up in the author's notes at the beginning of the story as an anti–Mary-Sue story, "Don't Panic!" begins with a description of what Boz4pm sees as the typical Mary Sue, the stereotype she will be writing against. The story opens with Penny dreaming about a Mary Sue named Roxana, who wakes up in a place she knows instantly to be Middle-earth:

> No, she was not dreaming: she was really here. Here, in Middle Earth, by some wonderful miracle. This was her destiny. Aged fourteen and with perfect skin, teeth and nose, she knew she was meant to be here. Her pointy ears had always meant she was picked on at school but here things would be different. She would fall in love with Legolas and the entire Fellowship would fall in love with her. She would save Boromir, warn them about the Balrog, perhaps persuade Theoden not to fight and die in battle.

Roxana is approached by Aragorn, Legolas, and Gimli, whom she addresses like old friends and flirts with, identifying herself as "Elrond's long lost niece." The three Tolkien characters come to a decision and Aragorn takes action: "He drew his sword. 'Die, Oh Mary-Sue, spawn of Morgoth!' Roxanna's head flew several yards before it rolled into a hollow. There was a snort of laughter from Penny as she turned over in her sleep. Yes, this was a very good dream" (Chapter 1).

This passage establishes a number of things. Firstly, it indicates the writer's, or at least the main character's, attitude toward Mary Sues: they are "spawns of Morgoth" (essentially Satan) and deserving of death. When Roxanna is beheaded, Penny laughs. By placing this Mary Sue example at the beginning of "Don't Panic!," Boz4pm highlights the contrast between Mary Sues and their stories and her own Penny Baker and her unusual journey. She is distancing Penny from Sues like Roxana.

Secondly, the passage provides a guideline to the characteristics of a Mary Sue story, the tropes that Boz4pm is working against. As the exact definition of *Mary Sue* is notoriously vague and idiosyncratic, it is helpful to have this example. The theme that runs through Boz4pm's depiction of the typical Mary Sue is idealism, both of the heroine and of her adventures. According to Roxana's expectations, being a modern Mary Sue dropped into Middle-earth is a jaunt in the park. Boz4pm takes care that Penny's experience will not be so idealized and self-indulgent, and therefore "unrealistic."

In order to avoid the lack of realism and the emotional overindulgence Boz4pm and other fans associate with Mary Sue stories, Boz puts Penny through an emotional hell. The emotions—or "feels"—produced by consuming fiction is very important in fandom and fanfiction: yet another characteristic of the genre that associates it with sentimental absorbed reading. One fan notes, "Does anyone else ever think about how traditional fiction is categorised by plot/setting (romance, crime, thriller, fantasy) but fanfiction is categorised by the emotions it's meant to give you (hurt/comfort, fluff, angst, smut)?" (Char). If Mary Sue stories are criticized for being idealized and therefore self-indulgent, then an author trying to avoid such criticisms may give the potential vessel for that self-indulgent wish-fulfilment a long string of terrible and uncomfortable experiences, which the reader might vicariously share. The absorbed reading experience is therefore believed to be far less self-indulgent for the reader.

Consequently, in "Don't Panic!," Boz4pm tries to perform a difficult balancing act between humor and light on one side and the excision of self-indulgent Mary-Sueism on the other. While Roxana expects nothing but delight from her visit to Middle-earth, Boz4PM describes Penny in terrible situations: in Middle-earth she must deal with a language barrier (the people of Middle-earth do not, as in the films and the Roxana example, speak English), Medieval sanitation, dreadful homesickness, the lack of modern medical technology, and more. The author takes every opportunity to keep accusations of self-indulgence at arm's length.

Unlike Roxana, who immediately recognizes her surroundings, identifies that she is in Middle-earth, and is thrilled to be there, Penny awakens in Middle-earth with no idea where she is or how she got there. It is some time before she realizes that her environment is meant to be Middle-earth and even longer before she realizes it's real rather than some *Candid Camera* set. When she does realize where she is, she believes for a time that she has gone insane, but ultimately cannot deny the terrifying reality of her situation: six thousand years in the past with a host of people who were meant to be fictional. At one point she counsels herself,

> She needed to just NOT think about the questions or implications of it all for a while. She just...
> What did she "just" need to do? Enjoy it? Hah! That was a laugh. Tolkien nut finally in Middle Earth yet too freaked out to enjoy it? Of course! How COULD she? It was all too weird. Too real. Too bloody terrifying.
> She thought of all those Mary Sue fics she had enjoyed loathing all these years. She chuckled. She'd like to see some fourteen year-old Orli[1] fancier cope with THIS lot. Could ANYONE cope with it? She seriously doubted it. SHE couldn't, that was for damn sure! [Chapter 10].

Boz4pm implies that part of the reason Mary Sue stories are unrealistic is because going to Middle-earth would not be an enjoyable experience: it would be terrifying, as it is for Penny.

Along with avoiding self-indulgence in the idealism of the Mary Sue's experiences, Boz4pm avoids it in the idealism of the Mary Sue character herself: she eschews each of the Mary Sue characteristics in the opening passage. The 14-year-old "Roxana" has an appropriately unusual name, a characteristic often identified in Mary Sues, while Penny Baker, at the more mature age of twenty-three, has a very common English name. Penny is described as merely passable in looks rather than having "perfect" features—in fact, the inhabitants of Middle-earth find her strange-looking, with hair considerably shorter than usual for their medieval culture. Penny is not an elf, like the pointy-eared Roxana, who recognizes main characters immediately and speaks to them like old friends, flirting with them and identifying herself as a person of social importance in Middle-earth: Elrond's long-lost niece. Instead, Penny is a human, who feels terribly outclassed by the noble Dúnedain (Men of the North) and the gorgeous elves around her. Boz4pm makes clear that flirting with or falling in love with any of the main characters, such as Aragorn or Legolas, would be madness, considering Penny is only a passably attractive mortal with no noble blood or social standing in Middle-earth culture.

Roxana also identifies Elrond as looking like Hugo Weaving, the actor who plays the character in the Peter Jackson movie. We know, therefore, that Boz4pm sees authors of Mary Sues as turning to the film adaptations for information about Middle-earth rather than the books. Some Tolkien purists and members of the fandom would consider this to demonstrate a lack of knowledge about or appreciation and respect for the canon. In contrast, "Don't Panic!" is clearly based on the details of the books. Here, the books are equated with realism, in contrast with the seemingly less canonical film adaptations.

Roxana knows that she is destined to fall in love with Legolas. *Lord of the Rings* fanfiction boomed in the wake of the release of the Peter Jackson film adaptations, in which the drool-worthy Orlando Bloom played Legolas. Consequently, Legolas became the most popular love interest in *Lord of the Rings* fanfic, a trope so common that there is term for Legolas romances: *Legomances*. Boz4pm is careful to subvert this trope. Penny does have a romance, but it is with a character Boz4pm invents for the story: Halladan, the son of Halbarad, who is himself both mortal and only a secondary canon character. The fic indicates strongly that Penny feels outclassed even by him. In all of these anti-Sue tactics, Boz4pm tries to eschew Mary-Sueish self-indulgence by making Penny's experience more realistic than Roxana's—and consequently, more uncomfortable, both for Penny and potentially for the absorbed reader. Though she may not be discouraging absorbed reading, Boz4pm does seem to be trying to make that reading more aesthetically acceptable by making it less self-indulgent.

Realism vs. Pleasure

As we can see in the contrasts between Roxana and Penny, if writing Mary Sues is self-indulgent "masturbation of the author's ego," a way for the reader to enjoy an experience that in real life would be terrifying, then an anti–Mary Sue reintroduces that terror and avoids self-indulgence. However, the very realism that "Don't Panic!" strives for seems to contradict the purpose of the fanfiction. In this fic, Boz4pm depicts reading as having two major functions: education and enjoyment/escape. Penny reads to learn the history and languages of Middle-earth. She also reads because she is such a fan of Tolkien's legendarium and enjoys immersing herself in beloved stories. On her return to the north in "Okay, NOW Panic!," Penny uses reading for the stated purpose of escaping from her own troubles:

> Meanwhile Penny got into bed with a lamp beside her and read some of her *Tuor*, allowing the story to transport her away from everything else trying to crowd in on her mind.
> If she had stopped to think about it, she would have noted the irony of how she was actually trying to escape the reality of something that previously would have been the very fantasy she would have escaped into.
> All very strange [Chapter 46].

The language Boz4pm uses here to describe Penny's pleasure reading—"transport her away"—indicates the escape from reality that results from absorption: often figured, as in Donaldson's poem, as traveling into the narrative. This is precisely what Penny herself has done with *Lord of the Rings*: she has traveled into the world of the narrative. Now, however, her experiences there are so uncomfortable that she is trying to travel out of it again, if only in her imagination.

It is appropriate that Penny Baker, the *Lord of the Rings* fan, should put so much emphasis on absorbed reading for pleasure and escape. Though the purposes of reading are many and varied, internet fanfiction itself is written primarily for the pleasure of the author and the readers. It is not particularly educational; it does not and cannot, for legal reasons, make money; and it does not raise one's social standing outside of fandom to quote fanfiction (quite the opposite, in fact). Fanfiction is therefore created and consumed primarily for pleasure: other benefits, such as the formation of fan communities around the stories, derive from this purpose. Fans come together around fanfictions because they all recognize that they are enjoying the story together, that they are all receiving pleasure from reading or writing it. Writer Emma Lord explains, "As a fan fiction author.... I can bet you on your life that none of us ... ever writes fan fiction with the intent of it becoming wildly profitable. We write because we love it. We write because we *must*. I think a huge part of what makes fan fiction so singularly special is that there is no ambition in it, only passion."

Incidentally, this is another characteristic of fanfiction that separates it in some people's minds from "great literature." In the academy, scholars write frequently about authors' intellectual reasons for writing fiction—to promulgate political opinions, for instance, or aesthetic philosophies—but very rarely discuss authors' emotional motivations. Scholars hardly ever seem to talk about the pleasure of creating and consuming literature, or its emotional effects on the audience, considering such pleasure to be too idiosyncratic to be analyzed. However, they seem to have no trouble discussing the equally idiosyncratic *thought* processes they believe these texts prompt in readers. Rational thought is thus established as the realm of academia and therefore the "great literature" it studies, while more emotional reactions like pleasure, escapism, and masochism are relegated to popular literature. The *Stanford Encyclopedia of Philosophy* notes, "Even to suggest, in the recent climate, that an artwork might be good because it is pleasurable, as opposed to cognitively, morally or politically beneficial, is to court derision" ("Aesthetic Judgment").

While it is true that there are surely many intellectual reasons that fans write fanfiction, they also tend to describe emotional reasons as being paramount: even the most thought-provoking changes fans make to the canon are often undertaken because they enjoy them. They want to introduce new political paradigms into the canon because it increases their pleasure in the story. They want involve themselves in the world-building of the canon because of the creative high it produces. They want to include erotic scenes with hot guys because ... why not? In fans' discussions of their work, fanfiction, like much of the absorbed reading that instigates it, is often depicted as being primarily about pleasure, in all its myriad forms.

In this story, Penny's reading (when it is not for education) is also for pleasure. But she herself states that too much reality in one's absorbed reading can rob it of its pleasure and escapism: can hinder the reader's attempts at absorption. She finds that the Tolkien stories she once used for that purpose are no longer adequate to the task now that she knows they are true stories:

> For a good half hour, then, Penny valiantly attempted to lose herself once more in the tale of Tuor, but her mind kept returning to the fact that both Galadriel and Celeborn had lived through those times, as well as a few other elves travelling with them. Glorfindel had known Tuor personally, of course, and indeed it was when she came to a paragraph describing Glorfindel that she felt that really what she was doing was no escape at all ["Okay, NOW Panic!" Chapter 46].

Once fiction becomes reality, Penny posits, it loses its value as escapism, and therefore some of its ability to bring pleasure and comfort to the absorbed reader.

By the same token, the depressing "realism" of Boz4pm's own story may ruin its potential for escapist pleasure reading. One survey conducted by the podcast *Fansplaining* has studied fan preferences for various emotional tones in fanfiction. Flourish Kink notes that there are clear preferences for certain tones over others:

> Fans prefer fluff to other types of fic. But angst (dramatic stories where characters have a wide range of emotions, including … angsty ones) comes in a close second. PWP stands for "plot, what plot?" or "porn without plot," and only comes in third…. There's a big drop-off between PWP and the final two fic tones. Crack is wilfully silly fanfic, stories that are intentionally ridiculous. (Parody and crack, similar types of story, both received many "Meh" votes.) But the least liked tone by far was darkfic—stories where everyone is miserable and there's nothing redeeming in the world. Not too surprising when you think about how many fanfiction readers say they enjoy fic as an escape from their everyday lives.

Flourish Kink concludes that while fans may enjoy some angsty drama in their fic, they tend to prefer stories that have the redeeming grace of a happy ending to works like darkfic that preclude those happy endings. If the drama becomes too dark or all-encompassing, many fans are turned off by the story: Flourish Kink notes, "one of the most-hated themes in fanfic is major character death, which usually prevents a happily-ever-after, and stories about negative events and situations (like rape, incest, eating disorders, and bullying) are also widely noped-out-of." It seems that most fans prefer that the angst of a story be limited, as well as balanced with and resolved by a happy ending.

By trying to avoid the supposed unrealism of self-indulgent and happy Mary Sue stories, "Don't Panic!" becomes a rather dark story that may not please these pleasure readers. The final chapter in particular is pretty pessimistic. Though Penny marries the man she loves and finds a home with the Dúnedain, there is good reason to doubt her ultimate happiness. Boz4pm makes sure to mention that Penny continues to suffer from homesickness and her husband Halladan from post-traumatic stress. A number of Penny's good friends among the elves depart Middle-earth forever, leaving her devastated. She nearly dies in childbirth, and Boz4pm relates, "Penny and Halladan had three children survive into adulthood: two sons and a girl. Two others, a boy and a girl, died in infancy, a fact that, for all she knew it was common enough in such a time, understandably distressed Penny greatly" ("Okay, NOW Panic!" Chapter 60). Boz4pm points out that true realism means tragedy.

Particularly alarming is Boz4pm's assertion that they were not an entirely happy couple:

> It would be wrong to say Halladan and Penny lived "happily ever after." They were happy enough for most of the time, it is true, but there were inevitably moments when the clash of cultures caused problems.... Thus there were inevitably times when he wondered why he had married a woman so different from his own kind.... On the whole, though, they rubbed along tolerably well—he with his gammy leg which would seize up sometimes in winter and her with her gradually improving culinary skills and steep learning curve for everything else. They certainly loved each other, for all their flaws, faults and problems [Chapter 60].

This is very tepid as happy endings go, and hedged around with "realistic" unhappiness and dissatisfaction. It returns the triumphant love story between Penny and Halladan to the somewhat depressing realism that was the impetus of the story in the first place. In the end, Boz4pm relates that Penny never discovers the reason why she was sent to Middle-earth, which leaves the reader with uncertainty and unanswered questions. Penny also turns out to be her own ancestor, and the final chapter ends with a lengthy description of Penny's reasonably satisfactory life in our time the night before she is transported into the past, ending the story at the same place it began: with Penny's dream about Roxanna, from which she awakens screaming when she realizes she is abandoned in the wilderness. Thus the emotional impact of the final chapter tends to be a negative one, emphasizing Penny's "realistic" dissatisfaction with her lot in Middle-earth and denying the reader closure, returning the story to the beginning of the emotional arc rather than finishing it up neatly on a high note.

While there are many readers who would disagree with Penny's dismissal of realism as ruining pleasure reading, who would view realistic and tragic works as absorbing, escapist, and enjoyable, the story here presents itself as problematic. It implies that the main point of non-educative reading is escapism and pleasure and that too much realism robs reading of its escapist function. Meanwhile, the story itself, which has been written for the same kind of enjoyment, specifically attempts to emphasize the realism of Penny's situation and down-play its escapism. In trying to make her story less self-indulgent for readers, Boz4pm may be going too far in removing the pleasure of reading it.

Furthermore, "Don't Panic!" finds itself in a double-bind on the question of realism itself. If the piece did not attempt to strenuously avoid self-indulgence, it could have laid itself open to accusations of Mary-Sueism. However, a commenter on the *TV Tropes* website suggest that in its extreme attempts to avoid self-indulgence, the story ceased to be realistic:

The story can come as too much: Too much drama, too much crying, too much angst that it robes [sic] the "Real Life" sense [it] is trying to implement and it seems to hurl it to parody. This troper [reader] couldn't finish because [he/she] ... was simply tired (not to mention disturbed by her lack of sickness) of her crying/screaming over the top at every single action around 15 to 20 times [per] chapter. I wouldn't recommend it unless you had seen too many Mary Sue Insert Fic and want something to mock them ["Fanfic Recs"].

This reader believes that the author has gone too far in her attempt to distance her work from "Mary Sue Insert Fics" and has inadvertently descended into parody. The piece could be seen, on the one hand, as too realistic to allow for escapism, and too extremely negative, on the other hand, to be realistic or to constitute an object of enjoyment. In both cases, the story is seen as unable to fulfill one of fanfiction's primary purposes, and one of the primary purposes the story gives for reading itself.

Realism vs. Changes to Canon

One final characteristic of Mary Sues that "Don't Panic!" inverts is Roxana's expectation of joining the Fellowship on their journey to destroy the Ring and her plans to change the plot of the story by saving the protagonists from death: Boromir, Gandalf, and Theoden will all live to the end of the story because of her. It is in the rejection of this trope that "Don't Panic!" finally goes so far in its critique of Mary Sue plots that it calls the very basis of fanfiction into question.

Boz4pm firmly rejects the trope of modern *Lord of the Rings* fans traveling to Middle-earth and interfering with the plot in order to save their favorite characters. Penny certainly understands the urge: she tells some of the main characters, "'Perhaps it is hard for you to understand but for me, for many like me, this story, the people in it,' she looked round at them for a moment, 'all of you ... it is like we know you. Of course we do not, but to those who know this story, we love it so, we feel for you, we ... *care*'" ("Okay, NOW Panic" Chapter 26). Penny, of course, comes to care for them even more than a typical reader would because she actually meets the characters and gets to know them personally. However, she is barred from saving any of the characters. While Penny is perfectly capable of warning various people about what will happen to them, she and Gandalf both firmly believe that if Penny changes any decision that the main characters make in their pursuit of the destruction of the One Ring or their defense of Middle-earth against the dark lord Sauron, the results could be disastrous, and the forces of good might lose the war. Penny is therefore helpless to save anyone, including Halbarad, of whom she has grown very fond, and who she knows will die at the Battle of Pelennor Fields.

Boz4pm links together the changes to the canon that Penny is too afraid to enact and the changes that fanfiction writers suggest in their work. At one point, Penny tells the main characters,

> "In my time, those that know this story well, sometimes ask 'what if' of many parts of it. It is true we can bend the story to fit so that Sauron still falls, but if we are honest, if we are really honest, then we know the slightest thing will have such a great effect that it puts it entirely at risk. It was a very slim chance indeed that [Frodo] would succeed, and it was only by the series of events as they occurred that it was possible. Perhaps by other events it may also have worked, but very likely not" ["Okay, NOW Panic!" Chapter 26].

This statement seems to imply not only that Mary Sues who enter and change the story are foolish to do so, but that fanfiction authors who change the plot of the story at all may be deluding themselves if they think it will still end happily. Penny's opinion may be strictly confined to fanfiction on *Lord of the Rings*, with its very small chance for the success of the protagonists. However, in many stories the protagonists have a small chance of success: if they did not there would be little suspense. Even if this is confined to *Lord of the Rings*, "Don't Panic!" still denies much of the fanfiction in its own fandom by elevating the canon so high that it cannot be changed.

While *fanfiction* might well be defined as a story that makes changes to the canon, it is not uncommon for members of a fandom to look askance at fanfictions that stray too far from the original text. In trying to avoid Mary-Sueism and improve the literary quality of her fanfic, Boz4pm has distanced her work from stories in which modern characters drastically alter canon plots. However, in doing so she seems to call the very basis of fanfiction—any changes to the plot whatsoever—into question. Chuck Wendig points out this paradox in a blog post:

> If we become too rigorous in our slavish devotion to canon, we lose the chance to tell stories…. The more we care about what's "true"—in a universe that has never been true and whose power lies in its fiction—we start denigrating those things that aren't…. We dismiss fan-fiction as just some wish fulfillment machine instead of what it often is: a way to tell cool new stories in a pre-existing pop culture framework that aren't beholden to the canonical straitjacket.

Penny's argument about the problems of Mary Sues changing the story to suit themselves could be extrapolated to condemn all fanfictions because all of them change the canon.

Interestingly, this focus on conserving the canon rather than altering it in order to create something new may be gendered in fandom circles. *Tumblr* user fozmeadows has suggested,

> The types of fandom that are most often considered traditional and acceptable, and which are often either male-dominated or coded as masculine, tend to be acquisitive, whether in terms of knowledge (obscure trivia) or merchandise (collectibles). Whereas, by contrast, the types of fandom most often considered insincere, non-serious or "unreal," and which are often either female-dominated or coded as feminine, tend to be creative, such as making costumes, writing fanfic and drawing fanart.

Fozmeadows attributes female fans' creativity in large part to their inability to see themselves in male-dominated narratives, and believes that their creativity is the result of attempting to insert representations of themselves into the story. She does not mention Mary Sues in this context, but they fit quite well: when all the heroes in one's favorite media are male, Mary Sues create a space for female fans to see themselves in heroic roles. Fan writers and critics who seem to overemphasize adherence to the canon might therefore be seen as valuing the masculine-gendered, highly structured, and rule-bound practices of knowledge-keeping fandom over feminine-gendered, "undisciplined and wild" creative fandom practices.

This rejection of the creative side of fandom and its association with femininity can be seen in the phenomenon of the "fake geek girl": some male fans may call female fans' genuine fannishness into question if they do not have certain facts about the canon memorized, if they have not seen or read the entirety of the canon, or if the men feel that these female fans are in some way dilettantes, only using small parts of the canon to create something that really isn't genuinely part of the fandom anymore. On the website *Black Girl Nerds*, contributor Alanna writes, "Being a woman in fandom means not being taken seriously and having to, at some point, 'prove yourself' as a geek.... 'You say you like Batman? Name every major story of his or you're not a true fan.' 'Oh, you like the Walking Dead? I bet you've never even read the comics.' It sounds ridiculous but it actually happens."

Such reactions from male—and even female—fans are often couched in microaggressions: seemingly innocent comments that are actually insulting or hostile. Dr. Andrea Letamendi gives a number of examples of these comments: "'You sure know a lot about Batman, for a girl.' 'You don't look like a geek.' 'That's nice of you to come to Star Wars celebration for your boyfriend.' 'Did your older brother get you into comics?' 'You're a nerd's wet dream.'" She points out that the hidden meanings of these microaggressions are not as harmless as the comments at first appear. What they actually communicate to women are messages like "'You do not belong.' 'You are abnormal.' 'You are intellectually inferior.' 'You cannot be trusted.' 'You are all the same.'"

The trope of the "fake geek girl" has been widely decried and mocked in female-dominated fandom spaces such as *Tumblr*. Laura Moss notes that young women are mocked for enjoying media aimed at them, but also distrusted when they express an interest in media aimed at men:

> "Sports, geekdom, and tech alike are positioned as male-dominated by default—girls aren't expected to be interested in them and accused of faking it when they are," [feminist writer Bailey] Poland said. As a teenager, she says her own interests in comics and "Lord of the Rings" were framed as bids for male attention or attempts to invade spaces where she wasn't welcome. "I felt pressure to downplay my interest in feminine things because they meant I was taken less seriously and pressure to prove myself to my male peers in other spaces and show that I was 'one of the guys.'"

Too much emphasis on staying true to the canon both closes off the narrative possibilities inherent in fanfiction and reinforces traditionally masculine fandom values, potentially disenfranchising female fans.

What's more, the concept of "canon" itself is problematic, as fans frequently debate the canon and what is actually considered canonical in any given fandom. There is much debate, for instance, in the *Star Wars* fandom over which of the many official spin-off materials, including tie-in novels, novelized adaptations of the films, radio dramas, comic books, and newspaper comic strips actually count as canon. Likewise, even if the materials that are considered canonical are firmly established, the facts of what actually happens in those materials are open to interpretation: *Tumblr* user monicam writes, "*whistles lowly* *pulls out magnifying glass* are we talkin subtext, implied, heavily implied, borderline, practically canon, not disproved by canon, creator-acknowledged, or actually canon[?]" Even one of the questions Penny asks the elves—"Do balrogs have wings?"—is based on a perennial fan debate about Tolkien's canon.

Fandom itself sometimes produces variants of the canon, known as fanon. These are things which frequently appear in fanfictions as either generally accepted facts or generally accepted variants. For instance, *Lord of the Rings* fanfictions frequently depict Elrond and his brother Elros as twins, even though Tolkien never said they were. Many fanfiction writers may not even realize that this trope isn't canonical. Likewise, in the *Harry Potter* fandom, Lucius Malfoy is frequently depicted as abusive toward his son Draco, even though there is no real basis for this assumption in the canon. Many fans simply acknowledge that this is an acceptable interpretation. What is canonical and what is not can be very difficult to establish, and sticking too closely to the canon cuts off a great many possibilities for fanfiction writers: if the rule of making fanfiction canonical were followed to its extreme, fanfiction would be completely impossible.

This seems obvious when it is stated clearly, but it can be easily forgotten that enjoyment is self-indulgent (even when masochistic), that escapism denies reality, and that fanfiction is predicated on changes to the canon. While fanfictions that do not try to limit self-indulgence, realism, and canonicity are at risk of criticism for their poor writing, fanfictions that try to limit them too much may risk becoming self-defeating. Where that line of good taste lies is, of course, a matter of individual opinion, and is an extremely difficult target to hit. By accepting unquestioningly the belief that self-indulgence in one's fanfiction is a sign of bad taste, Boz4pm may have set herself an impossibly small target.

Lost in Austen

The question of how much self-indulgence and escapism is too much is also clear in the British television miniseries *Lost in Austen*. While this is not a piece of internet fanfiction—that is, it did not arise from the online fandom community—it employs the common internet fanfiction trope of a modern absorbed reader traveling into a piece of fiction: in this case, Jane Austen's *Pride and Prejudice*. Furthermore, it clearly deals with the same problems of fannish, self-indulgent escapism and supposed lack of literary or moral value that internet fanfictions like *Don't Panic!* are in dialogue with. Like "Don't Panic!," *Lost in Austen* tries to limit its self-indulgence—and thereby avoid the criticisms Mary Sues suffer from—by depicting its main character, Amanda Price, as an extremely awkward outsider in Georgian culture. The series also demonstrates the danger to the canon when a modern reader interferes with the plot.

However, the most fascinating aspect of *Lost in Austen*'s dialogue with tropes of fanfiction is its discussion of escapism. Is escapist, absorbed reading too reality-denying? Can fandom ruin a fan's life by distracting her from real, everyday concerns? While the ostensible message at the end of the series is No, that escapism into fiction can inspire us to pursue what we really want from life, the ambiguity of the ending seems to indicate that the writers were ultimately unable to reconcile their twin goals of questioning and embracing escapist reading. Because escapism in pleasure reading is often set in a binary which contrasts it with mentally healthy adult reading practices, works like *Lost in Austen* which fail to question that underlying binary are unlikely to be able to fully defend escapist absorbed reading.

Celebrating Escapism

Lost in Austen begins with the question of escapism. The opening lines are spoken in voiceover by the main character Amanda Price while she pulls out *Pride and Prejudice* and begins to read: "It is a truth generally acknowledged that we are all longing to escape. I escape always to my favorite book: *Pride and Prejudice*. I've read it so many times now that the words just say themselves in my head and it's like a window opening. It's like I'm actually there." This description of reading is given over a series of shots, first of elements of upper-class Regency life, like carriages and balls, and then of Amanda herself in period clothing, running through a manicured garden: a visual representation of being imaginatively transported into the fictional world through absorbed reading. Amanda's absorbed reading is particularly intense: she continues, "It's become a place I know so—intimately. I can see that world, I can—touch it! I can see Darcy." The shot closes in on a man in period clothing with his back to the viewer. But as Darcy turns to face the camera, the shot cuts to Amanda, sitting on her couch, slamming the book shut. She closes her eyes and shakes her hair out of her face with a voiceovered "Whoaaaa!" as if to pull herself out of the story, which has become almost too real. But she opens the book again immediately with "Now, where was I?" Amanda's absorbed reading is so intense, her imaginative escape into Regency England so real to her, that she is almost frightened by it, a response conditioned in her by a culture that associates too absorbed a reading experience with a lack of grip on reality, a kind of madness. However, this fear does not stop her from reading on.

Amanda is set up in this scene as a fan and absorbed reader of *Pride and Prejudice*, just like presumed audience for the miniseries. The series therefore tries to establish a connection between its protagonist and its viewers by giving the audience a character they can identify with. Actor Hugh Bonneville (who plays Mr. Bennet) points out this fact of marketing in the "Behind the Scenes" featurette:

> I just thought it was such a wonderful idea and it seems to catch a televisual mood at the moment: this insatiable appetite for Jane Austen and the resurgence of time traveling ideas that there've been in the last five years or so. When we read the books we always think of ourselves probably as one of the characters or wonder what it would be like to be in that world, and this takes it to the logical conclusion of having a fan of the novel actually step into it ["*Lost in Austen:* Behind the Scenes"].

Likewise, actor Eliot Cowan (Mr. Darcy) indicates that the miniseries has been written specifically for Austen fans: "People who know about the story and are big fans of Austen will be the best people to watch this, because they'll be like the aficionados who get all the in-jokes, all the references" ("*Lost in Austen*: Behind the Scenes"). Clearly, Austen fans would be the target audience of this series.

Everyone interviewed in the "Behind the Scenes" featurette seems unified in describing the movement of Amanda, the stand-in for the watching Austen fans, into the novel as a fantastical representation of Austenites' absorbed reading and their fantasies based on such absorption. In the "Behind the Scenes" special feature on the *Lost in Austen* DVD, actress Alex Kingston (Mrs. Bennet) states that this is the universal desire of women reading *Pride and Prejudice*:

> We all know, any woman who reads *Pride and Prejudice* [she shrugs and smiles as if to put herself in that category] immediately will have a fantasy about, "Oh, if only, you know, I could go back in time and meet Mr. Darcy!" And the wonderful thing is, that is exactly what we're doing in this production. And Amanda Price and Jemima Rooper [the actress who plays Amanda] are able to go and have a snog with Darcy. It's fantastic! ["*Lost in Austen:* Behind the Scenes"].

Lost in Austen gives female fans of *Pride and Prejudice* a self-insert fic, so that through Amanda Price they can imaginatively experience what going into the novel and having a romance with Darcy would be like.

Because of their target audience of absorbed fans and their indulgence of these fans' tastes, the miniseries would seem to be celebrating absorbed and escapist reading with a character who gets to enact fans' fantasies and end up with Mr. Darcy. However, because this kind of absorption and escapism is so closely allied in our culture with a whole host of negative stereotypes, the mini-series must deal with criticisms of absorbed reading and escapism or be subject to complaints about its poor literary quality or its negative effects on absorbed female viewers, whom it may be seen as encouraging in their dangerous reading practices.

Questioning Escapism

In the second scene of the series, immediately after the opening credits, Amanda feels she needs to defend the absorbed and escapist reading of *Pride and Prejudice* she has described. In a voiceover laid over a montage of Amanda dealing with terrible clients at her job at a bank and of her uncomfortable commute home from work, she states, "I have no right to complain about my life. I mean, it's the same for everybody. And I do what we all do. I take it on the chin. And patch myself up with Jane Austen." Life, Amanda asserts, is unsatisfactory and painful for everyone. She sees escapism into *Pride and Prejudice* as a method of coping with universal, unpleasant realities: "patching herself up."

Nonetheless, she recognizes this escapism as socially suspect, likely to brand her as having no life. She continues self-deprecatingly, "I know I sound like this terrible loser. I mean, I do actually have a boyfriend. It's just, sometimes I'd rather stay in with Elizabeth Bennet." Amanda immediately feels the need to assert that her reading has not given her unrealistic expectations of life, and that her obsession with Mr. Darcy has not stopped her from developing a real-life romantic relationship. She does not need to "get a life" or get a boyfriend: she has one. She attempts to defend her escapist absorbed reading while still acknowledging how it is negatively perceived by the culture as reality-denying and socially and sexually isolating. Nonetheless, she speaks of Elizabeth Bennet like a real friend with an actual physical presence: a person with whom she can interact as much as she could with her boyfriend.

This state of mind, brought on by absorbed reading, becomes a reality one night after Amanda's reading of *Pride and Prejudice* is interrupted by an unwanted visit from her drunken and very unromantic boyfriend Michael. Hearing a strange noise, Amanda goes to investigate, only to find Elizabeth Bennet—whom she recognizes immediately—in her bathroom. Elizabeth claims to have come there through an impossible door in the attic of her house at Longbourn. When Amanda looks away for a moment, Elizabeth disappears.

"Okay," Amanda expresses in voiceover while she sits thinking at her desk at the bank. "Elizabeth Bennet in my bathroom. Clearly I'm hallucinating. Why? Too much Austen? My mother would say, Not enough boyfriend." The divorce from reality that would cause someone to think that a fictional character was real is here attributed to two causes: unhealthy obsession with a fictional narrative, and lack of social/romantic contact in the real world. Both of these are associated with absorbed reading. As established in Chapter 1, one perennial fear about women's absorbed consumption of media narratives, particularly romantic ones, is that women will absorb from these narratives a false and overly idealized view of romance and men, which will ruin all real relationships for them. Apparently, Amanda's mother would prescribe an actual romantic relationship as the cure for fiction-induced psychosis.

This conceptual connection between the absorbed consumption of fiction and the imbibing of unrealistic standards for romance is made clear in the next scene. Amanda's mother tries to convince Amanda to marry her boyfriend, describing him in terms that show an absence of negative traits rather than the presence of positive ones: "He doesn't take drugs! He doesn't knock you about!" When Amanda objects to her mother trying to "tell her who to marry," her mother retorts, "I'm reminding you, Amanda, that you are what you are. If you waste your life pretending to be something else, you'll regret it." Amanda's mother fears that her daughter's escape into the pages of fiction will ruin her grasp on reality, that her absorbed reading will lead her into *bovarysme*: into believing that she is like a fictional romantic heroine and will be treated like one. Because of this mindset her daughter may fail to take advantage of real-world opportunities, like marriage to her boyfriend.

Amanda replies, "I have this conversation with Pirhana [her roommate] on a regular basis and she never gets it. I'm not hung up about Darcy. I do not sit at home with the pause button and Colin Firth in clingy pants, okay? I love—the love story. I love Elizabeth. I love the manners and the language. And the courtesy. It's become part of who I am and what I want. I'm saying, Mum, that I have standards." Her mother concludes, "Well, you *have* standards, pet. Hope they help you on with your coat when you're seventy." Amanda asserts that she does not have an unhealthy sexual obsession with the fictional Mr. Darcy, personified by the actor Colin Firth in the famously prurient swimming-in-the-pond scene from the 1995 miniseries adaptation of *Pride and Prejudice*. She claims that her interest is not sexual, but that the courtesy and consideration of fictional Regency England has given her standards for the behavior of her romantic partners. Her mother, however, still fears that these standards will never be met, and that the everyday concerns of reality—who will be there for her when she is old?—will slip through the cracks. In particular, she thinks her obsession with fictional romance will leave Amanda an old maid.

This scene makes Amanda's life parallel Elizabeth Bennet's: each of them is a young woman whose mother wants her to marry for practical reasons. But like Elizabeth, Amanda intends to marry for love, not merely for comfort. Amanda's divorced and disillusioned mother clearly believes that Amanda's reading of *Pride and Prejudice* has given her unrealistic standards for romance, and that these standards will leave her an old maid. Though Austen's Mrs. Bennet does not blame Elizabeth's resistance to purely practical proposals like Mr. Collins' on the reading of fiction, novels were frequently blamed for unrealistic expectations of love in the period. In "Love and Marriage in 18th-Century Britain," Wendy Moore writes,

> the emphasis on self-expression, free will, and personal feelings in early 18th-century novels ... was blamed for undermining the concept of arranged marriages and fueling expectations of romantic love. Whether the rising popularity of novels really influenced views on marriage or simply reflected changing opinion can probably never be determined. But certainly the former was the perception among disapproving older generations [8].

Love matches rather than marriage for money became the norm by the mid–1700s. However, Moore states, "Yet if the typical romantic novel of the period ended happily, the outcome of this fundamental change in society's attitudes toward marriage did not bring universal joy.... The romantic hopefuls who now walked down the aisle in anticipation of marital bliss sometimes found their optimism sadly deluded. Reality, they discovered, did not necessarily reflect fiction" (8). Even after love matches became the norm, as they still are today, an excess of romantic reading was—and is—seen as dangerous to a young woman's grasp of the reality of love, and therefore to her ultimate happiness and satisfaction. Wendy Moore herself echoes these fears.

Likewise, in *The Family, Sex, and Marriage in England, 1500–1800* (published 1977), Lawrence Stone observes,

> The results of massive exposure to this pulp literature was clear enough to contemporaries. Thanks to notions imbibed from this reading, young people fell headlong into the arms of whoever took their fancy, and, if their parents raised objections, they ran away to Scotland to get married in a hurry. "Of all the arrows which Cupid has shot at youthful hearts," remarked *The Universal Magazine* as early as 1772, "[the modern novel] is the keenest. There is no resisting it. It is the literary opium that lulls every sense into delicious rapture." Not all young men or girls were, or are, so practical and sensible, and the romantic novel of the late eighteenth and early nineteenth centuries has much to answer for in the way of disastrous love affairs of imprudent and unhappy marriages [283–86].

Eighteenth-century commentators believed that absorbed reading of romantic novels would ruin young people's (and young women's, in particular) understanding of marriage. What is perhaps most fascinating in Stone's writing is that he seems to agree so strongly with eighteenth-century views of the novel: he seems to blame "pulp fiction" for "disastrous love affairs" and "imprudent and unhappy marriages." The fears of Elizabeth Bennet's era are being echoed by Lawrence Stone—and Amanda's mother—in our own.

Amanda's experiences and Elizabeth Bennet's are therefore linked. Like a moralist or a concerned parent from the Regency, Amanda's mother feels that she needs to temper her daughter's romance reading with the warning "You are what you are." Her mother believes that Amanda's reading of romances will induce unrealistic expectations and *bovarysme* and eventually cause deep disappointment when real life does not live up to the novels. Both Amanda's mother and Elizabeth's would rather their daughters forget their romantic dreams and focus on their socially assigned role: marriage to a merely adequate man.

Through this conversation, the miniseries sets itself up thematically to discuss the topic of absorbed reading's effects on the reader's real life, and by the outcome of Amanda's adventures the audience will be able to judge the series' stance on whether absorbed reading, *bovarysme*, and escapism are beneficial or harmful.

"Followed Their Road with Its Bumps and Bends"

At first, Amanda's attempts to make her life as fantastic as fiction appear to succeed: she switches places with Elizabeth Bennet and finds herself in Longbourn, Elizabeth's home in Georgian England. But almost immediately, things begin to go wrong. Amanda's presence in—and Elizabeth's absence from—the story, combined with Amanda's total inability to act with Georgian-level propriety, begins to skew the plot. Like "Don't Panic!," *Lost in Austen* seems to imply here that fans entering a story can only damage it by their presence: it might seem to be trying to invalidate fans' fantasies by demonstrating what might *really* happen if they got what they wished for. It is destroying an enjoyable fantasy by making it conform to an uncomfortable reality. *Lost in Austen* likewise attempts to avoid charges of self-indulgence by having Amanda embarrass herself at every turn: she has no idea how to behave in Georgian culture, showing up in leggings and a tunic, using unintelligible and even rude vocabulary, and giving Mr. Bingley a drunken kiss at a party after she steps outside for a smoke. In all of this, Amanda's foray into becoming a fictional heroine seems to be a total disaster, if a funny one.

Things become more complicated, however, when the element of romance is introduced. Throughout the first half of the miniseries, Amanda continually insists that she is not interested in Darcy, that she wants to set the plot to rights again, and that Darcy and Elizabeth need to end up together. But when Darcy declares his love to her at Pemberley, Amanda finally admits that she is in love with him. This love, she states, began before she entered the book, while she was still merely a fan. In terms that seem romantic from one perspective and deluded from another, Amanda declares, "I love you. I didn't know that. I didn't know that! But it is clear to me now that I have always loved you. Every time I've fallen for a man, I've closed my eyes and it's been you. Even Michael, and I pretty much lived with him for a year." Amanda and Darcy's love for one another *could* be seen as a positive result of absorbed, escapist reading. The narrative could be depicting the happiness that can come from following one's dreams, no matter how unlikely, rather than settling for something or someone one doesn't really want. Amanda declared that she had standards, and by holding out, she has finally found a man who can reach those standards. However, the miniseries could also be implying that fans really are deluded and setting themselves up for disappointment by falling in love with fictional men who cannot, by their very nature, ever love them back.

After their mutual declaration of love, Amanda implies that her escapist reading was ultimately empowering. She meets Mrs. Bennet on the grounds of Pemberley, weeping over Jane's disastrous (and noncanonical) marriage to Mr. Collins. Mrs. Bennet concludes bitterly, apparently partly thinking of her own situation, "Well, there's nothing to be done for it. The world is full of miserable, loveless marriages. She will find a way to endure it. Women do." This sounds like a very old-fashioned concept of love and marriage to a twenty-first-century audience, but the viewers may remember that Amanda has also been living for a year with a man she didn't love the way she loves Darcy. Even modern women, the miniseries reminds us, can end up in "miserable, loveless" relationships.

However, Amanda replies, "We are not condemned to endure our lives. We can change them! My life is about to change, Mrs Bennet. I am in love. And the man I love is in love with me. When I am married to him, I will be able to protect Jane. And I'll be able to help you and Mr. Bennet. I will buy Longbourn for you." Amanda's words here seem to imply that a belief in romantic love, brought about by absorbed and escapist reading of romances, so far from stopping women from pursuing their own good in life, actually inspires them to do so. If more women had the strength to say they were in love with Mr. Darcy and the way he treats Elizabeth Bennet, Amanda indicates, fewer women would make her own mistake of staying with men who don't treat them as they deserve and whom they do not truly love. Here, the miniseries seems to be asserting that the absorbed reading of romances and the resulting *bovarysme* is a tool for women's empowerment and true happiness, rather than their delusion and disillusionment: it gives them the strength to declare that they have standards and to stick to them.

However, this is not the happy ending that would tie up all the loose ends of the plot and place the final seal of approval on Amanda's absorbed reading of *Pride and Prejudice*. Instead, Darcy realizes that Amanda is not a virgin and breaks off their engagement. When, after a series of canon-skewing events, Mr. Bennet is badly injured, Amanda insists that she needs to find Elizabeth and bring her home. She rushes through a door and miraculously finds herself back in present-day London, where she meets up with her boyfriend again.

Michael's romantic behavior and his appreciation of Amanda seem to have improved: he has sold his beloved Ducati motorcycle in order to buy them a trip to Barbados. This is another place where the plot could have ended. If the story were to end at this point and Amanda took back up with her newly-reformed boyfriend, the theme of the miniseries might be that love for a fictional character, born out of obsession with a novel, cannot last, but that absorbed reading might still be a positive thing, if only because it leads us to have higher standards for our real lives once we have broken free of fiction's illusion.

However, the story still is not over. On her way to find Elizabeth, Amanda discovers that Darcy has followed her to modern London. Once reunited with Darcy, Amanda completely forgets about Michael and goes off hand-in-hand with the man she really loves. They find Elizabeth, now working as a nanny, and learn that she has adapted exceptionally well to the modern world. At one point she orders a taxi by text on her cell phone and pays for it ahead of time with a credit card, a procedure which Amanda seems to not even know exists. When Amanda goggles at her, making choking noises, Elizabeth says with a smile, "I was born out of time, Miss Price. Out of time and out of place."

Michael and Darcy take an instant dislike to one another, and Michael declares that if Amanda goes back through the door into the book, he will break up with her. However, the door will not open for Elizabeth and Darcy, but only for Amanda, so she escorts them back into their own time, officially accepting that Michael has dumped her. Back in Georgian England, she seems to be finally setting the narrative to rights, apparently following Mrs. Bennet's and her own mother's ideas of how marriage should work: she insists that it is Elizabeth's "duty" to marry Darcy, though they barely know one another and neither of them seems particularly thrilled at the idea. Amanda believes that in forcing them to marry, she will finally be setting the plot to rights. Darcy's imposing aunt Lady Catherine agrees to procure an annulment for Jane and Mr. Collins, so long as Amanda disappears entirely from her sight and from society, and Jane and Bingley are to be married and will emigrate to America. Amanda therefore prepares to return to her own time.

Everyone but Jane and Mr. Bingley is thoroughly depressed by this setting-to-rights. However, finding a note from Darcy which implies that he still loves her, Amanda changes her mind about returning to her own time and follows Darcy to Pemberley. Elizabeth also gets her father's permission to return to the modern world, where she feels happiest. This leaves us with the final romantic scene between Amanda and Darcy.

One looks for closure in the final scenes of a romantic comedy: some assurance that the romantic leads will live happily ever after. In this series in particular, one wants a final verdict on absorbed reading and escapism into romances. Do they really hinder the reader from finding true happiness in the real world? Or do they inspire her to follow her true happiness? The final scene is written with an ambiguity which refuses to answer the question. Amanda and Darcy are reunited, they share a kiss (over the swelling romantic music of the soundtrack), and the scene ends with them embracing and Amanda gazing smilingly into the future. But examining the actual dialogue, it is unclear whether they are going to marry or not—or, indeed, whether they can ultimately get along with one another.

MR. DARCY: Miss Price.
AMANDA: Yes. …We should celebrate. You asked me a question, I answered it, and we didn't have an argument about it.
MR. DARCY: [Smiling] I did not ask you a question. I made an observation: "Miss Price." The confirmation of your identity was entirely superfluous. As a result we are now arguing about it. And therefore, you are wrong.
AMANDA: [Smiling tearfully] That's so sweet. You're actually trying to make me laugh.
MR. DARCY: Yes. It shall not occur again.
AMANDA: And you're smiling.
MR. DARCY: No, no. I only smile in private. When nobody is looking. [They kiss].

The lines are delivered tenderly, but nothing is resolved. Are they actually going to marry one another, particularly considering that such an act would invalidate Amanda's deal with Lady Catherine? Darcy refused to marry Amanda before because she was not a virgin: is he now willing to overlook that? He has mentioned that his life is a very public one, and while Amanda's behavior has improved a great deal over the course of her adventure (her change in diction and improved curtsies are particularly noticeable), she is still very out-of-place in Georgian society and could reflect poorly on him if they married.

Their allegedly romantic dialogue here also references their inability to get along (probably partly inspired by Darcy and Elizabeth's initial dislike for one another in Austen's novel). Looking back over previous romantic scenes between them, one begins to doubt that their marriage will be a happy one. Even when he first declared his love for her, Amanda asked Darcy, "Which one of me do you love? The one you first met, when I was spiky and vulgar and I argued with you all the time? When you looked at me and felt all that abysmal disregard? Or the one I've been recently, simpering and fanning and trying so hard to fit in? Please, tell me you've noticed the difference." Darcy responds, "I found both incarnations of your character equally disagreeable. And yet I love you, Amanda Price. With all my heart." Not very reassuring, really.

In *Lost in Austen*, the lack of a convincing happy ending, of a satisfying solution to Amanda's problems both with her own time and with Austen's, leaves the question of escapism and absorbed reading unanswered. Did Amanda's escapist reading of *Pride and Prejudice* forever ruin her future happiness, or forever secure it? We don't know, because we have no idea whether she will be happy with Mr. Darcy. Because the series tries to create a celebration of absorbed reading for Austen fans without questioning the binary that identifies absorbed reading with passivity, gullibility, delusion, and dissatisfaction with reality, it ends in contradiction and ambiguity.

Both "Don't Panic!" and *Lost in Austen* are attempting to navigate between seemingly mutually exclusive goals. "Don't Panic!" wants to make an ostensibly Mary Sue story about a modern girl being "zatted" to Middle-earth without making it a Mary Sue; it wants the story to be realistic while still escapist, a self-indulgence for readers that avoids self-indulgence for the character they are absorbed into. *Lost in Austen*, likewise, wants to defend escapist and absorbed reading of romance while still holding tightly to realism (seen in Amanda's difficulties with Regency culture); it tries to appeal to an audience of Austen fans while making an Austen fan both a sympathetic character and an object of humor.

With such apparently contradictory goals, both stories seem to be setting themselves up for failure. In a subculture that considers all modern-girl-in-fictional-world stories to be Mary Sues and all Mary Sues to be self-indulgent, one cannot make a non-self-indulgent, non–Mary-Sue story on that plotline—at least, not without the risk of sacrificing a certain kind of readerly pleasure. In a culture that considers escapist reading to be *ipso facto* reality-denying and dangerous, one cannot make a story that is both escapist and realistic, a story that valorizes escapism as improving a woman's life. But if we see these as false binaries, then there is more space for overlap, for stories that can fulfill both sides of a supposed paradox: for stories that will not have to sabotage themselves with tonal problems, excessive awkwardness and negativity, plot holes, and ultimately self-contradiction, in order to escape criticism.

4

Scope for Discontent

Part of the criticism of absorbed reading—and thus genres like fanfiction that are closely connected to it—derives from the belief that those who read absorbedly will not read critically: that in thinking and feeling *with* the text they will fail to think *about* the text, and therefore will accept everything it says as truth. However, despite some strong distinctions between critical and absorbed reading, they are not mutually exclusive.

This is clearly visible in internet fanfiction. While fanfiction has its source in absorbed reading, critical reading also strongly affects the genre, and in fact, makes it possible. Implicit in many of fanfiction's changes to the canon are criticisms of that canon. Fans, though they are absorbed readers *par excellence*, disprove negative stereotypes of absorbed readers because they are constantly reading critically as well as absorbedly. Thus, while "absorbed reading" is a useful shorthand for describing some of the emotional aspects of fans' reading and their concept of fiction—as in absorbed reading's acceptance of the autonomy of the character from the work—the binary of a passive absorbed reading in contrast to an active critical reading is clearly a false one.

Furthermore, fans often use the critical reading implicit in their fanfiction to produce more opportunities for absorbed reading: they include more characters in their fanfiction that they and other fans can more easily be absorbed into. Not only does this kind of critical reading not inhibit absorbed reading, but in fanfiction, fans' critical reading can work to encourage absorbed reading.

Active Reading and Thinking in Fanfiction

Absorbed reading is often considered to be particularly passive—and therefore feminine—contrasted with active, masculine, critical reading. This view holds that while absorbed readers simply let the story wash over them, accepting any idea the author puts in their heads, critical readers set themselves apart from the text, constantly questioning its ideas and assumptions. But this binary is false. Absorbed reading is an active procedure: entering the story is an act of imagination and will. The creation of fanfiction—removing that story from its original narrative moorings and reshaping it—is also active. Many fanfictions are as long as or longer than novels; we certainly cannot call the reading that led to their creation inactive or passive. As *TV Tropes* points out, "The Subspace Emissary's Worlds Conquest" is a *Super Smash Bros.* fanfiction that may be the longest piece of fiction in the world, at more than four million words long (and still unfinished): in contrast, Proust's *À la recherche du temps perdu* is 1.2 million words and Tolstoy's *War and Peace* is only 587,000 ("Fan Fic: The Subspace Emissary's," "List of Longest Novels"). The act of creating fanfiction is simply that: an act, a result of the active use of the imagination in absorbed and creative reading.

Critics of young women's absorbed reading worry that they may accept everything presented to them in fiction as real and ruin their lives attempting to act out those unrealistic fictions. However, despite their enthusiastic embracing of fictions and the *bovarysme* they can experience through them, fans are very much aware of the differences between fiction and reality: as *Tumblr* user Konkoa points out in a Venn diagram, there are many "Things that I like in works of fiction" that are also "Things I would never approve of in real life." There is therefore no basis for critics' fears that fans will not be able to separate their reading from reality: they are perfectly capable of seeing this distinction and of thinking critically about fiction.

In fact, fans often engage in a kind of deep analysis of their favorite media that strongly resembles the "close reading" that is done by scholars in academic literary criticism: they pay attention to tiny details of language, movement, filmography, etc., to make arguments for certain interpretations of the text. Referred to in fandom as "meta," this kind of analysis can be very detailed, examining films and television shows almost frame by frame, teasing out the tiniest meanings in a short phrase, or spanning across an entire series of films or novels to pick out a theme or develop the understanding of a character. As Henry Jenkins has pointed out, fans are often criticized for applying the "reading practices (close scrutiny, elaborate exegesis, repeated and prolonged rereading, etc.) acceptable in confronting a work of 'serious merit'" to popular texts (*Textual Poachers* 17). This is not unthinking, hypnotized reading, but critical, scholarly reading. The biggest difference between fan meta and scholarly literary analysis is that while scholars often try to rid their writing of excessive emotion in order to depict themselves as rational and logical, fans often mix emotions directly into the analysis. They mix absorbed and critical reading, rational and passionate responses.

The reading that fans do in order to create fanfiction is also active in the way it implicitly criticizes the canon. In her description of the make-believe game that she likens to the first step in the creation of fanfiction, Sheenagh Pugh describes fan authors' desire not only to have more stories about their favorite characters, but to have different ones: she indicates that she, like many other fans, is engaged not only in absorbed reading of the canon, but also in critical reading. "Now and then, we departed from the canon altogether to produce a 'what if.' This tended to happen when the children, or I, didn't like some aspect of the canon. They disliked the sad ending of Robin's betrayal and death and preferred alternatives, while I got bored with the canonical Marian and liked to speculate that she was herself a mean hand with the bow and arrow and joined in the battles" (9).

Dissatisfaction with the canon is as much the impetus for fans to create fanfiction as enjoyment of the canon is. In an interview about his novel *The Magician King*, which has been compared to a fanfiction criticism of C. S. Lewis' Narnia series, Lev Grossman describes the criticism of canon inherent in much of Internet fanfiction:

> I adore the way fan fiction writers engage with and critique source texts, by manipulating them and breaking their rules.... Some of it is straight-up homage, but a lot of [fan fiction] is really aggressive towards the source text. One tends to think of it as written by total fanboys and fangirls as a kind of worshipful act, but a lot of times you'll read these stories and it'll be like "What if *Star Trek* had an openly gay character on the bridge?" And of course the point is that they don't, and they wouldn't, because they don't have the balls, or they are beholden to their advertisers, or whatever. There's a powerful critique, almost punk-like anger, being expressed there—which I find fascinating and interesting and cool [qtd. in Canavan].

Fanfiction implicitly criticizes the canon by doing things with the story that the creators of the canon did not.

Entire fanfictions can be devoted specifically to fixing what fans perceive as flaws in the canon: such fanfictions constitute the genre of "fix-it fics." In such fanfictions, fans can change those things in the original canon that they dislike, including unhappy endings, problematic relationships, unsatisfactory themes, etc. *Archive of Our Own* hosts over ten thousand fanfictions tagged "Fix-it." I've written a fix-it fic myself: unhappy with the sad ending in the final season of BBC's *Merlin*, I rewrote the entire fifth season: I included larger parts for sidelined female characters, reincorporated some Arthurian legends the writers skipped, added a Mary Sue, gave my favorite character Gwaine (played by the gorgeous Eoin Macken) a happy ending with said Mary Sue, saved Britain from the Anglo-Saxons, and redeemed Morgana—none of which the canon had done (see Barner "New Faces"). The very fact that fans have invented this term for fanfictions that "fix" the canon indicates how often they have used fanfiction as a form of critical reading, to repair the narratives they love but can still criticize.

Fanfiction and Representation

Fans frequently display their powers of critical reading and literary evaluation in discussions of the canon that occur on *Tumblr*. These discussions often involve fans criticizing the media they consume on the basis of liberal-progressive politics. One political criticism that appears frequently in fan discussions of media narratives, as exemplified in Grossman's statements, is their lack of diversity and minority characters. This criticism is strongly connected to fans' absorbed reading: fans who do not see characters like themselves represented as protagonists in the media they consume have greater difficulty in finding characters to imaginatively inhabit.

Representation of minorities in media give members of those minorities their own Mary Sues: their own ways to imagine themselves as heroes of their own lives. For example, Whoopi Goldberg once famously described how seeing the black female character of Uhura as an officer on *Star Trek* inspired her: "When I was nine-years-old *Star Trek* came on, I looked at it and I went screaming through the house, 'Come here, mom, everybody, come quick, come quick, there's a black lady on television and she ain't no maid!' I knew right then and there I could be anything I wanted to be" (qtd. in Brunner). Nichelle Nichols' depiction of Uhura inspired many women and minorities besides Goldberg: working with NASA's Women In Motion program, Nichols helped to boost the number of applications to NASA from women and minorities from 1500 to over 8000 in six months, receiving the American Society of Aerospace Education's Friend of the Year award for "outstanding contributions to the promotion of aviation and space" (Greenberger). Mae Jemison, the first African American female astronaut, credited Nichols with "the inspiration to begin [her] career" ("Nichelle Nichols"). Jemison has explicated the relationship between seeing people of color pursue science careers in fiction and the belief that she could do the same:

> What was really great about *Star Trek* when I was growing up as a little girl is not only did they have Lt. Uhura played by Nichelle Nichols as a technical officer.... At the same time, they had this crew that was composed of people from all around the world and they were working together to learn more about the universe. So that helped to fuel my whole idea that I could be involved in space exploration as well as in the sciences [qtd. in O'Keefe].

We can see in the example of Uhura that positive fictional representations of minorities can have a very great emotional and practical impact on readers and viewers. Asian American *Star Wars* fan Jessica Lachenal describes how much of a revelation it was to see a female Asian X-Wing pilot in *Star Wars VII*, to be able to experience that *bovarysme* herself through this small example of representation in the film:

> It hit me right then and there: this is how good it can feel to see someone like yourself represented on screen. Finding someone I finally, *truly* identified with was such a huge moment for me. Sure, I can find bits and pieces of myself in other characters, and I'd be lying if I said I didn't look up to a few fictional characters as role models, but this is different, you see.
>
> This might seem very self-inserting and awkward, but.... I felt like I was watching someone who could be me up there on the screen. I was watching an example of the type of character *I* could be. And that was *magic*. I don't know that I've ever connected or resonated so much with a character–and she's not even in a majority of the movie! That's how powerful that moment was. More than that, seeing and identifying with her felt *empowering*.
>
> That's how meaningful it was to find someone like myself in something I love so dearly. Hell, I'm getting choked up just thinking about it again.

Because this kind of representation is so important to fans, they frequently criticize media narratives that do not demonstrate character diversity in terms of gender, sexuality, race/ethnicity, etc. And of course, if the narratives fans read do not have something they want, they create fan works that do: lack of interesting female characters in the canon, for instance, is part of the impetus for fans, frequently female, to create Mary Sues. Along with adding characters to their fanfictions, fans often change the characteristics of the canon characters in order better to represent a diverse readership: fanfictions may change characters' races and ethnicities, their genders, their sexualities. Characters whose genders or races/ethnicities have been changed in fanfictions are described as "genderbent" or "racebent." Changing the sexuality of a canonically straight character is very common, as is "shipping" two same-sex characters who are depicted as straight in the canon. Fans often make these changes to characters in order to make the canon more diverse and offer more opportunities for *bovarysme* through expanded representation of minorities.

Racebending in fanfiction and fanart can have an immense impact on fans of color, who consequently have the opportunity to immerse themselves imaginatively in a wider variety of characters. Recently, a number of fan artists have taken screenshots of Disney princesses and change their races and ethnicities (see lettherebedoodles). Lilian-Ann Bonaparte describes the emotional and political impact of such representation in her article, "For Black Girls Who Considered Esmerelda Black When Cinderella Wasn't Enuf":

> To behold an Aurora, with dark skin and a wide nose like mine, is an act of revolution.... A brown Rapunzel, wrapped in a marigold sari is revolutionary.... These crucial depictions remind women and people of color of their beauty, existence and visibility. Black girls need not limit themselves to Princess Tiana. Latina girls need not limit themselves to Sophia the Great. Southeast Asian girls need not limit themselves to Mulan. Middle Eastern girls need not limit themselves to Jasmine. Native American (NDN or indigenous Americans) need not limit themselves to Pocahontas.

By racebending characters, fan writers and artists can provide more opportunities for fans of color to see themselves in their favorite characters.

One demonstration of how a lack of representation in popular media can affect fans appears briefly in *Lost in Austen*. When Amanda returns to Georgian England with Darcy and Elizabeth she suggests that her roommate Pirhana come along, at least to see it if not to stay. Pirhana answers, "Amanda, I'm black. What's more, I cannot live without chocolate, electricity, or bog paper." This brings up an interesting question: To what extent are people of color—or, indeed, people with disabilities and other differences—barred from absorbed reading into certain canon texts? How would a black Mary Sue fare at Longbourn, or a woman in a wheelchair in Middle-earth? Fanfictions which alter main characters to be more inclusive can offer role models, increased self-esteem, and the enjoyment of absorption to readers of various minorities who were not represented in the canon.

When a minority character would encounter great resistance, such as a black Elizabeth Bennet or Mary Sue in Austen's Georgian England, a fanfiction can deal with the conflict in a number of ways. A realistic exploration of what a black Mary Sue would experience in that culture could present a criticism and analysis of racism in the period—and remind readers that members of minorities did live in these time periods and participate in history, thus reversing their erasure from popular memory.[1] A version of Regency England in which race is dealt with more healthily than it actually was can offer an image of what a society without racism could look like. Or, an "alternate universe" fic in which the story is transplanted to some other place, time, culture, etc., can eliminate the problem altogether. In all of these ways, fanfiction can include representation of minorities in works that ignored them, giving members of those minorities the opportunity for *bovarysme* and perhaps a vision of the world, not as it is, but as it could be.

Wish-Fulfillment for Minorities

This ability of fanfiction's to provide unrealistically positive experiences for minority characters is not universally praised, especially by canon creators. Annie Proulx, author of the short story "Brokeback Mountain" (later adapted as a film of the same name), complains in an interview with Chris Cox for *The Paris Review* that critical fans keep writing fanfiction that changes her story. She implies that she would not mind if the fans merely used absorbed reading to "fill in spaces" left in the text, or to see themselves and their experiences in the narrative, but she objects to fanfiction that has used critical reading to change the text in what she sees as fundamental ways:

> I think it's important to leave spaces in a story for readers to fill in from their own experience, but unfortunately the audience that "Brokeback" reached most strongly have powerful fantasy lives. And one of the reasons we keep the gates locked here is that a lot of men have decided that the story should have had a happy ending. They can't bear the way it ends—they just can't stand it. So they rewrite the story, including all kinds of boyfriends and new lovers and so forth after Jack is killed. And it just drives me wild. They can't understand that the story isn't about Jack and Ennis. It's about homophobia; it's about a social situation; it's about a place and a particular mindset and morality. They just don't get it [qtd. in Cox].

Proulx wanted to depict the conflicts gay people encounter in a homophobic culture: her fans want to be absorbed into a more positive story with a happy ending for a gay couple. As *bovarystes*, they want to fantasize about what *could* be, about possibilities, not have a homosexual romance made impossible by a canonically tragic ending. There is space for both of these in liberal political movements: fiction that presents the problems in our culture as it is, and fiction that demonstrates how our culture could be. Fanfiction has a tendency to lean toward the latter, particularly because of fans' affinity for absorbed reading. If a fan is reading him- or herself into the character's situation, that character's tragedies may have a more painful effect on the reader. *Tumblr* user skywalkers reminds readers that literary criticism of happy endings can have real emotional effects on readers, especially those with mood disorders or other painful real-life struggles:

> **edgelord™:** the worst way to end something is "everyone is happy in the end!" like how boring can you be???
> **me, with my crippling mental health cocktail, clinging desperately to the idea that survivors can find happiness someday and aren't forever plagued by their problems:** ...okay

Though works like "Brokeback Mountain" may criticize the ways our culture oppresses minorities by depicting that oppression, many fans want to see more depictions of happy endings for these characters. *Tumblr* user mildmanneredmuse points out in "The Importance of Writing Carefree Blackness™" that while struggle-driven narratives are common in black-centric literature and film, there is a great benefit to happy and whimsical depictions of black people. She acknowledges,

> Writing black characters has become a reflection on the pain associated with blackness.... It's also true that many of our well-known pieces of literature are struggle-driven narratives. The Color Purple. A Raisin in the Sun. Beloved. Native Son. Literary culture (with its broad, white base) is endeared to them for their dramatic profundity, the skill with which these authors paint true ugliness so deep it becomes beautiful. And for some reason, we are stuck in this place. The only stories people know to tell about us, are about our pain.

In contrast, mildmanneredmuse praises works like NBC's *The Wiz Live!* for presenting "images of black whimsy," since black people "are seldom represented outside of [their] own circles as people capable of happiness or frivolity.... It's why Lupita going from Patsey in 12 Years a Slave to Maz Kanata in The Force Awakens ... gave black girl nerds LIFE.... What a novelty to not see ourselves in roles where blackness isn't an armor or a tragic diary entry. This is what it looks like to have fun." Such positive representation, she reminds the reader, is not only enjoyable for black audiences, but educates white audiences by further humanizing blackness: by demonstrating that black people can do more than struggle against racial inequality. She concludes, "If you're going to write diverse characters, that means giving them the full spectrum of humanity and not just using them as statements and plot devices. And humanity for black characters—women and girls especially—means letting them dance or build airships or be alien pirate matriarchs or battle dragons for once instead of the patriarchy."

Giving minority characters happy endings in fiction can lift the spirits of those who are oppressed in their daily lives: a particularly helpful and healthy kind of "escapism." One example of fan criticism of tragic stories for minorities appears in the fan backlash toward the writers of *The 100*, a CW television series about one hundred juvenile criminals sent to repopulate a post-nuclear earth. The show depicts a much-beloved lesbian couple, Clarke and Lexa. After seasons of tension, the two finally have sex in Season 3, Episode 7 … followed almost immediately by Lexa being accidentally killed.

Enraged fans pointed out that this fell into a terrible trope in which lesbian and bisexual women characters are frequently killed off in fictional narratives. Just like many nineteenth-century novels killed off "fallen women" characters so that the narrative could display some sort of divine justice toward the wicked, these modern narratives seem to punish lesbian characters for not being straight. *Autostraddle*, a website for lesbian and bi women, demonstrated the enormity of the problematic trope in contributor Riese's article "All 160 Dead Lesbian and Bisexual Characters on TV, and How They Died." The writers of *The 100* had stumbled right into this trope, and without even having the option of claiming that they were depicting the problems of homophobia in our present culture, as the television series was set in a fictional post-apocalyptic future.

Fans had hoped that *The 100* would provide a more thoughtful, hopeful, and helpful depiction of a lesbian couple, and were extremely upset by the series' callous use of the "dead lesbian" trope. In response, *The 100* fans raised over $100,000 for The Trevor Project, which provides suicide prevention services for LGBTQ youth, and created websites such as *We Deserved Better* "to advocate for positive change in media engagement and representation" ("Clarke/Lexa," "About *The 100* and Its Controversy"). Of course, they also created reparative fanfictions. In fact, the *Fanlore* article on the Clarke/Lexa ship points out that the fan-created alternate universe ship "Lexark," which allows these characters to continue to be together and alive, became so popular among *100* fans that *Archive of Our Own* categorized it as a canonical ship ("Clarke/Lexa"). When the canon has ruined an example of minority representation, fans are there, not only to protest, but to step in and fix it.

Many fans, like those of *The 100*, are clamoring for more positive and hopeful representations of minorities in media, believing that such representations are mentally healthy for members of those minorities and that they may have a transformative effect on the culture in general. They want to harness the powers of positive representation and *bovarysme*: they engage in critical reading and transform the canon itself in order to create more opportunities for enjoyable absorbed reading.

Caveats

This is not to say that fandom is an ideal community for minorities. Fans do not leave their cultural assumptions at the door when they enter fandom, and minority fans still experience discrimination in fandom settings. For example, Centrumlumina has pointed out that for the last four years, "the top pairings on [Archive Of Our Own]—the shipping juggernauts of fandom—are overwhelmingly white" ("Fandom's Race Problem"). And these top pairings represent a huge percentage of the fanfiction on the site: Centrumlumina notes, "in This Year's list, the top 10 spots account for 29% of the fanworks covered, and 6% are for the #1 pairing."

Centrumlumina sums up her data findings:

> More than half of the POC [people of color] on This Year's list are from Anime and K-Pop fandoms [These are generally fandoms for Asian-produced media in which the vast majority of characters or band members are Japanese or Korean]. Limiting the list to only Western media fandoms, only 12.5% of characters are POC. Half of the POC in Western media fandom are either mixed race or fantasy races. Compared to Western media in general, the fandom list has less POC representation, more mixed race characters, and fewer black characters. For reference, the US census gives the proportion of POC as 38.4%. Of the POC on the list, I have observed a bias towards light-skinned characters who are subsequently whitewashed by fandom....
>
> I feel it is plainly evident from this analysis that fandom—or at least, fic-writing Western media fandom based on AO3—has a significant issue with racism.... Fandom has gradually been edging towards greater inclusion of POC, but the pace of change is slow, and there are still huge barriers to overcome.... For fandom to make

good on its promises of diversity, we must all contemplate the part we play in supporting or erasing characters of colour in our fics and other fanworks ["Fandom's Race Problem"].

While fanfiction holds the possibility of offering representation for minority readers who were not represented by the original work, this does not mean that fanfiction as a whole is always good at producing as many examples of that representation as it reasonably should. Fans carry their prejudices with them into fandom, and these prejudices can be seen in such quantitative studies.

As the Mary Sue phenomenon indicates, fanfiction often gives female characters larger roles—but even here, fandom does not offer a utopian gender equality. For example, while male-male homosexual pairings (M/M slash) is wildly popular in fanfiction, female-female pairings (F/F or "femslash") is not. *Tumblr* user destinationtoast noted in June 2013 that 42.57 percent of all fanfictions on AO3 were labeled M/M and 15.39 percent were F/M, while only 3.53 percent were labeled F/F ("AO3: Relationships").

Many fans have attributed this discrepancy between male slash and female slash fics to a larger percentage of slash writers who are heterosexual women who enjoy reading about men's intimate lives. However, Centrumlumina has pointed out that more (female) readers and writers of M/M slash are lesbian, bi, or pan than straight ("M/M Fans"). Another possibility is that a great deal of media does not have enough representation of fully developed female characters to create F/F stories about. But it is also possible that this is an example of unconscious sexism: that fans, like other media consumers, have been taught to value and discuss men's experiences, both social and sexual, more than women's. However, the percentage of F/F fanfictions is on the rise: Destination Toast noted in February 2016 that it had risen to approximately 9 percent ("F/F Stats"). Fanfiction may slowly be improving its record as a place to repair the lack of representation in popular media.

Cumulative Revision

Fanfiction is only made possible by a combination of critical and absorbed reading: fans must feel that the characters have enough seeming reality that they can put them in new situations and watch them react. But the changes to canon involved in fanfiction also imply that fans want both something more and something different than what was given to them in the canon: their critical reading, their thinking about the story, is as important as their thinking with the story.

One fan, glitterarygetsit, expresses her appreciation of the fan criticism implicit in fanfiction and the improved narratives fans produce: "The fact is that you've got thousands of intelligent people thinking about a problem, and statistically speaking some of them are likely to come up with something more clever than the creators.... There comes a point at which, frankly, fandom IS better than the creators. We have more minds, more cumulative talent, more voices arguing for different kinds of representation, more backstory" (qtd. in imorca). More people are involved in the creation of fanfiction, and they produce more possible versions of the narrative than the canon ever could. Cumulatively, they can transform and improve that canon in innumerable ways.

However, while some kinds of critical reading enable the creation of fanfiction, other kinds can limit and threaten this creation. Fanfiction displays fans' critical reading, not only of canon, but of other fanfictions. Fanfiction is a genre highly informed by a web of multidirectional criticism from both within fandom and from outside of it. The next chapter examines some of the less-than-constructive forms that fans' criticism of other fans can take.

5

Please Don't Kill the Author

As Chapter 4 demonstrates, fans engage in both absorbed and critical reading of canon, producing fanfictions that implicitly—or explicitly—criticize the source material on which they are based. But fans do not just apply their critical reading to canon: they also apply it to one another's fanfictions. Just as absorbed reading is not a purely harmful approach to texts, critical reading is not a purely beneficial one. Fans criticizing one another's work often repeat many of the same criticisms of fanfiction that the culture has used against them. Unfortunately, therefore, fans' criticisms of one another's texts can easily devolve into bullying, hair-splitting, and internalized discrimination. Assuming that there are objective criteria for discriminating between "good writing" and "bad writing"—and that most of fanfiction falls into the latter category—fan criticism often reinforces false and highly critical messages about fanfiction as a genre.

As the example of "Don't Panic!" demonstrates, fans are careful in their work to conform to the fandom community's standards of good taste as they understand them. However, because there is no restriction on the writing and publishing of fanfiction online, many writers publish their fan writings before they are fully cognizant of or capable of conforming to the standards for acceptable writing held by the wider fanfiction community. They may write Mary Sues, alter or misunderstand aspects of the canon, or leave important information out of their narratives. In some cases, this breach of communal standards of literary quality happens because these fan writers haven't read widely enough in the fandom; in others, it's simply because they are very young and are still developing their writing skills. Sometimes they are aware of the standards but choose to write against them for their own and their friends' enjoyment.

Because there is no mechanism to stop these fans from publishing their fanfiction online, other fans sometimes step in to try to police the quality of work emerging from the community. This is an aspect of communal social control: as Henry Jenkins observes in *Textual Poachers*, "Taste is always in crisis; taste can never remain stable, because it is challenged by the existence of other tastes that often seem just as 'natural' to their proponents. The boundaries of 'good taste,' then, must constantly be policed; proper tastes must be separated from improper tastes; those who possess the wrong tastes must be distinguished from those whose tastes conform more closely to our own expectations" (16).

Internalized Discrimination

Part of the reason for fans' preoccupation with literary quality is fanfiction's poor reputation with critics. In an article on *Bustle*, Emma Lord notes, "Unfortunately, fan fiction writers are in a constant stream of ... judgment on all sides.... Even in the last week, I had a friend *seven years older than me* tag me in a mocking tweet that revealed that he and two other of my friends had been poking fun at my fan fiction behind my back." This kind of mockery can ruin fans' fun by making them feel bad about their writing. Fans want to take what steps they can to defend their fanfiction: Lord writes, "I think the reason people feel so comfortable mocking fan fiction authors is because we're somehow less 'real' or 'legitimate' than other writers in their minds, and they don't think we'll take personal offense to them mocking our work." Because fans and fanfiction are so often mocked for poor taste, fan critics may become sensitive to such criticisms and therefore harsh in their condemnations of what they see as other fans' poor writing. In trying to defend fanfiction, they end up reinforcing the arguments that denigrate it.

This is actually an example of internalized discrimination. *Community Tool Box*, a website promoting healthier communities and social change, explains the term: "When people are targeted, discriminated against, or oppressed over a period of time, they often internalize (believe and make part of their self-image—their internal view of themselves) the myths and misinformation that society communicates to them about their group" ("Chapter 27, Section 3"). While this can happen on an individual basis, causing members of a discriminated-against group to act out stereotypes, it also happens between members of the same cultural group:

> People in the same group believe (often unconsciously) the misinformation and stereotypes that society communicates about other members of their group. People turn the oppression on one another, instead of addressing larger problems in society.... Often people from the same cultural group hurt, undermine, criticize, mistrust, fight with, or isolate themselves from one another ["Chapter 27, Section 3"].

This is the mechanism that appears so often in fan writers' criticism of one another's work. Some fans have internalized the stereotypes that fan writing is self-indulgent, *bovaryste*, of poor quality, disgusting, oversexed, immature, ridiculous, and poorly written. Instead of directly attacking these stereotypes, these fans direct them toward one another, harshly criticizing and putting down other fans whom they feel may harm the public reputation of fanfiction still further.

Henry Jenkins notes in *Textual Poachers* how fans will direct criticisms toward others in order to defend themselves:

> There is always someone more extreme whose otherness can justify the relative normality of one's own cultural choices and practices. As C. E. Amesley (1989) notes, "I have yet to find a self-identified 'hardcore Trekkie.'" Whether fans watch the show every night, miss other events to come home to watch, go to conventions, participate in contests, collect all the novels or study Klingon, they always know others who, unlike them, are 'really hardcore'" [20].

Similarly, "Don't Panic!," with its Mary-Sueish premise, firmly assigns the label of Mary Sue to other stories, while Boz4pm declares in her story descriptions, "NOT a Mary Sue!" This internalized and displaced discrimination appears throughout fandom and fanfiction, and frequently in other denigrated, absorbedly-read genres, as well. Jane Austen tries to escape criticisms of her own genre, the novel, by displacing them onto the even more devalued Gothic novel.

Internalized Misogyny

Since the great majority of fans who write and consume fanfiction are women, and given that fanfiction and the absorbed consumption that produces it are considered feminine, the internalized discrimination of fans is likely to be at least partly caused by internalized misogyny. Writer Suzannah Weiss for *Bustle* points out that "internalized misogyny does not refer outright to a belief in the inferiority of women. It refers to the byproducts of this societal view that cause women to shame, doubt, and undervalue themselves and others of their gender." For instance, internalized misogyny often leads to mocking and policing other women's behavior. Erin Tatum for *Everyday Feminist* explains that to women suffering from internalized misogyny, "every woman is a potential threat to your security and your sense of self. You have to belittle them to reaffirm your superiority." This kind of behavior is clearly seen in how some fans police one another's writing and fandom interactions. Just as some women, suffering under a belief in the negative stereotypes about their gender, may claim "I'm not like other women," some fans may try to claim "I'm not like other fangirls."

Internalized misogyny also explains why even some feminists attack absorbed reading, feminine genres like romances, and fan behavior: they are trying to advance themselves and their beliefs by attacking other women and their "feminine" behavior. Mary Wollstonecraft's objections to sentimental literature and George Eliot's to "silly novels by lady novelists" on the grounds that they set back the cause of women's education by proving to men that women are not worthy of such education fall into this category of internalized misogyny. Instead, Wollstonecraft and Eliot could have tried combating negative stereotypes about female readers and writers, valorizing those reading and writing behaviors that were called feminine and inferior, and deconstructing the cultural constructs that considered them pathetic and dangerous. Unfortunately, this is the much more difficult path to convincing a patriarchal society to accept women as equals, as it involves transforming the culture's unspoken assumptions about gender.

Another sign of internalized misogyny that appears in discussions of fanfiction and other absorbed genres is exaggerated feelings of guilt. Weiss points out that women feel guilty more frequently than men, partly because women are attempting to conform to a nearly impossible standard of acceptably feminine behavior. Weiss comments, "The more I learn that guilt is a gendered phenomenon, the more I notice the ridiculous things women feel guilty about: eating, saying 'no,' asking for what they want in bed—the list goes on." Some things we can certainly add to that list of things women feel unnecessarily guilty about are becoming emotionally attached to fictional characters, writing and reading fanfiction, enjoying "bad" movies, and reading romances and escapist literature. The guilt in these guilty pleasures is largely a product of internalized misogyny.

The Example of Twilight

Twilight is, once again, a good example of how fans, suffering under internalized discrimination and misogyny, use the culture's hierarchies of taste to place themselves above, in opposition to, other fans. In "'The Rabid Fans That Take [Twilight] Much Too Seriously': The Construction and Rejection of Excess in *Twilight* Antifandom," Jacqueline M. Pinkowitz describes the anti–*Twilight* movement among fans, noting particularly how *Twilight* antifans adopt a masculine and scholarly-critical stance as opposed to the *Twilight* fans' supposedly feminine, emotional and obsessed attitude toward the series:

> The group of Twilight antifans known as the Anti-Twilight Movement has constructed themselves as a safe "us" in relation to the threatening and inappropriate Other that they have defined through their characterization of "rabid" Twilight fans and antifans' "them." Fearful of a low ranking on the cultural hierarchy, they have created their own internal fan hierarchy that, according to cultural notions about the superiority of class, education, and the elite over the uneducated and the popular, as well as of the dismissability of girl culture, ensures the dominance and safety of their own affected rationality over the characterized emotional and excessive behavior of rabid Twilight fans and antifans.

We can see this gendered hierarchy at work in online fan discussions of the series. When *Twilight* became popular, the media frequently compared it to the *Harry Potter* series. Since *Twilight* gained such a poor public reputation, it soon became common for fans of the *Harry Potter* books and films to try to distance themselves from the *Twilight* franchise, arguing for the greater merit of the Potter stories. One writer, Tim Gomez, writes, "What I saw onscreen [in the first *Twilight* film] was soap opera trash for the tween nation. It didn't bear anywhere near the universal appeal of the *Harry Potter* series.... So how is *Potter* better than *Twilight*? Well, for one, it's not *Twilight*." Gomez goes on to enumerate the many ways he considers his favorite fiction more meritorious, and thus more culturally acceptable, than the much-reviled *Twilight* series it was being compared to. Gomez describes *Potter* fans as "dweebs" and *Twilight* fans as "emos," claiming that while both are "pretty lame," "at least dweebs are usually smart, right?"

Using stereotypes about *Twilight* fans, Gomez attempts to attribute greater intelligence and education to one group of fans over another. Commenters on his writing continue this pattern: "After going through some of the comments I've noticed a trend. Most of the Harry Potter fans use proper grammar and spelling, where as the Twilight fans stick to tacky 'text talk.' This alone says a lot about the given audience for each." "I'm kinda generalising here, but one thing I have noticed is that Twihaters or lolfans [people who just enjoy *Twilight* because they enjoy making fun of it] are usually smarter than the average fangirl, who has trouble stringing together a coherent sentence. Also, fangirls often come out with recycled, overused garbage during arguments." These fans attempt to distance themselves from others whose media choices, level and kind of engagement with the text, and social reputation they do not wish to be associated with. In order to protect themselves from common criticisms of fans, they project the criticisms of fandom in general and female fans in particular onto others whom they see as even more socially unacceptable than themselves.

Even some *Twilight* fans try to distance themselves from the series and to hierarchize the *Twilight* fandom so as to protect themselves. One such fan is Cleolinda Jones, author of the popular website *Movies in Fifteen Minutes*. Jones attempts to distance herself from her own interest in *Twilight* by claiming that she is reading with an emotional distance that allows her to laugh at the books. She created the term "lolfan" to describe those who engage in this emotionally distant fandom practice: "I pretty much made up this word just now to describe the kind of people (i.e., me) who read these books for the sole purpose of snarking on them ~~and yet cannot stop oh God please send help~~. Levels of affection for the subject matter may vary." Though she admits to a kind of obsession with the series, Jones' use of the term *lolfan* to describe her interest allows her to distinguish herself from other, even more emotionally invested and accepting fans.

Distancing oneself emotionally from a work by laughing at it or making fun of it is often suggested as an antidote to dangerously absorbed reading: blogger James Bow writes of *Twilight*, "While I would not seek to keep this book out of anybody's hands, I would be, frankly, disturbed if my daughters were to take it up. Unless, of course, it was their intent to point at it and laugh." Bow unconsciously echoes Mary Wollstonecraft's opinion of novels in general: "The best method, I believe, that can be adopted to correct a fondness for novels is to ridicule them.... If a judicious person, with some turn for humour, would read several to a young girl, and point out, both by tones and apt comparisons with pathetic incidents and heroic characters in history, how foolishly and ridiculously they caricatured human nature, just opinions might be substituted instead of romantic sentiments" (Section 13.2).

Fan Policing

In the fanfiction community, this policing of taste can come in a number of forms, not just in mocking conversations about *Twilight*. Most sites that host fanfiction, including *FanFiction.Net* and *Archive of Our Own* have some sort of mechanism for reviews and feedback, and sometimes fans leave "concrit" (constructive criticism) or "flames" (harsh, over-the-top criticism) for the authors through these forums. Fans may try to help other fans to achieve better writing through educating them on fandom's standards of literary quality, or may punish the writers through negative feedback when they transgress those standards.

However, fans not only criticize other fans through reviews: they do it through their own fanfictions. Sometimes fanfictions merely allude to tropes (such as Mary Sues) that they consider to be in poor taste; we saw this in the first chapter of "Don't Panic!" However, sometimes these criticizing fanfics can be more pointed. Two series of fanfictions that criticize other fanfictions and their writers are the Protectors of the Plot Continuum (PPC) and "The Official Fanfiction University of Middle-earth" (OFUM).

The Protectors of the Plot Continuum demonstrates that fanfictions that act as criticism struggle with another problem as well: namely, the difficulty of criticizing Mary Sues without attacking the writers who create them. Because Mary Sues are seen as self-inserts of the author, attacking the character often shades into attacking the author, which is considered bullying.

Another issue in fan criticism is that taste is, at bottom, subjective, while any criticism about literary quality must be based on a shared or ostensibly objective standard. This problem is particularly noticeable in "The Official Fanfiction University," where the students constantly transgress the rules laid down for them by their teachers. However, the PPC demonstrates that absorbed reading can actually give fan critics a common value to appeal to in their criticism. If fan critics assume that all fan readers are reading absorbedly, anything in the story that is likely to disrupt that absorbed experience can be attacked with some appearance of objectivity. The Protectors of the Plot Continuum appeal to the disruption of the shared absorbed reading experience in their condemnations of "badfics." The PPC's relationship to absorbed reading is therefore a contradictory one, as the community's fanfictions both uphold absorbed reading as a test of literary quality and condemn Mary Sues, which are a result of that absorbed reading.

PPC and Bullying

The Protectors of the Plot Continuum, or the PPC, is a shared metafictional universe, begun by fans Jay and Acacia after the explosion of *Lord of the Rings* fanfiction subsequent to the release of the Peter Jackson film *The Fellowship of the Ring* in December of 2001 ("History of the PPC"). The PPC is an agency that sends "assassins" (later "agents") into bad fanfiction. The assassins draw up a list of charges against the Mary Sue character of the fic and execute her, often in poetically just fashion.

The concept of the PPC became very popular, leading to a large number of other fans writing stories about their own assassins/agents. In March of 2003 the *PPC Posting Board* was founded, where those who wrote PPC fanfiction could meet for discussion and to share fanfiction. PPC writers have organized meetings IRL (In Real Life) a number of times, from 2004 to 2009 ("History of the PPC"). This group also boasts a wiki, started in December of 2007, which contains 2,603 pages of information about the PPC. PPC stories continue to be published: according to the "Latest Story Releases" on the front page of the PPC wiki, as of early April 2015 members were still collectively publishing an average of two stories a week (*PPC Wiki*).

As there would be no possible way for me to study all of the PPC stories, I have chosen to look at the original series by Jay and Acacia, and also one later set of stories by the fan Tungsten Monk. Both the original series and the Tungsten Monk series focus on Mary Sues rather than on other "badfic" genres such as bad slash. Despite their claims that they do not engage in bullying or personal attacks on authors, the PPC seems unable, because of the concept of the Mary Sue as an author avatar, to avoid criticizing the author rather than the fic.

Each PPC story begins with the agents in "headquarters," a strange and Escher-like building. (HQ is run, for reasons unknown, by giant sentient flowers.) The agents live together in pairs in "response centers," and are alerted electronically when a "badfic" is identified. The agents then don disguises appropriate to the situation they will be facing and enter the badfic.[1] While inside, experiencing the fanfiction from within, they draw up a list of charges against the Mary Sue of the fanfiction and then execute her in poetically-just fashion. For example, one of the Tungsten Monk stories involves a Mary Sue who claims to be the daughter of the Egyptian goddess Sekhmet, so the agents decide that the most poetically just end for her would be to be dumped into the Hindu legend in which the goddess Kali becomes drunk on the blood of demons and destroys everyone in her path. One of the most disturbing executions of a Mary Sue in the original PPC series is in "Protector of the Ringbearer," in which the Mary Sue takes the form of a unicorn. After killing the Mary Sue by shooting it through the eye, the assassins saw off its horn with a hacksaw and take the carcass to a fellow agent who is skilled in taxidermy. While they chat, she pumps out its blood and skins it to make a throw rug, after which she mounts its head on the wall.

The execution of the Mary Sue character is highly problematic because of the PPC's inability to separate the writing from the writer. Because Mary Sues are believed to be fictionalized versions of the authors, attacking a Mary Sue is tantamount to imaginatively killing the author of the fanfiction. Though the PPC has a policy against directly attacking authors, their stories constantly transgress this boundary because of the difficulty of separating attacks on the work from attacks on the author.

PPC Policies

The PPC as an organization attempts to limit direct attacks on fan authors. The "Mission Writing Guide" on the PPC wiki states,

> Sporking [mocking badfic] is NEVER about the fic's AUTHOR. This point cannot be emphasised enough. Authors of a badfic are not equal to the badfic. Moaning and complaining about the badfic should *never* turn into insulting the author. It's rude, it's cruel, and it's created far too many dramas already. Leave authors out of it. Don't even mention them in your mission if you can possibly avoid it. Yes, that can be hard. Yes, we used to call the possessing force that makes canon characters OOC [Out Of Character] "author-wraiths"—they're now called Sue-wraiths … for a reason. You can mention the author if you have to (e.g., when complaining about author's notes), but no bad-mouthing them. Aim it at the fic itself. Please. Trust me. It's better that way.

Clearly, the PPC has already had to deal with complaints from authors on this subject and would like to avoid the problem in the future.

Similarly, in the article on authors, the PPC wiki states that killing the author is murder because authors are sapient creatures, but fictional characters are not. (One wonders, then whether the fictional agents are considered to be sapient creatures?) The article also argues that "Killing authors is unnecessary" because "Institutions like OFUM and its sister schools have proven that badfic authors can be turned into goodfic authors.... This was also the purpose of the former Department of Author Correspondence." Finally, the article states,

> For similar reasons, PPC writers are strongly discouraged from flaming, bad-mouthing, casting aspersions on, or otherwise insulting badfic writers. The PPC's problem with bad writers is their badness, not the character of the writer him/herself: more often than not in a mission, the Mary Sue or the Sue-wraith can be deemed the manifestation of this badness, containing all of the shortsighted stupidity that the author may temporarily be under the influence of. This is why Mary Sues are charged with the crimes of badfic, rather than the authors being charged ["Author"].

Despite these rules, the PPC still has trouble separating authors from their works: the previous existence of the "author wraith" trope and the hair-splitting involved in designating the Mary Sue the "manifestation of [the author's] badness" and "all of the shortsighted stupidity that the author may temporarily be under the influence of" are evidence of this trouble. The original stories themselves include attacks on the authors, most memorably in "To Know Where You Are Going," in which the character of Legolas becomes suicidal after the death of the Mary Sue character with whom he was in love. The agents deem him to have been possessed by the spirit of the author. One of them exclaims, "What have they done [to Legolas], the author deserves to die for torturing him!" They then "exorcise" Legolas of the fic author's influence:

> She took a copy of *Return of the King* from her pouch, opened it, and held it up to the air. "Begone foul authoress from this place! You have no more control here!" The circle started to glow and a gust of wind went through it, blowing out the candles (for dramatic purposes).
> The Authoress's essence coalesced above the grave. "Noooo! My Story Is Just Beginning! All will know the tragedy of Damien, second daughter of Elrond! And her doomed love of Legola—!"
> "Oh, quiet," Jay said, and slammed her over the head with *The Two Towers*. The authoress/Damien crumpled in a heap. The grave shivered, and collapsed dramatically in on itself.

Clearly it is the author who has made Legolas behave as he has and who has changed the canon of the story. The usage of "the authoress/Damien" indicates how difficult it is for the PPC stories to separate the Mary Sue character from the supposedly self-inserting author.

Even when the agents do not directly reference the author, many of the "crimes" that are charged to the Mary Sue are clearly the actions of the author, not the character. In the first mission by Tungsten Monk, the list of charges is extensive. Almost all of the twenty-six charges are clearly the fault of the author, not the character. A character could do terrible things—murder, rape, steal, lie, hurt others physically or emotionally—but the charges listed in the story are far different. Making other characters love the Mary Sue, "making Boromir a sexist bastard," "gratuitous angst," and "lack of paragraph differentiation," just to name a few, are clearly acts that the author committed, not the character. It doesn't help that the PPC claim that the Mary Sue is the vessel of the author's badness: what the PPC is attacking is the author's writing, the author's actions.

It is obvious that the Mary Sue is here standing in for the author, an association made even more obvious by the longstanding belief that Mary Sues are fictional author avatars. When the PPC agents kill the Mary Sue, therefore, it is clear to the readers that the one they are "bludgeoning into oblivion" is symbolically the author, not the character. Because Mary Sues are so widely considered to be self-inserts, the PPC cannot attack a Mary Sue character, especially for the author's "crimes," without breaking their own policy and symbolically attacking the author of the story.

PPC Writers in Doubt

Some members of the PPC are not unaware of the problematic nature of the organization's mission and methods, and implied criticisms of their own work appear in some PPC stories. One example shows up in the Department of Author Correspondence, or the DAC: "The Department of Author Correspondence was set up to deal with those badfic authors who were deemed salvageable; the agents of the DAC talked to and emailed these authors, encouraging them to improve their writing habits" ("Department of Author Correspondence"). However, the wiki notes that this department has been defunct since 2008. In one dystopian, noncanonical fic about the future of the PPC,

> the DAC appears to be revived as the Department of Author Correction, which punishes—and sometimes kills—badfic authors and eventually … grows to rule over the PPC with iron leaves.[2] The circumstances of its rise to power are unknown, however; [sic] what is known is the DAC … [is] overthrown in a fourth PPC civil war, after which the PPC as an organisation scatters ["Dept. of Author Correspondence"].

The Department of Author Correction's behavior is taken very seriously in this futuristic dystopian fic. A character defending the DAC in this piece points out how killing Mary Sues in PPC stories is only a short step away from killing the authors who created them. When one character argues that the DAC is evil for torturing "girls in their teens, who've done nothing more than a bit of bad writing," the DAC apologist answers, "And we kill Mary-Sues who've done nothing more than try to seduce a canon character" ("Thirty Years Hence"). This author clearly recognizes the problematic nature of the PPC, its extreme and violent reactions to charges that are really very trivial, and the near-inseparability of violence against the Mary Sue character and violence against the creator of the character. By imagining a dystopia in which this bullying aspect of the PPC's mode of operation becomes more serious—a literary attack on the Sue becomes a physical attack on the Sue's creator—the author draws attention to the problematic behavior of the PPC and asserts that it could become the downfall of the organization.

Another example of the PPC's acknowledgment of its own problematic nature appears when writers spork their own fics. The PPC wiki has an entry on "author-requested missions": "a mission in which the author of the fic requests the PPC's attention, aids the PPC in their work, or otherwise becomes involved in the sporking of his or her own work." The wiki article claims, "Author-requested missions are not actually a very rare phenomenon. With news of the PPC spreading across the Internet and many serious fanfiction writers having grown out of their Mary Sue phases, there are more than a few people with the desire to teach others how not to write a Mary Sue" ("Author-Requested Mission").

The article gives three examples of such author-requested missions. In two of them, the author of the PPC story was actually mocking her own former work. "Mission: Swim" features an agent named July, who is hunting down the author's own former Mary Sue character, JulyFlame. The problems in this mission are clear when July and JulyFlame come face-to-face:

> The reason for July's insanity was now apparent; the author looked exactly like July, but younger.
> Library looked at her partner in concern. "This was your story?"
> "Yep." July nodded in confirmation. "And now I'm taking care of it." She turned back to the avatar girl and aimed the gun. "Now, where was I? JulyFlame, with no space between the two words pointedly noted, for all of this, your sentence is death" [Julyflame "Mission: Swim"].

However, July's partner, Library, tries to stop her from killing the Mary Sue.

5. Please Don't Kill the Author

> [Library] looked at her partner with a look of disgust. "I can't believe you! That—she's basically you! You were trying to kill yourself! What on earth is wrong with you, July?"
>
> July eyed the avatar with a look of extreme hate. "That's not me," the Agent said. "It's just a stupid avatar I once made. For fun."

There is an argument here over whether this earlier version of the fictional PPC agent is really the same person as the agent. It is not difficult to draw a parallel to the debate over whether the author avatar is really the same person as the author, or whether the author is still responsible for her former writing. Even the Mary Sue herself argues that she is in some form sentient and therefore, like a badfic author, should not be killed: she responds to July, "I'm a person, not an it."

July is forced by her partner to spare the Mary Sue, which over the course of a series of fics, leads July to attempt to murder the Mary Sue, to run away, alienate her friends and family, and spend some time in the psych ward of the PPC. The painfulness of having to acknowledge one's former Mary Sues—and the difficult moral tangle one finds oneself in in the attempt to murder one's own former author-avatar—is clearly depicted in the July stories. In contradiction of the PPC's official position on Mary Sues, the author of the July stories acknowledges the Mary Sue as some form of herself, albeit her younger self, and when the agent July attacks the Mary Sue JulyFlame, her partner seems appalled at her victimization of herself. Here the Mary Sue is close enough to the author that the execution of a Mary Sue in a mission becomes a difficult and murky moral problem.

OFUM and Subjectivity

The *ad hominem* attacks of Mary Sue assassinations are not the only problem with fan criticism. The problem of individual taste in the creation of a universal standard of literary quality is made obvious in Camilla Sandman's[3] "The Official Fanfiction University of Middle-earth," frequently referred to as "OFUM," and its sequel, "Once More into the Urple Depths of OFUM." The story begins with Lina Holling, a girl who is writing *Lord of the Rings* fanfiction late at night. Three men in suits suddenly appear in her bedroom and inform her that she is not allowed to write any more *Lord of the Rings* fanfic unless she successfully graduates from the Official Fanfiction University of Middle-earth and receives her license. They give her enrollment papers and disappear. Believing that she is hallucinating, Lina fills them in and falls asleep—only to awaken the next morning in Middle-earth on her way to OFUM (Sandman Chapter 1).

OFUM, under the command of the self-inserted headmistress Miss Cam, is much like a real university, with dormitories, roommates, classes, assignments, and exams—but with a few differences. All the classes are intended to improve the students' fanfiction, with subjects like Platonic Love (so they will stop writing slash—homoerotic fic—about Frodo and Sam), Striding (to teach them what hardships rangers actually face), and Evil Is as Evil Does (to make their villains more realistic). The classes are taught by Tolkien's characters, who live in the staff section. This section is strictly off-limits to students and is guarded by mini-balrogs,[4] created spontaneously whenever a fanfiction misspells a proper name. When the more "drool-worthy" characters—Legolas in particular—appear outside the staff section, they are at risk of being stampeded by lustful students. Students who have claimed a different race (elf, hobbit, ent) on their enrollment papers are actually given the appearance they requested. And finally, most of the education at OFUM comes through misery of some form or another: long reading lists, difficult assignments, and corporal punishment, often from the mini-balrogs, when students attempt to attract the notice of their "lust-objects." Most of the students in OFUM are real fans who have filled out the "enrollment papers" that Miss Cam posted online after the immediate clamor among readers to be included in the story (Miss Cam).

Though OFUM's ostensible purpose is to educate its students (and the readers) in better fanfiction writing, this task is complicated by the association of fanfiction with pure pleasure reading and the idiosyncrasies of taste. For example, in year two ("Once More"), Túrin (a character from Tolkien's *Silmarillion*) teaches "Angst and Proper Woes 101" and imitates some angsty fanfiction in hopes of demonstrating to students how exaggerated fanfiction angst often is:

> He fell to his knees, now sobbing heavily. "Thingol hit me because my ears were round! Then he raped me! And I accidentally killed my friend! My one true love turned out to be my sister! A dragon outsmarted me! Wah! My life is horrid! And to think all that was needed to save me was hot, healing sex with my one true love! Woe, woe, woe is me!... Now this is how you don't do it. You see how silly that was, all overblown and much too dramatic?" Túrin asked.
>
> There was a silence.
>
> "That was so hot," Bjam muttered finally.

"Oh, shut up," Túrin broke in, sounding annoyed. "You honestly found that pathetic self-pity display hot?"
"Yes," Evil Munky replied after a moment. "Could you do it again?" ["Once More" Chapter 32].

Though the fanfiction is gently making fun of fans and their tastes, this scene and similar ones point out the problems of taste-based judgements. Túrin's only argument against supposedly excessive angst is based on his expectation that readers will find it silly when they see it. However, they disarm his argument by finding it attractive, instead.

The Subjectivity of Literary Enjoyment

Judgments of taste are, at bottom, subjective judgments. The *Stanford Encyclopedia of Philosophy* states, "The first necessary condition of a judgment of taste is that it is essentially *subjective*. What this means is that the judgment of taste is based on a feeling of pleasure or displeasure. It is this that distinguishes a judgment of taste from an empirical judgment" ("Aesthetic Judgment"). Of course, the *Encyclopedia* notes, more goes into our judgments of taste than our personal feelings. Tastes are also socially constructed: we can see this in Jeanne's essay on "Shameless Setteis." A culture or a subgroup of that culture has its own ideas about what is aesthetically good and bad. Since these cultures often disagree, it is clear that there is no universal or truly objective standard of good taste—though we often act as if there is. Therefore, any argument about good and bad art or literature must appeal to a shared concept of good and bad taste existing within the community.

However, there seems to be no absolute shared standard from which a fan critic can argue about matters of taste in a genre that is so closely allied with reading for pure pleasure. As a matter of fact, personal taste is so important in fandom that the community has its own ethical standards based on it. One *Tumblr* user, ozhawkauthor, wrote a post titled "The Three Laws of Fandom," which has become so popular in the community that it has its own page on *Fanlore*. Ozhawkauthor writes, "If you wish to take part in any fandom, you need to accept and respect these three laws. If you aren't able to do that, then you need to realise that your actions are making fandom unsafe for creators. That you are stifling creativity."

The three laws that ozhawkauthor suggests and that have been widely hailed by other fans all relate to the importance of accepting others' personal tastes. The first law, "Don't Like; Don't Read (DL;DR)," is a slogan that fan writers have used for many years in response to extremely negative reviews from others. No one forces a fan to read any particular piece of fanfiction, so if the fan does not like what they are reading, they should stop and go read something else rather than leaving angry, dismissive, or cruel reviews. As *Tumblr* user wellhalesbells reminds her followers, "Fanfiction isn't written *for* you, it's shared *with* you."

The second law is "Your Kink Is Not My Kink (YKINMK)." A "kink" is one's own idiosyncratic fetish or sexual interest, but the term is frequently used by fans to mean anything that a fan particularly likes. When one fan is judgmental about another fan's tastes, this is referred to as "kinkshaming." Ozhawkauthor explains the second law: "Simply put, this means that everyone likes different things. It's not up to you to determine what creators are allowed to create. It's not up to you to police fandom." This is not to say that you are not allowed to have and voice your opinions: Ozhawkauthor adds, "If you don't like something, you can post meta about it or create contrarian content yourself, seek to convert other fans to your way of thinking. But you have no right to say to any creator 'I do not like this, therefore you should not create it. Nobody should like this. It should not exist.' It's not up to you to decide what other people are allowed to like or not like, to create or not to create. That's censorship. Don't do it."

Finally, the third law states, "Ship and Let Ship (SALS)." When fans want two characters to be in a relation*ship*, they are said to *ship* them. Sometimes members of the same fandom come into conflict with one another because they are rooting for different ships. The third law reminds fans, "It's not up to you to police ships or to determine what other people are allowed to ship. Just because you find that one particular ship problematic or disgusting, does not mean that other people are not allowed to explore its possibilities in their fanworks." Taken together, these three laws essentially state that everyone is allowed to have and express their own tastes, as long as they are not impolite to other fans or curtail other fans' rights to the same. Fandom is all about what one likes: what one is a fan of. It is therefore the height of absurdity for fans not to allow one another the freedom of liking what they like.

Many fans have suggested amendments to these laws, generally along ethical or political lines, but Ozhawkauthor's supporters have found flaws in all of these arguments. For example, *Tumblr* user sarcasm-

who added, "Agree but please do not ship ILLEGAL otp's (pedophilia, incest, etc)." Meedee responded with tongue-in-cheek humor: "Homosexuality is still illegal in 79 countries. So that would rule out slash. Incest laws also vary from country to country, so best to obtain legal advice before shipping." Ozhawkauthor added, "Well said! The age of consent varies between countries as well, and even between different STATES in the USA" (qtd. in "The Three Laws of Fandom").

As mentioned earlier, the literary quality of a work has long been closely tied to its perceived level of morality, and works that are believed to be of poor aesthetic quality are often credited with negative moral and psychological effects on absorbed readers. In order to break apart the ideas of political or moral correctness and personal enjoyment, writer Lindsay Ellis urges fans to stop questioning whether their favorite films and books are feminist or not before they decide to claim enjoyment of them. She explains,

> Don't ask "is this feminist?: as a means of giving yourself permission to like something. Media is designed to elicit an emotional response. You are not a bad person for having an emotional response to problematic media; you are not being attacked if someone examines the racial politics of your favorite movie. Media criticism is not about you. Nothing is exempt from critique. You don't get a gold star for liking the "right" things, and for the love of Christ stop trying to qualify your enjoyment of a thing by whether or not it's feminist enough. Go, go, and love what thou wilt.

While it is not bad for viewers and readers to consider and analyze the morals and politics of the media they consume, to think about that media critically, this does not mean that we should curtail our enjoyment of that media based entirely on that analysis. For example, the Centrumlumina survey discussed in Chapter 4 that revealed that fanfiction as a whole tends to demonstrate some racism in its choice of popular ships is not arguing that the fans who wrote that fanfiction are bad people or should feel badly about their fanfiction or their shipping preferences. What it is saying is that these statistics reveal something about trends in the community's preferred fiction, trends that represent widespread unconscious prejudices. These statistics are a thermometer, not a stick to beat fans with. Demanding that we enjoy "better" morality or politics in our media returns us to the old subconscious beliefs that literary quality and morality are somehow correlated.

As a matter of fact, it may be that pleasure readers find the supposed literary quality (in terms of style) or merit (in terms of subject) of a work inversely proportionate to the pleasure they gain from it. Victor

Nell, in "The Psychology of Reading for Pleasure: Needs and Gratifications" (1988), notes that this is true of many "ludic readers" (that is, spontaneous pleasure readers): "When the 33 ludic readers in this study were asked what percentage of their pleasure reading would be rated as 'trash' by a suitably austere representative of elite culture, such as their high school English teacher, their mean rating was 42.6%; 12 subjects rated 75% or more of their pleasure reading as trash" (20–21). Nell adds, "It is a strange reflection on our culture that pleasure reading, so zealously inculcated by school reading programs, may later be judged by the products of this education as aesthetically worthless, in society's eyes if not their own" (21).

Nell performed an experiment in which students, librarians, and professional academic literary critics were asked to rank extracts from unknown books in order of the pleasure they thought they would take in reading the book. The three groups were then also asked to rank those same extracts in terms of literary merit. As Nell sums up his findings, "Readers perceive literary merit to be inversely related to reading pleasure" (6). If one of fanfiction's primary purposes is pleasure reading, then its writers and readers may to some extent be purposefully dispensing with supposed literary quality or merit.

Fan critics may be able to understand the pitfalls of attempting criticism of fanfiction better than those outside of the community, who might not understand the nearly unlimited power of pleasure reading within the genre, or share fans' value for the absorbed reading experience. In "Why Is It So Hard to Talk About Fanfiction?," Undie Girl discusses the problem of judging fanfiction. She writes, "Here's the thing about fanfiction that everyone within the community instinctually understands: some of it is hilariously absurd. Fanfic is all about asking 'what if' and the answer is always yes, which leads to some pretty bizarre stuff. Limitless possibility is what makes fanfiction so amazing but it's also pretty funny sometimes…. It's part of enjoying fanfic." Undie Girl acknowledges that fanfiction has no absolute, authoritative rules, and that this is part of the appeal.

OFUM's Failure

While OFUM suggests arguments for and against certain forms of expression in fanfiction, the work is highly cognizant of the sovereignty of personal taste in fandom. It signals the impossibility of policing tastes through indicating OFUM's failure as an educational institution. As in the overblown angst example, the university seems capable only of teaching the students the "rules" of good taste: not of encouraging the students to stick to them. One sign of OFUM's failure is its inability to stop "lusters" among the students from fantasizing about their objects of affection among the staff. Intense lusting after one of Tolkien's characters is seen as the first step of Mary-Sue-ism, and is therefore one of the things that OFUM is trying to train their students out of. The students all have their favorite "lust objects," and despite lessons on how the characters are not interested in them and repeated threats of punishment from Miss Cam, the students continue to fantasize about them. Even the narrator can't stop fantasizing: at the beginning of the second semester she writes,

> Male Bonding had created a stir, for all the Legolas-droolers couldn't wait to have a class with him and [What did I say about thinking such things? Signed, Miss Cam]. On the other hand, the Aragorn-should-be-single club was in mourning ... and consoled themselves thinking of Aragorn in [Must I censor every sentence? Do-not-think-such-things! Signed, Miss Cam]. And the hobbits were heartbroken.... The Sam Stampeders had been known to lurk in the gardens hoping to catch their favourite gardener and [Oh, for the love of Galadriel,[5] stop! Signed, Miss Cam] ["OFUM" Chapter 32].

The story implies that even the narrator herself cannot stop the character-lust from leaking into the story, signaling the University's total failure to eliminate it.

In fact, many of the standards of good writing that are taught by the University are subverted by the fic, as the students only follow the rules laid down for them because they are under the threat of extreme pain. One of the most obvious subversions is that students are told not to write self-insert fic, but when the main character, Lina, has finished her education, she writes the story of how she has fallen in love with one of the staff members (albeit not a traditionally attractive one): Gimli the dwarf. She is then offered a position on the staff. Because of fanfiction's basis in personal pleasure—and the fic's attitude toward fans' foibles as fun and amusing—"poor writing" is depicted as impossible to eradicate. "OFUM" demonstrates how difficult it is to educate fans out of what are actually their personal tastes.

Even Miss Cam admits to having literary tastes she is not proud of—the kinds of tastes she seems to be trying to educate her students out of. Seeing Lina and the dwarf Gimli together as a couple toward the end of the year, she cannot stop herself: "'Aaaaw,' said a muffled voice and they both turned to stare at Miss Cam. 'Oh, shut up,' Miss Cam said briskly. 'I'm a sucker for romances.... Excuse me, I think I'll go watch *Bridget Jones's Diary* again—and oh yes, mention this to *anyone* and I'm frying you both on a McDonald's fryer and drowning you in salt'" ("OFUM" Chapter 62). OFUM cannot eradicate personal tastes, even those that are considered guilty pleasures, such as women's frank expressions of sexuality. It is impossible to lay down rules on such a subjective basis: OFUM has more success educating students about spelling and grammar, which are seen as more objective.

Realistic? Really?

Another standard of "good taste" in writing that OFUM frequently refers to is one based on realism. For example, students are taught to write fanfictions with more realistic depictions of the Fellowship's grueling trek through the wilderness by being forced to perform part of this trek themselves ("OFUM" Chapter 27). However, realism does not ultimately work as a criterion of literary quality in OFUM because Miss Cam's fanfiction itself is deeply unrealistic, with its metafictional setting, the cartoon-like ability of characters to bounce back from injury, and the general silliness of the premise and the writing. Nor is realism a good objective criterion for *Lord of the Rings* fanfiction in general, because the magic and supernatural powers on which Tolkien's plot is based are themselves unrealistic.

Realism is a problematic criterion for literary quality in general. After all, most fictional stories are not really realistic: they leave out details, condense events, and contain wildly improbable coincidences. Realism only emerged as a requirement for good writing in the eighteenth century, under the same system of social control that condemned *bovarysme*. In *The True Story of the Novel*, Margaret Anne Doody explains "the increasing pressure to produce novels that are lifelike, probable, [and] verisimilar" in this period, which she attributes to a political "desire on the part of the authorities to sustain the *status quo*" and to the call for more morally acceptable "exemplary tales."

Bovarysme was dangerous to the status quo because it inspired the disenfranchised to see themselves as heroic. Likewise, stories set in exotic cultures and time periods could lead readers to rethink British imperialism, and tales of the world as it *could be* might teach the disenfranchised to question whether political and social change were really as impossible as they seemed. Safer by far to stick to stories that showed the everyday English society as it was, that taught readers moral lessons about accepting their lot in life and in society. Doody concludes, "'Probability' and 'verisimilitude' had been introduced to save the day, to discipline the [novel] and make it acceptable.... At the price of getting rid of its medieval phase, the Novel ... could enter the Kingdom of Literature" (285–86).

We can see even today that genres of literature that do not stick so closely to this socially constructed (certainly not absolute) idea of probability and verisimilitude—such as science fiction and fantasy—are accorded less respect in our culture than more "realistic" genres. And of course, as fanzine/internet fanfiction began in the *Star Trek* fandom and arose from the sci-fi fanzine culture, much of fanfiction has been written from science fiction and fantasy fandoms ever since. Fandom, as a genre that asks "What if?" is a genre based on unrealism and departure from the "truth" of the canon. Miss Cam's university proves the impossibility of policing fanfiction based on the unstable and subjective grounds of taste and realism.

Finding a Basis for Criticism

Absorbed reading thus appears to make the fan critic's job considerably harder, since the personal tastes of pleasure reading do not provide an objective basis for criticism, and attacks on Mary Sue characters can be seen as bullying attacks on authors. However, while implicitly criticizing the absorbed reading goes into the creation of Mary Sues, the PPC finds a way to deploy absorbed reading itself as a seemingly objective basis for fan criticism. Because absorbed reading is so closely allied with fanfiction, fan critics can assume that this is how the vast majority of their fellow fans read works in the genre. Therefore, as we will see, PPC missions can claim that a fanfiction is poorly written when something in the writing is likely to confuse an absorbed reader and interfere with the cohesive absorbed reading experience.

The PPC recognizes that in order for their criticism to function, they must not be seen to be making purely subjective critiques. Personal taste cannot be the basis for fan criticism, or their entire mission is pointless. The PPC thus make sure to claim that their opinions on the quality of other fans' writing is, in some sense, objective: they write, "We are also here because we despise bad writing, but let us make it clear that this definition has to be applied more or less objectively—it's not a matter of taste" ("Guide to the PPC").

Objectivity in the judgments of the agents is necessary to make the PPC proceedings seem at all fair. After all, PPC agents draw up and announce a list of "charges" against fics, indicating that they have broken some kind of objective "laws," and that the PPC are the proper body to determine when such laws have been broken. The agents' authority is so unquestionable that there is never even a trial: characters are executed immediately after being charged. The PPC stories must therefore depict the agents as objective judges of literary quality.

The PPC utilizes a number of approaches to give the impression of objectivity. For instance, they make new members go through a sort of apprenticeship and a permission requirement before they are authorized by the PPC to write missions. The organization cites the fact that if one is going to write stories attacking other works for errors and poor writing, that the stories themselves should be well-written: "We take pride in the fact that our stories are well-written. If someone asks for permission to PPC, and that person's post is riddled with bad spelling, grammar, and logic, permission will not be granted. What right do we have to mock people's stories if our own writings are just as bad? Additionally, it would be super-hypocritical if the PPC ended up full of Sue and Stu agents who are not reformed" ("Permission").

The process for becoming a PPC writer is surprisingly difficult. In order to establish familiarity with the PPC universe, new writers are encouraged to spend time on the PPC message boards and read through the Original Series as well as other supplemental reading. Finally, they are asked to "create two writing samples based on the 36 Permission Prompts. You'll use one control prompt of your choice and one random prompt you'll get based on a dice roll" ("Permission"). The writer must then apply to one of a select group of "Permission Givers," turning in a short biography of their new agents, the two small writing samples, and the badfic they plan to "spork" for their first mission. Then the Permission Giver will let them know whether their work looks good enough for the PPC.

The PPC agents also support their claim to objectivity with fictional scientific devices, such as the Canon Analysis Device and the Character

Analysis Device. An agent can simply use the numbers the Canon Analysis Device spits out to determine by what percentage a canon character is out of character, and point to that number as a (fictional) "objective" measurement. All these things seem to support the PPC's claim to critical objectivity. However, their greatest tool for this purpose is the value they share with other fan readers for a coherent and smooth absorbed reading experience.

The experience of the agents entering the story is in many ways like that of an absorbed reader entering a fictional world. This is obvious in many aspects of PPC stories, including how these fics deal with "the words." Just as an absorbed reader can focus on the images the reading experience creates, the words themselves on the page, or both, agents can focus on the words that create the fictional worlds they enter, sometimes glancing ahead at future events. The wiki states,

> Agents can see the Words that make the world while in a fic if they squint, let their eyes unfocus, gaze at the sky, or do some other trick they've invented; seeing the Words appears to be akin to seeing a Magic Eye picture. Reading the Words can be useful when agents don't want to be exposed to traumatizing or dangerous situations or when it would be impossible to observe the action without being caught. However, it is PPC policy to observe badfic in person rather than just reading the Words; charges are based on how the fic affects the canon, not on the agents' judgment of how bad the writing is.... Agents have been known to read ahead in the Words to warn themselves of approaching danger. This is by no means foolproof, since the exact way the Words play out cannot be known until they actually express themselves ["Word World"].

The "badness" of the fic cannot truly be experienced or judged through a more emotionally and intellectually distanced critical reading, focusing merely on the words themselves on the page. It isn't until the agents experience the action of the story through absorbed reading of the text that it is clear what effects the writing will have within the fictional reality. Fanfictions are thus judged by the negative effects the writing may have on the absorbed reader, who is experiencing the story like an agent entering into a metafictional world.

With a shared value for the absorbed reading experience, fan critics like the PPC have a foundation from which to make criticisms about the literary quality of fanfictions. Any problems in the writing that might jolt an absorbed reader out of their absorption or create bizarre mental images can be decried. In the PPC, the consequences of writing flaws are literal and obvious. For instance, in one of Tungsten Monk's stories, set in the magical school Hogwarts from J. K. Rowling's

Harry Potter series, the author misspells *silverware* as *silverwear*. The bizarre mental image this misspelling might create in the mind of a reader is, in this story, real: the tables of the Great Hall of Hogwarts are suddenly covered in silver clothing. The agents pause the story, steal the valuable apparel, and charge the author with "mistreatment of clothing." In the same story, the author leaves the character of Dumbledore alive, despite the fact that the fic is set in year seven of the Harry Potter series, and the canonical Dumbledore died at the end of year six. In the PPC story, this means that Dumbledore appears as a walking corpse: an *inferius*, as zombies are called in the *Harry Potter* universe (Tungsten Monk "Ow, Ow, and Ow Again"). The bizarre mental images that an absorbed reader might experience when reading such spelling and canonical mistakes is made literal in PPC stories.

Misspellings of proper names cause even greater problems in PPC missions. Every time a proper name is misspelled, the misspelling spawns a miniature monster. (This trope originated in OFUM, which exists in the same fictional universe as the PPC, and the trope was adopted by PPC writers.) The form of the monster depends on which fandom the fic is in: misspellings in Middle-earth create minibalrogs, in Narnia mini-dragons, in Harry Potter mini-Aragogs,[6] etc. In one memorable Tungsten Monk story, the misspelling of an Egyptian goddess' name spawns an adorable mini-Ammit, a monster from Egyptian mythology.[7] These minis are frequently kept by the agents as pets.

Other errors that would make for distracting reading also have objective results. Inaccuracies about the passage of time or distances within the canon can cause temporal/spatial distortions which may give the agents hangover-like headaches (Tungsten Monk "Ranariel"). Notes from the author inserted directly into the text can boom down from the sky like the voice of God, or even cause injury as they fly past: "Rowen was prevented from outright attacking the Sue when she was hit with a flying author's note. *(IMPORTANT A/N—DRACOna is not named after Draco Malfoy, I just changed the spelling of DRAGON abit ... just so you know!)* ... Rowen sputtered incoherently and gingerly touched her nose. There hadn't been a crack, but it hurt like hell getting hit in the face with an author's note" (Tungsten Monk "Ow, Ow, and Ow Again"). Agents can also be injured by unannounced scene changes.

All of these errors or infelicities of style can distract an absorbed reader, pulling them out of the fic they are reading. In the world of the PPC their distracting and bizarre effects are made literal and even injurious to the agents, who can add them to the list of charges against the author. Thus, PPC criticisms against what they see as poor writing can be considered in some way objective, because of the shared experience of absorbed reading amongst fans and the shared value for a cohesive absorbed reading experience.

Ironically, the shared experience that PPC stories rely on as an objective basis for literary criticism—absorbed reading—is the very basis of the Mary Sues they so abhor. While members of the PPC could argue that the unrealistic nature of the Mary Sue character or her uncanonicity may be disrupting the absorbed reading experience of the fanfiction, it is clear that the fan who created the Mary Sue found her to be a useful and enjoyable tool to enhance her own absorbed reading experience. If the basis for judgments of taste in fandom is the shared valuation of the undisturbed absorbed reading experience, then Mary Sues should not be a problem.

Battling Internalized Discrimination

The centrality of absorbed reading in the creation and consumption of fanfiction can make fan literary critique more difficult, in that the pleasure reading of fanfiction provides no objective standard for literary quality, and the close association of the writer with her self-inserted Mary Sue characters can easily turn fan criticism into bullying. The shared experience of absorbed reading itself can provide a basis for a different kind of literary critique, which judges fics according to how much the errors or infelicities in the writing disrupt a cohesive absorbed reading experience. Unfortunately, despite this seemingly objective basis for fan criticism in PPC stories, the act of criticism itself can still be hurtful to the authors of the so-called badfics and reinforce patterns of discrimination against fans and other absorbed readers.

Instead of seeking for an objective basis for fan criticism directed against one another, fans should be working together to defeat the internalized discrimination and misogyny that informs such criticism. *Community Tool Box* insists, "Internalized oppression is not the fault of people whom it affects. No one should be blamed or blame themselves for having been affected by discrimination. Nevertheless, as community members, we have to face these barriers in order to achieve our goals" ("Chapter 27, Section 3"). As fans, we need to abandon in-fighting and unasked-for "quality control" and turn our attention toward breaking down the negative stereotypes of fans and fanfiction that harm us all. To quote Jane Austen, "Let us not desert one another; we are an injured body."

6

Follow the Money

No discussion of fanfiction's reputation as a guilty pleasure would be complete without a discussion of copyright law. One of the major reasons why fanfiction is tainted with a feeling of illegitimacy is because many people believe that it is illegal and in violation of copyright. This supposed illegality also connects with what many critics consider fanfiction's lack of originality. Why write fanfiction with someone else's characters, they ask, when you could simply invent your own? A desire for originality in art and literature is deeply embedded in modern culture: as author Patricia C. Wrede observes, "Originality is held up as an absolute, fundamental prerequisite for high quality writing (and this is further reinforced by the attitude of modern society toward plagiarism)." Fanfiction, by using other writers' characters, settings, and even fanfiction premises, appears to violate this concept of originality, along with the copyright laws so closely connected with it.

What many people do not realize is where the modern value for originality came from. Originality, like realism, only began to be upheld as a sign of literary quality in the early eighteenth century, with the advent of Britain's first copyright law. This copyright law and the concept of intellectual property that developed from it were concerned mainly with protecting authors financially. Even today, the application of copyright law is strongly concerned with finance. Internet fanfiction, because it does not—and under copyright law generally *cannot*—make money, is divorced from this financially motivated concept of originality. This chapter examines how copyright law makes fanfiction appear to be a guilty pleasure, and how the genre stands in opposition to a system that considers monetary value to be an indispensable part of literary quality.

A History of Derivative Literature

To fully understand fanfiction's current position under copyright law, it is helpful to gain a broad view of the genre, and especially its connection with a much longer and broader history of literature. Modern fanfiction is merely the most recent manifestation of an ancient literary tradition of derivative literature. Myths and legends were often the products of a large group of storytellers, all embellishing and altering stories as they passed them down to others. When stories moved from oral to written dissemination, this pattern continued. For example, ancient Greek tragedies were fanfictions, "almost always inspired by episodes from Greek mythology" (Cartwright). Similarly, many ancient writers would write within the same "cycle" of myths and legends. Virgil's celebrated *Aeneid*, for example, picks up where Homer's *Iliad* left off.

This creation of derivative literature within a mythic cycle continued on into the medieval era. One instance of this occurs in the "Theban Cycle." This consisted of four poems, possibly by four different writers, about the mythical history of Thebes. The Latin author Statius created the *Thebaid* based on these stories in the first century BCE. In the fourteenth century the Italian poet Boccaccio based his *Teseida* on the *Thebaid*, and then the English poet Chaucer based his *Anelida and Arcite* and "The Knight's Tale" on the *Teseida*. In fact, in his introduction to Chaucer's famous *Troilus and Criseyde*, Stephen A. Barney writes,

> Boccaccio stimulated a new tradition that flourished in the fourteenth century—taking a small episode or group of episodes from the great chronicles and treating them in more elaborate detail, just as the Greeks had elaborated segments of the Homeric cycles as independent works. Like the romances of Chrétien de Troyes and his followers, these new works could explore nuances of human relations, develop moral and philosophical themes, rearrange and give point and conclusiveness to the structure of events, and represent details of settings, conversations, private complaints, public speeches, and the subtlest gestures [471].

Such medieval writing displays the results of absorbed reading. These authors imagined the characters of Greek myths and Homeric epics as having real, human interactions, emotions, and motives, and illustrated them more fully in derivative expansions. These medieval expansions of famous stories were actually fanfiction.

There was a strong tradition of derivative literature in general in the European Middle Ages because such works were seen as relying on already-established authority. This appeal to authority was important in Medieval culture: even works that weren't derivative were often introduced with comments from the authors claiming that they were translations of rediscovered ancient writings (see Pugh 13). Similarly, the tales of Robin Hood or of King Arthur that flourished at that time and continue to proliferate are all fanfictions—Marie de France; Chrétien de Troyes; Sir Thomas Malory; Alfred, Lord Tennyson; and Marion Zimmer Bradley included. And it did not stop with the Middle Ages. Many of Shakespeare's plots came from history, Ovid, and Chaucer, among many other sources (see "Narrative and Dramatic Sources"). And what is Milton's *Paradise Lost* but Biblical fanfiction?

Even in the eighteenth century, when originality began to be upheld as a required characteristic for great literature, unauthorized rewritings, sequels, and dramatic adaptations flourished, as has been well documented by David A. Brewer in *The Afterlife of Character, 1726-1825*. The late nineteenth century saw the rise of one of the first recognizable modern fandoms: the fans of Arthur Conan Doyle's Sherlock Holmes stories. Anastasia Klimchynskaya describes the immense popularity of Conan Doyle's short stories and the way Holmes fans, as absorbed readers, blurred the lines between reality and fiction: "Doyle began to receive massive amounts of fan mail—addressed to Mr. Sherlock Holmes, asking him to find their stolen purse or their lost dog. They asked for copies of the stories to be signed by 'Sherlock Holmes.' Women wrote to Holmes asking to be his housekeeper. Letters were written to 221b Baker Street (which was a problem, since Baker Street numbers didn't go up that high at the time)." When Conan Doyle finally killed off the immensely popular character in 1893, the public outcry was massive: Klimchynskaya writes, "British society dressed in mourning. Black armbands were worn to commemorate the great detective's passing. People cancelled their subscriptions to *The Strand* (the newspaper that then published the Holmes stories), but not before sending piles of angry letters. Even more piles of pleas and petitions arrived on Doyle's doorstep. Obituaries appeared in newspapers. Accusations of murder flew through the air."

The twentieth century, which featured the originality-obsessed modernist movement, has also produced Tom Stoppard's *Rosencrantz and Guildenstern Are Dead* and Jean Rhys' *Wide Sargasso Sea*, based on *Hamlet* and *Jane Eyre*, respectively, as well as many other great works of literature that are actually fanfictions. Fan Aja Romano has compiled a list of "professional" works that would qualify as fanfiction, including a number of Pulitzer-Prize winning works: the list is extremely long, and commenters add to it constantly. And in the twenty-first century, we have the *Wicked* phenomenon: L. Frank Baum wrote *The Wizard of Oz*, which was adapted as the film of the same name by Metro-Goldwyn-Mayer in 1939, which was rewritten in the fanfiction novel *Wicked: The Life and Times of the Wicked Witch of the West* by Gregory Maguire in 1995, which was adapted as a stage musical (*Wicked: The Untold Story of the Witches of Oz*) in 2003 by Universal Studios, who are now planning to create a film version (Madison). All of these works of literature from Sophocles and Shakespeare to Stoppard, qualify as fanfiction.

The internet/fanzine fanfiction that this book has mostly focused on constitutes a subgenre in this wider tradition of derivative literature. The distinction is that internet/fanzine fanfiction is written within and for a community of fans—a "fandom"—rather than by individual fans for a more widespread audience. While works like Jane Austen's novels and Arthur Conan Doyle's Sherlock Holmes stories have long had organizations and clubs of fans, internet/fanzine fanfiction can really be said to have originated with the *Star Trek* fandom in the 1960s. Prior to this time, the term "fan fiction" meant only amateur science fiction, published in magazines by groups of science fiction fans: it was not written using the characters and settings of other writers' works ("Fanfiction"). As was noted earlier, science fiction for clubs had met together since the 1920s and published fanzines since the 1930s. These clubs were a major component of the audience that first saw the pilot of *Star Trek* at the World Science Fiction Convention in Cleveland in 1966 and formed a large part of the show's later fanbase. A group of these fans subsequently produced a fanzine dedicated exclusively to *Star Trek* fiction.

The fanzine *Spockanalia*, published in September of 1967, at the beginning of the television show's second season, contained the first fanzine fanfiction based on someone else's characters: the first works of this new subgenre of derivative fiction. Many others followed. As Alice Bell notes, "This series not only inspired fans, but it offered a whole infrastructure with which they could interact. There were conventions to attend and magazines where they could be published." *Star Trek* fans soon began writing fanfiction about other series they enjoyed, like *Doctor Who*, and fanzine fanfiction became its own genre with its own style, tropes, and conventions (Bell).

Eventually fan writers moved from hardcopy fanzines to the internet. Bell writes, "First there were news groups and then mailing lists, followed by a short period on blogs. People soon moved to *LiveJournal* because it offered such a great comments structure. More recently, *Twitter* and *Tumblr* have become key community places." Fanfiction is published online on privately-owned fan websites, usually structured to support only one fandom, or on sites set up to host fanfiction in multiple fandoms, such as *FanFiction.Net* and *Archive of Our Own* (AO3).

Modern internet fanfiction follows a tradition of derivative literature that was ostensibly abandoned with the advent of the financially motivated copyright laws in the early eighteenth century. However, as Romano's list of great literary fanfictions indicates, this derivative concept is not gone. It is merely embattled, especially when it is created by young women and based on popular texts rather than classical ones. The fact that fanfiction continues to be written and enjoyed even after the rise of originality in the eighteenth century demonstrates the strength and resilience of absorbed reading as a practice of media consumption and readers' persistence in thinking about fictional characters like real people. Fanfiction is part of a much longer tradition of derivative literature, one that existed long before the advent of copyright law and that has refused to be eradicated.

Originality and the Advent of Copyright Law

Modern culture's value for originality, which has helped to create the stigma attached to the apparently unoriginal genre of fanfiction, is inextricably tied to the concept of legal copyright. In *Nobody's Story: The Vanishing Acts of Women Writers in the Marketplace, 1670–1820*, Catherine Gallagher gives a brief overview of the first law to protect intellectual property: the Statute of Anne, 1710. Before that time, rights to written works belonged to the publishers. Gallagher explains that the Statue of Anne was the first law in England to grant the right of ownership to the author, linking together ideas of intellectual property and profit:

> The Licensing Act that had lapsed in 1695 had granted the "copy," or right to print a book, to the member of the Stationers' Company who registered its title.... No law for the regulation of the press previous to 1710 made any mention of an author's rights or property, and hence the Statute of Anne might be said to have initiated the idea that texts, as opposed to manuscripts, were exchangeable commodities belonging ultimately to their authors by virtue of being "the product of their learning and labour" [155–56].

This concept of an author's ownership of his or her text and the elements therein, Gallagher explains, led directly to a new emphasis on originality, as originality was the criterion on which the right of ownership could be legally determined:

> When one looks at the decisions handed down under the Statute of Anne in early copyright disputes, one is struck by the emphasis the courts placed on "invention" or "originality" as the definitive characteristic of authorship. Determining "wherein consists the identity of a book" became a task of discovering authorship, which in large part became the task of discovering "invention." As the century progressed, copyright disputes became occasions for articulating even more radical notions of originality than have ever been incorporated in the law itself. In 1769, for example, one justice suggested copyright should protect the *ideas* of the work, and hence that the requirement of invention might not be satisfied by mere reformation or rewording, although he simultaneously admitted that ideas, divorced from the particulars of their expression, "were 'quite wild' and incapable of *indicia certa*." The question whether an author was commonly, if not legally, definable as someone whose thoughts are original had, however, been broached, and the affirmative response was to gain wider acceptance over the next two centuries [157–58].

This concept of the author as the originator—and thus sole rightful proprietor—of his or her own ideas progressed from the realm of law to the realm of literary criticism. To have the legal right to one's work, one needed to make sure that work demonstrates original invention. Gallagher observes that it was a small step from there to the idea that good literature must be original: "It is not surprising, then, that a similar valorization of unprecedented, unique conceptualization appeared in numerous discussions of literature. Indeed, literary criticism at midcentury was often an inquiry into what could properly be attributed to various writers as their own inventions, as if the critics, like the courts, had been set the task of ferreting out infringements of literary property" (158). The veneration of originality which has since become most prominent as a hallmark of modernism and which still dominates in the area of literary criticism today—the veneration that causes our culture to look askance at derivative literature and to exclaim against works like fanfiction—thus originated a mere three hundred years ago with the advent of copyright law.

Complicating the issue is the fact that, like "realism," "originality" in literature is not an absolute. In his essay "On Fairy Stories," J. R. R. Tolkien compares all stories to a pot of soup, a mishmash of materials and of sources in older stories: "The Pot of Soup, the Cauldron of Story, has always been boiling, and to it have continually been added new bits, dainty and undainty." Every plot point or aspect of formal structure that an author could use has been used already: originality lies in authors' recombinations of those plot events or formal techniques in aesthetically, emotionally, and mentally pleasing ways—a recombination that fanfiction writers perform just as "original fiction" writers do.

Derivative literature has always been a norm in human culture, and though copyright law has made writing derivative literature more complicated, it has not put a stop to it. As Henry Jenkins points out in "Digital Land Grab," an article on the internet and the legal concerns of fan culture,

> For most of human history, the storyteller was the inheritor and protector of a shared cultural tradition.... The great works of the western tradition were polished like stones in a brook as they were handed off from bard to bard.... Contemporary Web culture is the traditional folk process working at lightning speed on a global scale. The difference is that our core myths now belong to corporations, rather than the folk.

Profit-based copyright concerns and the resulting valorization of originality have handicapped this ancient tradition of derivative and transformative literature.

In fact, U.S. copyright law has become significantly more restrictive during the twentieth century due to the Disney corporation's legal actions to keep their characters out of the public domain. Steve Schlackman for *Art Law Journal* explains this slow transformation. The original American copyright law, the Copyright Act of 1790, guaranteed a creators of maps, charts, and books the rights to his or her work for fourteen years, a term which could be renewed once during the creator's lifetime for an additional four-year term. These creators were required to register their copyright and use a copyright notice in order for this law to apply. Any work that was not registered for copyright or that had outlived its fourteen- or twenty-eight-year copyright automatically entered the public domain, where anyone was free to copy, alter, and distribute the original material. This original short term did expand: Schlackman writes, "By 1831 it was changed to 28 years with a 14 year renewal and in 1909, copyright duration became 28 years with a 28 year renewal. Very few works actually maintained those copyright durations as only a small percentage of people even bothered to register copyrights in the first place, and of those that did, only a tiny fraction renewed them." So even after these expansions to the term of copyright, the vast majority of works were available in the public domain in less than thirty years.

Mickey Mouse first appeared in the short animation "Steamboat

Willy" in 1928. As the expiration of the character's copyright in 1984 neared, "Disney is said to have begun serious lobbying push for changes to the Copyright Act." Due to the company's actions, "in 1976, Congress authorized a major overhaul of the copyright system assuring Disney extended production." The new law followed the European norm of granting individual authors copyright protection for their life plus fifty years. Furthermore, "for works authored by corporations, the 1976 legislation also granted a retroactive extension for works published before the new system took effect. The maximum term for already-published works was lengthened from 56 years to 75 years[,] pushing Mickey protection out to 2003." This meant that any works published before 1923 are in the public domain, but anything published since that time may still be protected by copyright.

However, Disney still didn't want to let go of their copyright to Mickey Mouse and all their subsequent character designs, and five years before Mickey's term of copyright expired, Congress passed the Sonny Bono Copyright Term Extension Act of 1998, which guaranteed works created after 1977 protection for the "'life of the author plus 70 years,'" and extends copyrights for corporate works to 95 years from the year of first publication, or 120 years from the year of creation, whichever expires first.

In other words, as Duke law professor James Boyle concludes, "We are the first generation to deny our own culture to ourselves.... No work created during your lifetime will, without conscious action by its creator, become available for you to build upon." Disney's prominent role in expanding copyright law to keep its own characters out of the public domain seems particularly hypocritical, considering how many Disney films are based on fairy tales and classic books like *Alice in Wonderland*, *Pinocchio*, and *The Hunchback of Notre Dame*, which they were able to use specifically because those works were in the public domain. Twentieth-century expansions to U.S. copyright law demonstrate nothing so much as corporations' use of monetary power to protect their profits at the expense of other creators.

Money Matters: Fanfic vs. Profic

Copyright law, which assigns a monetary value to originality, derives from profit concerns: violations of copyright are illegal because violating works may take a share of or otherwise harm the profits that should belong to another writer. Derivative genres like internet fanfiction give rise to ethical qualms that arise partly from this legal concern for profit. Authors also object to fanfiction because they feel it "steals" or "kidnaps" their characters, corrupts their authorial reputations, and violates their intellectual rights. Though these feelings about having their characters appropriated by others are not directly financially motivated, they derive from the concept of literary rights and property instituted by financially motivated copyright laws. The financial and legal definition of originality has become so deeply embedded in western culture that more original literary works are considered to be of higher quality than more obviously derivative works—and derivative works are often believed to demonstrate a lack of moral fiber on the part of their authors. Ethical, legal, and financial motives combine to award the greatest accolades of originality to texts that can legally make money.

It may seem strange to assert that works that can gain a profit for the author are considered to be of higher literary quality than works that are created simply for pleasure. There is a concept in our culture that a "true artist" does not consider profit when creating art, and that the more divorced the art is from profit concerns, the freer and more "genuine" it will be. However, there is another impulse in our culture to value those things which have monetary worth more than those things which do not. We can see this second impulse in some of the discussion surrounding *profic*: professional fanfictions that can make money, such as tie-in novels.

Fanlore defines a tie-in as "a published work meant to complement (and derive a profit from) another published work. In general, tie-ins are novels or graphic novels that spring from a movie or television show" ("Tie-in"). Widely known examples include the hundreds upon hundreds of *Star Trek* and *Star Wars* tie-in novels (see "List of *Star Trek* Novels," "List of *Star Wars* Books"). Lee Goldberg, who writes tie-in novels for television series like *Diagnosis Murder* and *Monk*, defends his writing and attacks amateur fan writers partly on the grounds that his work is paid and their work is unpaid. Goldberg states, "licensed tie-in fiction, which I have written, differs significantly on ethical and legal grounds from fanfiction because it is done with the consent, participation and supervision of the original author or rights holder" (qtd. in Young, "Lee Goldberg's War on Fanfic"). Goldberg separates fanfiction from tie-in fiction on the grounds of legal copyright and permission (ignoring the fact that many authors have allowed and even encouraged fans in general to write fanfiction of their works, though they are not directly supervising those fan writers).

Goldberg's definition of fanfiction depends on legal considerations of copyright, and as a result, his arguments against the genre frequently revolve around money:

> [S]omeone asked what the difference is between someone who writes tie-ins and someone who writes fanfic... beyond the fact that tie-ins are written with the consent of the author/right's [sic] holder.
> There's a big difference.
> I was *hired* to write *Diagnosis Murder* and *Monk* novels. It's something I am being paid to do. It's not like I woke up one morning with a burning desire to write *Diagnosis Murder* novels, wrote one up, and sent it off to a publisher (or, as a fanficcer would do, posted it on the web). The publisher came to me and *asked* me to write them.
> I would never write a book using someone else's characters *unless* I was hired to do so. It would never even occur to me *because the characters aren't mine.*
> Given a choice, I would *only* write novels and TV shows of my own creation. But I have to make a living and I take the work that comes my way ... and that includes writing-for-hire, whether it's on someone else's TV show or original tie-in novels based on characters I didn't create. Ultimately, however, what motivates me as a writer is to express *myself* ... not the work of someone else.
> That's the big difference between me and a fanficcer.
> Given a choice, fanficcers "write" fanfic [qtd. in Young "Lee Goldberg's War on Fanfic"].

Goldberg seems to be trying to argue that originality is his lodestar, so that he would never consider writing in someone else's "world" without their express request. However, his argument does come off as a rejection of the idea that he enjoys creating the tie-in novels that he writes. Enjoyment of writing in someone else's world, he seems to assert, belongs to fanfiction, whereas he writes only because he was hired to. Though this is probably not how he would like to summarize his arguments, it did lead blogger Cathy Young to state that Goldberg defends the contradiction between attacking fanfiction while writing fanfiction "on the grounds that he does it only for the money" ("Lee Goldberg's War on Fanfic").

Clearly, even in the case of tie-in novels, the commercialization of fanfiction seems problematic, due to both the copyright-motivated (and therefore profit-motivated) taboos on writing about someone else's characters, and the contrasts that our culture has established between creating art for its own sake and creating art for money. Nonetheless, while art is considered less pure if it is done for money, there is also a general feeling that a piece of art must be worth money to be "any good."

Fanfic Making Money

There have, of course, been attempts to monetize internet fanfiction. One of the most obvious ways this is done is by "filing off the serial numbers": this means "taking a piece of existing fan fiction and removing any details that tie it to a copyrighted source" ("Filing Off"). One of the most widely known examples of this is the bestselling erotic novel *Fifty Shades of Grey* by E. L. James, a piece which began its life as a *Twilight* fanfiction. "Originally self-published as an ebook and a print-on-demand," *Fifty Shades* "has sold over 100 million copies worldwide" after "publishing rights were acquired by Vintage Books in March 2012 … and set a record in the United Kingdom as the fastest-selling paperback of all time" (*"Fifty Shades of Grey"*).

Metro notes that other fanfics-turned-original-fics have been picked up by publishers since:

> Berkley Books recently paid a seven-figure sum for Sylvain Reynard's *Gabriel's Inferno*, which also started life as *Twilight* fan fiction and has been hyped as the next *Fifty Shades*. Similarly, Harper Collins has snapped up *The Dark Heroine* by teenage author Abigail Gibbs, which is heavily influenced by the Twilight saga, although not strictly a work of fan fiction. Gibbs received 17 million hits on publishing website *Wattpad* before she stopped posting just before her story's conclusion: within 24 hours of the ebook's release, it was at No. 22 in the Kindle charts [Metrowebukmetro].

In the cases of fanfictions "crossing over" from free online fandom to commercial publication, fanfictions in a sense cease to be fanfiction, as the derivative elements have to be removed. And readers of the fanfiction may resent having to pay for a work which they were earlier able to read for free. *Fanlore* notes,

> In recent years, fewer fans are supportive of these pro publishing activities. Ironically, this comes at a time where fans are finding it much easier to self-publish their fanfic or work through smaller, non-traditional presses. Fans may not appreciate having a beloved, or worse, unfinished WIP [Work In Progress] suddenly disappear so an author can publish it. Other fans have expressed dissatisfaction at buying a professional [male slash] work, only to discover they've already read the story in its earlier fanfic guise ["Filing Off the Serial Numbers"].

The only cases in which amateur fanfiction can become profic without these problems are in fandoms like *Pride and Prejudice*, where the canon is out of copyright. The huge number of professionally published *Pride and Prejudice* fanfictions attests to the success of this approach (see "A Comprehensive Guide to Austenesque Novels"). Unfortunately, it only works if the canon has managed to remain popular for more than several decades, and if the fanfiction has not been published online before being published for profit, lest it run into the same problems as fics which have had their serial numbers filed off.

Kindle has attempted to cash in on fanfiction though the publisher service Kindle Worlds, which hosts fanfictions, accessible to subscribers for a fee. The original premise was that "writers will receive a 35 percent royalty for stories of over 10,000 words, or 20 percent for shorter fanfics" (Baker-Whitelaw). However, the fanfictions have to be within sponsored "worlds," including "Warner Bros. shows *Gossip Girl, Pretty Little Liars,* and *The Vampire Diaries*" (Baker-Whitelaw).

Unfortunately the full list of worlds mostly consists of Warner Bros. titles and is hardly comprehensive. The other problem fans have with this platform is that "once your story's been published, Kindle Worlds gives Warner Bros 'a license to use your new elements and incorporate them into other works without further compensation to you.' So if you introduce a new character to the Vampire Diaries cast, and that character somehow shows up in the actual show… you won't be getting any extra money for inventing them" (Baker-Whitelaw). Kindle Worlds and Warner Bros. are thus trying to profit off of fanfiction not only by making readers pay for it but by potentially using the ideas in the fanfictions to enhance the canon works.

Unsurprisingly, Kindle Worlds has not prospered. Journalist Jeff Roberts points out that in June of 2014, fan writers published 46 fanfictions to the *Pretty Little Liars* category on Kindle Worlds, as compared to the six thousand fanfics in that fandom that were published on two other fan fiction sites during the same month. Roberts continues, "More broadly, on one of those sites, *FanFiction.net*, fans posted 100 new stories every hour across all categories. And [Kindle]? Its entire output for all 24 'Worlds' of content, which also includes franchises like *Gossip Girl* and *Vampire Diaries*, was just 538 stories over the course of more than a year."

The problems with Kindle Worlds are manifold. The most obvious is that readers must pay for the fanfiction they can get for free elsewhere. There are also strict rules on content: for example, crossovers are not allowed (Baker-Whitelaw). Characters also "can't use drugs or employ profane language. And gay, bisexual or deviant sexual behavior might be off-limits too" (Roberts). The fan writers on Kindle Worlds make a small profit, but Kindle makes a much larger one, and Warner Bros. can capitalize on fans' ideas without remunerating or crediting them for their intellectual property. If the laws regarding the monetization of literature are meant to protect authors' rights to their work, they are failing magnificently in the case of Kindle Worlds.

Fan scholar Karen Hellekson argues that the commercialization of fanfiction will never be fully successful because fandom operates on a gift economy rather than a commercial one. Her analysis neatly explains the failure of Kindle Worlds: "Attempts to monetize fan activity rely on commercial ventures that will work for some fans but not others—often at the expense of unfettered fan creativity, as commercial ventures limit fannish expression in terms of explicitness and what is considered appropriate. In addition, all too often, this legitimacy is granted on terms that do not benefit the fan" (127).

However, Hellekson argues, the conflict between fandom and money goes deeper than a commercial platform merely failing to attract all of fandom. Hellekson states, "Making money to create value merely applies the dominant paradigm—that of commerce—to what makes something worthwhile. The attempt to switch the fannish mode from gift to commerce is simply a way to legitimize fan activity by subsuming it under the dominant paradigm that fandom is so frequently held up as working against" (127). Non-monetized internet fandom offers an alternative to the commercialization of literature, which means that attempts to monetize it may alienate the very fans that publishers are attempting to attract.

Is Fanfiction Legal?

So is fanfiction itself legal under copyright law? That is a very difficult question, one that Aaron Schwabach discusses at length in the comprehensive *Fanfiction and Copyright: Outsider Works and Intellectual Property Protection*. The first question is whether fanfiction is legally "derivative" or "transformative." If fanfiction is merely derivative, then it is illegal, because "the copyright owner has the sole right to control the making and distribution of derivative works" (59). However, even then, "certain uses that might seem infringing, even if they incorporate protected characters or are otherwise derivative, may be protected as fair use, as parody, or if the use is otherwise sufficiently transformative" (59). Schwabach notes that fanfiction is never *simply* derivative in the way that adaptations to a new medium are: "Fanfic rarely infringes by direct imitation of the work; that would defeat the purpose of fanfic. Instead, fanfic takes familiar story elements and combines them in unfamiliar ways."

However, this does not mean that fanfiction is immediately off the hook. Examining Section 101 of the Copyright Act, which defines a derivative work, Schwabach draws three conclusions: Section 101 tells us only that "an adaptation from one medium, form, or language to another is a derivative work, as are shortened versions" or "fictionalizations" (60); that "a work can be derivative even though it is 'an original work of authorship'—that is, even though the secondary work itself would otherwise be eligible for copyright protection" (61); and that even derivative works could still be protected under the fair use clause, especially if their creators do not profit from them (63). So adaptations, translations, and abridgements are derivative, but works like fanfiction are not specifically addressed. Fanfiction could be legal if it is considered transformative, or if it is derivative but still considered fair use.

Many fans believe that fanfiction is legal under copyright law because it is transformative and because it is protected by this fair use doctrine. Fair use is defined in 17 U.S.C. § 107:

> The fair use of a copyrighted work, including such use by reproduction in copies or phonorecords or by any other means specified by that section, for purposes such as criticism, comment, news reporting, teaching (including multiple copies for classroom use), scholarship, or research, is not an infringement of copyright. In determining whether the use made of a work in any particular case is a fair use the factors to be considered shall include—
> (1) the purposes and character of the use, including whether such use is of a commercial nature or is for nonprofit educational purposes;
> (2) the nature of the copyrighted work
> (3) the amount and substantiality of the portion used in relation to the copyrighted work as a whole; and
> (4) the effect of the use upon the potential market for or value of the copyrighted work [qtd. in Schwabach 63].

One group that believes fanfiction to be legal under the fair use clause is the Organization for Transformative Works (OTW), "a nonprofit organization run by and for fans to provide access to and preserve the history of fanworks and fan cultures" ("What We Believe"). The

OTW created *Archive of Our Own* (AO3), one of the most popular fanfiction websites online, as well as the wiki *Fanlore* and the online scholarly journal *Transformative Works and Cultures.*

The OTW website provides a number of articles regarding the legality of fanfiction, in which the OTW argues that fanfiction falls under the category of fair use: they state,

> Fair use favors uses that (1) are noncommercial and not sold for a profit; (2) are transformative, adding new meaning and messages to the original; (3) are limited, not copying the entirety of the original; and (4) do not substitute for the original work. None of these factors is absolutely necessary for fair use, but they all help, and we believe that fanworks like those in the archive [*AO3*] easily qualify as fair uses based on all these factors" ["What Exactly Is Fair Use?"].

In particular, the OTW emphasizes the absence of profit as one of the most important aspects of fair use:

> *If fanfiction is legitimate, wouldn't that also mean that publishers or studios could produce derivative works without compensating the original authors?*
> No. Profit matters, and the degree of transformative quality matters: telling stories around a campfire, freely sharing nonprofit fanfiction, summarizing plot in a book review, or making a documentary film about fans is not the same as a major commercial derivative enterprise like making a major TV miniseries out of a novel ["If Fanfiction Is Legitimate"].

Internet fanfiction, the OTW maintains, is legal under fair use because it transforms rather than simply copying or retelling the original work and because fan writers do not profit from their fics.

Schwabach does not venture to judge whether most fanfiction passes the four criteria—indeed one could argue that fanfictions might have to be judged on these criteria on a case-by-case basis—but his discussion of the four criteria in the case of the fanvid "They're Taking the Hobbits to Isengard" by Erwin Beekveld can be extrapolated to discuss fanfictions.

On the first factor, most fanfiction is neutral: "The use is not commercial, except insofar as it increases traffic to [the fan creator's] website and enhances his professional reputation, but neither is it for a nonprofit educational purpose ... it seems designed primarily to entertain fans of the underlying work, and to give its creator the pleasure of creating it" (86). On the second criterion, Schwabach notes that "movies and music are traditionally accorded a high level of protection," so that fanvids that utilize portions of films or songs are at risk for litigation, but prose fanfiction seems to be substantially less risky. The amount of the original work utilized in a fanfiction will of course differ from work to work, but many (certainly not all) fanfictions are substantially shorter than the canon works, and most do not incorporate more than a few lines of directly quoted text from the canon, usually in the form of dialogue.[1] "The fourth factor, market effect," Schwabach writes,

> is widely regarded as the most important and, in the opinion of many, should trump the other three. This factor also weighs in Beekveld's favor: the video of "They're Taking the Hobbits to Isengard" does not and cannot compete in the marketplace with the Lord of the Rings movie trilogy. No one will watch "They're Taking the Hobbits to Isengard" as a substitute for the movie; among other things, it lacks the plot and quite a few of the characters [87].

While many prose fanfictions do contain a large portion of the plot and numerous characters from the canon, one could also argue that fanfiction is not generally mistaken for or substituted for the original work (but more on this in Chapter 7).

Ultimately, neither Schwabach nor anyone else can answer definitively whether fanfiction in general is protected by fair use. "The factors are factors," Schwabach states: "despite the paramountcy often accorded to the fourth factor by the courts, Congress has given no clear guidance on how the factors are to be weighted and applied. There is no way to know for sure whether this use, or a similar use of this sort, is fair until the parties go to court. This—the necessity of litigation in order to declare a use fair—is often criticized as having a chilling effect on uses that would otherwise be protected as fair use" (87). As there has as yet been no major case regarding the possible copyright infringements of internet fanfictions, there is no precedent from which to judge fanfiction's legality.

In the absence of any certainty regarding the legal status of fanfiction, nonprofit fanfiction is not likely to be in any danger from litigation, as it is partly protected by its nonprofit status and by the fact that it would simply be too costly for the original content owner to begin suing the huge numbers of fans who have written such fanfiction. Furthermore, doing so would risk alienating the fans who are author's main source of income. Schwabach notes that when Warner Brothers, who own the copyrights to the Harry Potter films, began cracking down on Harry Potter fansites, their actions enraged the fans who were the very people they were attempting to sell film merchandise to. Schwabach argues, "Such actions against noncommercial Harry Potter fandom seem shortsighted; they show a misunderstanding of where Harry's money comes from, and of the value of fandom as free advertising and marketing far more effective than any marketing campaign Warner Brothers could actually buy" (119).

In sum, noncommercial internet fanfiction would *probably* be protected by fair use or its transformative status, but is much more protected by the cost copyright owners would pay, in both court costs and lost fandom, if they actually chose to take fanfiction writers to court.

The MZB Debacle

One legal objection to fanfiction that writers commonly raise is the question of whether fanfiction could economically harm an author who was still in the process of creating works based on the characters in question. Schwabach writes, "Owners assert a more clearly economic interest when they object because fan fiction may anticipate elements of an author's own future works, precluding the author from publishing them. Although this ... is an economic interest, it is not necessarily a protected one" (2).

This is partially in reference to a widely-known case regarding fanfiction of Marion Zimmer Bradley's Darkover series. Bradley, commonly referred to as MZB, initially welcomed fanfiction and criticized writers who did not allow fanfictions to be made of their works (Schwabach 110–111). Scholar Catherine Coker notes, "Bradley actively engaged with her fans by editing their stories and publishing them in fanzines, holding contests for fan works created in her universe, and finally professionally publishing, with DAW Books, 12 anthologies of fan-written stories." However, the plot for one of her novels, *Contraband*, was similar to that of the fanfiction "Masks," published by fan author Jean Lamb in *Moon Phases*, one of the twelve anthologies of fanfictions.

What actually occurred between Lamb and Bradley is the subject of debate. George R. R. Martin, author of the *Song of Ice and Fire* series, expresses the most commonly disseminated version of events:

> MZB had been an author who not only allowed fan fiction based on her Darkover series, but actively encouraged it ... even read and critiqued the stories of her fans. All was happiness and joy, until one day she encountered in one such fan story an idea similar to one she was using in her current Darkover novel-in-progress. MZB wrote to the fan, explained the situation, even offered a token payment and an acknowledgement in the book. The fan replied that she wanted full co-authorship of said book, and half the money, or she would sue. MZB scrapped the novel instead, rather than risk a lawsuit. She also stopped encouraging and reading fan

fiction, and wrote an account of this incident for the SFWA [Science Fiction and Fantasy Writers of America] FORUM to warn other writers of the potential pitfalls of same ["Someone Is Angry"].

Martin's version indicates that Bradley and Lamb had written similar stories through sheer coincidence. However, other sources indicate that this may not be the case. Lamb herself states,

> Here's what happened. It *was* fanfic, but published under MZB's more or less aegis as a permitted issue of MOON PHASES (Nina Boal, editor). It was a book entitled MASKS set entirely within Darkover.
>
> I received a letter offering me a sum and a dedication for all rights to the text. I attempted at that point to *very politely* negotiate a better deal. I was told that I had better take what I was offered, that much better authors than I had not been paid as much (we're talking a few hundred dollars here) and had gotten the same sort of "credit" (this was in the summer of 1992).
>
> At that point I did not threaten any sort of suit whatsoever; in fact, a few months later I received a letter from Ms. Bradley's lawyer threatening me with a suit should I be a bit too frank about Ms. Bradley's um, writing methods, and who her current collaborators were at the time (at least that is how I took the lawyer's phrasing). Needless to say, I could not afford to defend myself if sued. Winning with the truth could have bankrupted me (and probably still could) [Lamb].

Lamb indicates that it was not a case of coincidental inspiration, but that she believes that Bradley was actually using her fanfiction—and possibly other fan writers' work—as inspiration for her own.

Mercedes Lackey, a well known sci-fi/fantasy author and a good friend of Bradley's, seems to back up that portion of Lamb's version of events:

> I actually am privy to and part of the "Marion Zimmer Bradley situation" and I can state with confidence the facts of the matter.
>
> Marion had begun to write a Darkover book about Regis Hastur. She liked the "take" a particular fan author had on the situations and asked to use that spin on things for her book in return for the usual acknowledgement in the front of the book. She had done this before with other fan authors (even though she didn't have to, after all, you can't "own" an idea[2]).
>
> However in this case, the next party heard from was the author's agent, who demanded cover credit and co-authorship, or there would be a lawsuit.... She elected not to finish or publish the book. So that book will never see the light of day [Lackey].

Though Lamb and Lackey disagree on Lamb's terms and whether Lamb threatened a lawsuit, they both seem to agree, Lackey with great openness, that Bradley was in the habit of using fanfiction plots as inspiration for her works. Of course, it is possible that a situation of coincidental inspiration could occur and could cause legal problems for the canon writer, one of the reasons why many authors, including Lackey, do not read fanfiction about their works in order to protect themselves legally. Whether such an occurrence is *likely* is another question. But this most widely known case is actually not about coincidental inspiration but about a canon writer who wanted to use an idea that was originated by a fan writer.

Changing Minds

Bradley went from enthusiastically encouraging fanfiction to forbidding it, an action on which Schwabach blames the dwindling and near-disappearance of the Darkover fandom (Schwabach 114–16). In contrast to this, however, many authors move from forbidding fanfiction to embracing it—or at least allowing it. As internet fanfiction becomes more popular and more and more people join in fandom activities, understanding of fanfiction increases and authors' opinions on it change. Activities like playing *Dungeons & Dragons*, going to sci-fi conventions, and creating costumes based on fictional characters are all becoming more widespread and slowly gaining ground in mainstream culture. Meanwhile, fanfiction itself is booming. In 2000, statistician Mary Ellen Curtin estimated there were something like two million pieces of fanfiction online. As of June 25, 2010, FFN Research indicates that there were 3.2 million fanfictions on *FanFiction.Net* alone (FFN Research, "*FanFiction.net* Story Totals"). As of July 2016, *Archive of Our Own* states that it hosts almost 2.4 million fanfictions, so from those two websites alone the number is over five million, not to mention the dozens, perhaps hundreds, of smaller fanfiction collections online (*Archive of Our Own*).

Partially in response to this boom in fanfiction and its increase in visibility and defenders, many authors are beginning to rethink their position on fanfiction's legal, aesthetic, and moral acceptability. One example is Orson Scott Card, author of *Ender's Game*. On his official website, Card wrote in 1997,

> **Question**
> How do you feel about your fans writing "fanfiction" using characters that are already established by you (e.g., Ender, Valentine, etc.)?
>
> **OSC Answers**
> I'm flattered; and then, if they try to publish it (including on the net) except in very restricted circumstances, I will sue, because if I do NOT act vigorously to

protect my copyright, I will lose that copyright—and that is the only inheritance I have to leave my family. So fan fiction, while flattering, is also an attack on my means of livelihood. It is also a poor substitute for the writers' inventing their own characters and situations. It does not help them as writers; it can easily harm me; and those who care about my stories and characters know that what I write is "real" and has authority, and what fans write is not and does not.

However, Card eventually changed his tune. The *Wall Street Journal* reported in 2012 that "after spending years fending off fan fiction, and occasionally sending out 'cease and desist' letters through his lawyer to block potential copyright violations," Card was "planning to host a contest for 'Ender's Game' fan fiction.... Fans will be able to submit their work to his Web site. The winning stories will be published as an anthology that will become part of the official 'canon' of the 'Ender's Game' series. 'Every piece of fan fiction is an ad for my book,' Mr. Card says. 'What kind of idiot would I be to want that to disappear?'" (Alter).

Other authors have had similar revolutions of thought on the subject. Jasper Fforde, author of the Thursday Next books, wrote on his website, "It seems strange to want to copy or 'augment' someone else's work when you could expend just as much energy and have a lot more fun making up your own.... Clearly I can't stop you writing and playing what you want in private, and am very flattered that you wish to do so. But anything published in any form whatsoever—and that specifically includes the internet—I cannot encourage, nor approve of" (Fforde).

This seems a particularly bizarre position for Fforde, given the nature of the Thursday Next books themselves. They are set in an alternate universe where art and literature are taken far more seriously than in ours, and in which some people have the ability to read so intensely that they can physically enter works of fiction: a premise which by now should sound familiar. Thursday Next, a former soldier, is an agent with JurisFiction, which polices the book world. Just as readers can enter books, the self-aware fictional characters can jump from book to book and even commit crimes in each others' texts. This PPC-like premise ensures that large parts of the Thursday Next series could actually be considered fanfiction. Fforde seems to have come to the same conclusion, writing in December of 2010,

> After speaking to many Fanfictioneers and understanding the genre a little better, I have modified my opinion since writing [my original statement on fanfiction]. I still have no interest in reading any of it, but would regard it more as a celebration

of writing rather than simple copying. The bottom line is that all creative writing is good, wherever it is, whoever does it, and whatever the subject, and nobody should attempt either conciously or unconciously [sic] to discourage those who wish to express themselves. Question: Is the Thursday Next series itself Fanfiction? Does the act of publication define Fanfiction? And how do we properly define publication?

I have featured Fanfiction in *One of Our Thursdays is Missing* [the sixth Thursday Next book] [Fforde].

One of the more dramatic revisions of opinion on fanfiction that an author has undergone is in the case of Anne Rice, author of the Vampire Chronicles series. For many years, Anne Rice strongly disapproved of fan writers creating fanfiction based on her work. Her official website contained the warning, "I do not allow fan fiction. The characters are copyrighted. It upsets me terribly to even think about fan fiction with my characters. I advise my readers to write your own original stories with your own characters. It is absolutely essential that you respect my wishes" (qtd. in "Anne Rice"). Rice may even have gone a step or several beyond this: the website *Croatoan Fanfic* alleges,

> This statement was then followed up by attacks on Anne Rice fanfic authors. The attacks consisted of, amongst other things, e-mailed threats regarding not only the writing of fanfiction but any writing that any fanfic author attempted to engage in (regardless of who owned the copyright), attacks on businesses that the fanfic authors owned and weeks of harassing personal letters sent to fanfic author's e-mail addresses and guestbooks. Personal information about fanfic authors was also dug up by Anne Rice employees and used as part of the harassment ["Where Has Anne Rice"].

In response, *FanFiction.Net* deleted all fanfictions based on Rice's work ("Anne Rice").

But even Anne Rice has modified her position on fanfiction in recent years. In an interview with *Metro* in 2012, Rice observed, "I got upset about 20 years ago because I thought it [fanfiction] would block me.... However, it's been very easy to avoid reading any, so live and let live. If I were a young writer, I'd want to own my own ideas. But maybe fan fiction is a transitional phase: whatever gets you there, gets you there" (qtd. in metrowebukmetro). While some fans might be offended that Rice considers fanfiction a "transitional phase" to writing "better," more original fiction rather than an end in itself, Rice has clearly adopted the fanfiction philosophy of "Don't like, don't read."

In all these examples, it seems that more and more authors are coming to realize that fanfiction is unlikely to cause authors legal or monetary problems, and frequently functions for them as free advertising. If fanfiction really were a threat to their profits, these authors would not be revising their opinions on the subject, much less embracing and encouraging fanfiction of their work. Though free internet fanfiction is far from universally accepted by published authors, its increasingly positive reputation among them is a sign of how little of a legal threat this genre actually poses.

7

Damaging the Brand

One legal concern that some authors have about fanfiction is whether fanfiction may be mistaken for their canonical writing. If it is, they worry that such fanfiction may damage the reputation of their work. A number of authors have voiced this fear, despite the relatively small—and usually canonically-educated—audience any particular fanfiction may have. For this reason, perhaps it is not internet fanfictions that authors should fear, but commercialized fanfictions and adaptations. Authors frequently have little control over how their work is changed in film or television adaptations once they have signed away their adaptation rights to a filmmaker, and a frequent area of debate for book fans, even those outside of internet fandom, is the changes which those filmmakers almost always make in the process of adaptation to a different medium.

While writers and creators of commercial fanfictions and adaptations enjoy a greater prestige because of their greater fame and the association of profit with legitimacy, they do have to contend with concerns over things that may harm their profits, what their work may be doing to the reputation of the canon work, and greater fan opposition to the changes they introduce. One commercial fanfiction adaptation that has had to contend with these issues is the BBC's television series *Sherlock*. *Sherlock* strongly resembles internet fanfiction in its basic premise, but was created for profit rather than simply "for love." In the example of *Sherlock*, we can see that consideration of profit can cause profic authors to worry about whether other fan writers in the same fandom will outcompete them or otherwise harm their sales. The commercial fan writers who created *Sherlock* demonstrate in their work a great anxiety about what their fanfiction and others' will do to the reputation of the canon work—in financial terms, "the brand." It is ultimately the commercial fanfictions like *Sherlock* itself, not the internet fanfictions, that can do the most damage to an original work's reputation.

Confusion with Canon

If we define fanfiction as a literary category consisting of new stories centering on characters and settings established in other authors' works, then it is clear that many film and television adaptations of written works could also be termed fanfiction because they so frequently change the material they adapt. We can see the contrast between adaptation and fanfiction in film versions of *A Little Princess*. The 1986 miniseries *A Little Princess*, starring Amelia Shankley, is a pretty direct adaptation that would probably not count as a fanfiction. Although it adds scenes and dialogue that were not present in the 1905 Hodgson Burnett novel, the details and characters of the story are little changed, except for a slight telescoping of the time frame so that the production would not have to hire two actresses of different ages to play Sara Crewe.

However, the 1995 film adaptation, directed by Alfonso Cuarón, could be accurately called a fanfiction because it displaces the narrative in time and space: the story is set in the early twentieth century instead of the late nineteenth, Sara goes to school in New York instead of London, and her father "dies" in World War I in Europe rather than of disease in India. This adaptation could thus be called an "alternate universe" (AU) fic in internet fanfiction terms. The plot is also altered: while Sara's father dies in the Hodgson Burnett novel, in the 1995 adaptation Sara's father is not actually killed in action, as reported, but blinded and afflicted with temporary amnesia. The two are reunited at the end of the story.[1] One character is also racebent in this adaptation: the scullery maid Becky is depicted as black, and is adopted as Sara's sister at the end rather than employed as her private maid. The 1995 version stays close enough to the novel to clearly be an adaptation rather than an original work, but it also makes enough changes to be termed a fanfiction.

Original fiction, commercialized fanfiction, and internet fanfiction all hold slightly different places in the network of concepts surrounding copyright: originality, profits, legal protections, personal property, literary quality, etc. One way in particular in which internet fanfiction differs from commercialized fanfiction is in the effect these two kinds of fanfictions can have on the reputation of the canon work. Because commercialized fanfiction can be published in traditional and widespread media like books, television shows, and films, and internet fanfiction (for the most part) cannot, commercialized fanfiction can reach a larger audience, and one that is less likely to be educated about the canon work.

Online fanfiction is unlikely to be mistaken for the original work, partly because it is mostly consumed by people who are either in the fandom and are therefore already familiar with the original work, or by people who are in fandom in general and recognize fanfiction for what it is. Though authors have expressed fears of internet fanfiction's ability to "masquerade" as the original work, at least in fans' memories, it is commercialized fanfiction and adaptations that pose the greatest threat to the public concept of the canon work.

Diana Gabaldon, author of the popular *Outlander* series (which has now been adapted for television by Starz) has objected to fanfiction being written on her work, partly because of the possibility that fans might mistake fanfictions for her own canon text. She writes that during the long gaps between the publication of the books in her *Outlander* series, she often likes to post excerpts of upcoming novels, and states that "people do pick them up without permission and repost them on fan-sites, though. Because of this, readers occasionally *do* stumble over bits of fan-fiction, and—while they realize they're reading fan-fiction at the time—still incorporate these *faux* stories into their comprehension and memory of the real series" (qtd. in Nepveu). Gabaldon goes on to tell a story in which her assistant argued with a fan for a long time on a discussion board about whether a particular scene had actually occurred in one of the published *Outlander* novels. It eventually turned out that the scene had been posted on a fanfiction site. Gabaldon concludes, "I can't blame people for getting confused as to what they've read where. But it's one really good reason for not wanting fan-fiction to intrude—however innocently—on 'the canon'" (qtd. in Nepveu).

Gabaldon does note that the fanfiction in question was posted on a "properly labeled" fan-site," so the fan writer did all she could to avoid the possibility that her work would be mistaken for the canon. Nonetheless, it is understandable that original authors might worry about the reputations of their works because of such mistakes. Indeed, as mentioned earlier, the fanfiction term "fanon" refers to tropes that are so widespread in fanfiction that they may be mistaken for (or intentionally taken as) canon by fans ("Fanon"). For instance, many fans will assert that Sherlock Holmes and Dr. Watson were closer than mere platonic friends, and were actually lovers. This concept appears nowhere in the canon work, though the incidents from which the fans drew this inference do. However, it should be pointed out that fanon concepts are not just disseminated through fanfiction, but through simple conversations among fans about the canon work. Fanon could not be eliminated, even if fanfiction were.

The "proper label" Gabaldon refers to was at one time a common part, not just of fanfiction websites, but of the fanfictions themselves: most fan authors put disclaimers at the beginning of their fanfictions, believing that these would protect them from being sued by overzealous canon authors:

> Disclaimer: I own none of it. Except Penny. I do own her (well, someone's got to). The rest is all the property of The Great Man Himself (JRRT) before whom we are not worthy. I hope I do not get him turning over too fast: a gentle rotation, perhaps, rather than an out-and-out spin [Boz4PM "Don't Panic!"].
>
> Disclaimer: All Tolkien's. I don't own Middle-earth or its characters, but they're happy [sic] to camp out at my place any time they like [Sandman "The Official Fanfiction University of Middle-earth"].
>
> My stories are inspired by the world of the Southern Vampire Mysteries created by Charlaine Harris. Any SVM characters, plots and settings are her property.
>
> Her characters and mine are dancing to the same band [Vaughan "Index"].
>
> I own nothing. Wheee [Rivard "A Very Mary Sequel" Chapter 6].

However, of late years such disclaimers seem to have fallen out of use, especially with many fan writers moving from *FanFiction.Net* to the OTW-run *Archive of Our Own*. As author threats to sue fan writers have become less common, and with the OTW assuring fan writers that their work is fair use, fans have become less paranoid about labeling their work with disclaimers. They trust that online readers will recognize fanfiction when they see it.

Many commentators believe that, even without these labels, fanfictions are not in the least likely to be mistaken in any widespread way for the original works. Cathy Young opines, "[Author Robin] Hobb's idea that readers may mistake Robin Hobb fan fiction for her own work borders on the paranoid." Aaron Schwabach also believes that there is little likelihood that anyone will mistake the fanfiction for the work of the canon author. He writes, "Even without the disclaimers many fanfics contain, it seems highly unlikely that any readers will believe them to be created or authorized by the owners of the marks. Here, too, is where those disclaimers—so meaningless for copyright purposes—actually have some use; they serve to reduce the likelihood of confusion yet further" (74).

Not only is fanfiction unlikely to be taken as canon, but the main audience for fanfiction consists of people who are already members of the fandom for the canon work (and therefore should know what is canon and what is not). Internet fanfictions are quite likely to be at least partially unintelligible to non-fans, for whom they may act more as an advertisement for the canon work than a replacement. Internet fanfiction is therefore little to no threat to the reputation of the canon work.

Sherlock *and "The Brand"*

However, just because internet fanfiction, read mostly by fellow fans, does not pose a major threat to the canon work, profics, which are consumed by fans and nonfans alike, might. One particularly interesting example of a profic which demonstrates a preoccupation with the public reputation of its source material is *Sherlock*, a BBC television adaptation of Sir Arthur Conan Doyle's Sherlock Holmes stories. The producers of *Sherlock* have been particularly touchy about the details of other, similar Holmesian profics and have expressed concerns about what these other adaptations might do to *Sherlock*'s profits. But even beyond this, the show itself demonstrated an overriding concern in its first two seasons about the version of Holmes' story it was choosing to tell and how this retelling might affect the reputation of the entire Holmes "brand."

Sherlock makes a common fanfiction move with a "modern-day AU": the story is set in modern, rather than 1890s, Britain. The series was a cult hit in the U.S., "where it is screened on the PBS network" (Sherwin). Adam Sherwin, a journalist for *The Independent*, reports that CBS approached the BBC with a plan to remake the series for American audiences, but they were turned down. So CBS decided to make their own modern-day adaptation of *Sherlock*—and Hartswood Films, which produced the British series, threatened to sue.

It goes almost without saying that legal action over a similar AU premise would not occur in internet fandom, though someone *might* criticize the second writer for a lack of originality or for not giving credit to the source of her inspiration. But with the consideration of profit comes a more hard-nosed approach to intellectual property. The response from Hartswood Films was a mixture of drawing careful legal lines and asserting emotional attachment to their intellectual property by speaking of it as a child:

> Sue Vertue, *Sherlock* Executive Producer at Hartswood Films, said: "We understand that CBS are doing their own version of an updated Sherlock Holmes. It's interest-

ing, as they approached us a while back about remaking our show. At the time, they made great assurances about their integrity, so we have to assume that their modernised Sherlock Holmes doesn't resemble ours in any way, as that would be extremely worrying." She added: "We are very proud of our show and like any proud parent, will protect the interest and wellbeing of our offspring" [Sherwin].

Hartswood Films could not claim the characters Sherlock Holmes and John Watson as their children—after all, they were the creations of Sir Arthur Conan Doyle. However, they could legally claim their particular show as their property, and couched that in the emotional terms of parenthood.

The idiosyncratic visual elements in particular of the BBC show could have been defended legally. *The Independent* reported, "Margaret Tofalides, a copyright specialist at law firm Manches, said: 'The concept of a new Sherlock Holmes is unprotectable. But if the unusual elements of the BBC series—the modern settings, characters, clothes, plots and distinctive visual style—were closely reproduced in the CBS version, that could form the basis of a potential copyright claim'" (Sherwin). However, the concept of a modern-day AU adaptation of a story could not be claimed as the artistic property of Hartswood Films, despite Sue Vertue's acidic tweet when she found out about CBS' new series: "Mmm interesting @CBS, I'm surprised no one has thought of making a modern day version of #Sherlock before, oh hang on, we have!" (qtd. in Moore, Trent).

As a matter of fact, *Sherlock* was certainly not the first Holmes adaptation to "update" Conan Doyle's source material. What is possibly the most famous series of film adaptations, the fourteen Basil Rathbone films released between 1939 and 1946, were set during the time they were produced: Rathbone's Sherlock Holmes investigated the Nazis ("Sherlock Holmes [1939 Film Series]"). More recently, CBS produced the television movies *The Return of Sherlock Holmes* and *1994 Baker Street: Sherlock Holmes Returns* in 1987 and 1993, respectively ("*The Return of Sherlock Holmes*," "*1994 Baker Street*"). Both versions involved a cryogenically frozen Sherlock Holmes being revived by a female sidekick (private detective Jane Watson in the first and Dr. Amy Winslow in the second) in modern-day America. So CBS already had a history of writing modern-day AU adaptations of Sherlock Holmes. And when they resurrected Holmes again in the series *Elementary*, they stayed true to form, though there were no cryogenics involved this time. Sherlock Holmes in this version is a modern British private detective who is now working in New York City with a "genderbent" Dr. Joan Watson.

Apparently these changes were enough for Hartswood Films. In fact, Nathalie Caron points out that Steven Moffat, the *Sherlock* showrunner, moved on from complaining that *Elementary* was too close to their own take on Conan Doyle's material to complaining that it was too far away from the canon. Caron quotes Moffat as saying,

> What we did with our *Sherlock* was just take it from Victorian times into modern day. They've [*Elementary*] got three big changes: it's Sherlock Holmes in America, it's Sherlock Holmes updated and it's Sherlock Holmes with a female Watson. I wonder if he's Sherlock Holmes in any sense other than he's called Sherlock Holmes. It's almost like they should have made Watson a woman but kept the show in Victorian times. Actually ... that would actually be quite interesting [Caron].

This sounds a little like fans debating whether a piece is true to the canon or not, except that fans would probably not object to three common fanfiction changes being made rather than only one. However, Moffat's objections remained commercial ones: he stated, "I don't want it to sound like Mark [Gatiss, a co-producer] and I don't want other people to try this. We welcome it, but don't damage the brand" (qtd. in Caron). The problem for Moffat and Gatiss is not really the fannish issue that they feel the source material wasn't being treated respectfully; their worry is that they may lose income if people do not like *Elementary* and then associate it with *Sherlock*.

As a matter of fact, some fans turned out to prefer *Elementary* to *Sherlock*, and appreciated some of the extra changes. *Whatculture.com* ran an article by Brian Chapman on "10 Reasons Why *Elementary* Is Better than *Sherlock*." Among Chapman's reasons for his preference was that *Sherlock* only runs three (lengthy) episodes every two-ish years, as compared to *Elementary*'s approximately 24 episodes a year, which means that *Elementary* must invent more original storylines (whereas *Sherlock* tends to do adaptations of Conan Doyle stories). With more time, the supporting characters in *Elementary*—including Joan Watson—are more developed, and therefore seem to be shown more respect by the show. Holmes' drug problem, only hinted at in the first couple of seasons of *Sherlock*, is made a major plot point in *Elementary*, making Holmes more interesting and less of an unrealistic superhero. The *Elementary* cast is also far more diverse, with an Asian Joan, a black police detective (Marcus Bell), a black Latino sober sponsor (Alfredo Llamosa), and a transgender Mrs. Hudson (played by a transgender actress, no less). *Whatculture* notes, "What's more, *Elementary* manages to deal with these diversity issues without wandering into gay jokes like BBC's *Sherlock* does" (Chapman). And finally, the Moriarty arc is more original and shocking in *Elementary*, as Irene Adler, the love of Holmes' life, turns out to also be Moriarty (Chapman). It seems that the creators of *Sherlock* had nothing to fear about *Elementary* "damaging the brand."

However, this is not the end of *Sherlock*'s concerns about how Holmes fanfictions and adaptations may be affecting the reputation of the canon, and thus their profits. *Sherlock* demonstrates anxiety about what fanfictions—their own and others'—may do to the reputation of the Sherlock Holmes stories, thus "damaging the brand." This concern can be seen in how the show's plot handles the idea of Sherlock's fame. The first two seasons of *Sherlock* express a deep anxiety regarding the reputation of Sherlock Holmes and how the show, as a fanfiction itself, is either protecting or harming that reputation.

Sherlock's Storytellers

In the very first episode, *Sherlock* sets itself up to talk about its own mediation. The series begins with Dr. John Watson, who has returned from a tour of Afghanistan with a psychosomatic limp and a diagnosis of Post-Traumatic Stress Disorder. His therapist has required him to set up a blog to write about his experiences, but he finds himself unable to write anything. However, after meeting Sherlock Holmes, John does have something to put on his blog: information about his new friend and roommate.

The importance of such information is highlighted when John encounters Mycroft Holmes, Sherlock's brother, for the first time in episode 1. Mycroft does not give John his name, and instead has him picked up in a private car and brought to meet Mycroft in an empty warehouse. Mycroft, who works for the British government, offers John money for information on Sherlock: "Nothing indiscreet. Nothing you'd feel uncomfortable with. Just tell me what he's up to" ("A Study in Pink"). John refuses, feeling that this is disloyal and suspect. Though John considers sharing information on Sherlock with Mycroft potentially dangerous, he later writes up accounts of his cases with Sherlock on his blog. Sherlock himself has a website, called *The Science of Deduction*, but it has significantly fewer readers because it is not written in an engaging narrative fashion, like John's.

7. Damaging the Brand   153

John's website as a vector for the spread of information about Sherlock Holmes is a reference to the Conan Doyle stories, in which Dr. Watson served as the narrator. Conan Doyle's stories repeatedly commented metafictionally on Watson's budding literary career writing up Holmes' case studies. In the television series *Sherlock*, John publishes these case studies in his blog. The first episode of series 2 emphasizes this point with a montage that shows a number of their cases and gives their titles: "The Geek Interpreter" for "The Greek Interpreter," "The Speckled Blonde" for "The Speckled Band," "The Navel Treatment" for "The Naval Treaty" ("The Great Game"). Sherlock also states on the show, "I'd be lost without my blogger," a reference to a line about Watson in the original stories: "I am lost without my Boswell"—referring to Jonson's famous biographer ("A Scandal in Belgravia," Conan Doyle "A Scandal in Bohemia"). Therefore, just as in Conan Doyle's writings, the episodes themselves are in a sense John's stories. Although the television series is not synonymous with John's blog, the showrunners also run John's blog in real life, at http://www.johnwatsonblog.co.uk/. Likewise, Holmes' more scientific but less popular website is also a reference to the original stories, in which Holmes had published a monograph on 140 different types of tobacco ash (on the *Science of Deduction* website it is 240 types) (Conan Doyle *The Sign of Four*, "A Scandal in Belgravia"). This too was produced as a real website by the showrunners, at http://www.thescienceofdeduction.co.uk/.

John's website, run by the producers of the television series, is both an in-story source of information on Sherlock Holmes and a real-world metaphor for the series itself. The other major source of information on Sherlock is his brother Mycroft who, in a fascinating twist, also functions as a metaphor for the series. Mycroft is played by Mark Gatiss, who is co-creator and co-producer of the series, along with Steven Moffat. He has also written a number of episodes, including "The Great Game" (S1E3) and "The Hounds of Baskerville" (S2E2) ("Mark Gatiss" *Wikipedia*). Gatiss is also himself a Sherlock Holmes fan. In fact, four years before *Sherlock* aired, Gatiss, a "well-known Holmes enthusiast ... was asked to address the Sherlock Holmes Society's annual dinner at the Houses of Parliament. Gatiss, who brought along Steven Moffat as his guest, told the audience about a meeting at the BBC to discuss the possibility of resurrecting Arthur Conan Doyle's creation for a Christmas special" (Ross Jones).

Gatiss has also been a tie-in writer. One fansite notes, "Thanks to a childhood interest in *Doctor Who*, [Gatiss's] early writing was devoted to the series. His earliest published fiction was a sequence of novels in Virgin Publishing's New Adventures series of *Doctor Who* stories" ("Mark Gatiss" *Sherlockology*). In these novels,

> [Gatiss] attempted to correct the problems that had killed the show off in the late Eighties. "I thought I knew how it should be done," he says.... And the first TV scripts he ever wrote were for his own series of cheap, short [Doctor] Who spin-off films with titles such as *The Devil Of Winterbourne* and *The Zero Imperative*, which were shot on video and featured ex-Doctors Jon Pertwee, Colin Baker and Peter Davison [Phelan].

After creating these professional "fix-it fics," Gatiss later helped to revive the television series *Doctor Who*, writing several episodes himself.

As Gatiss is a writer, producer, and actor in *Sherlock*, Gatiss' Mycroft might be considered something of a self-insertion: a role written for him to allow him to participate in the story. As in the original stories, Mycroft holds an important, if unspecified, position in the British government. That position is all about the movement of information. In the Conan Doyle stories, Holmes tells Watson,

> The conclusions of every department are passed to him, and he is the central exchange, the clearinghouse, which makes out the balance. All other men are specialists, but his specialism is omniscience. We will suppose that a minister needs information as to a point which involves the Navy, India, Canada and the bimetallic question; he could get his separate advices from various departments upon each, but only Mycroft can focus them all, and say offhand how each factor would affect the other [*The Adventure of the Bruce-Partington Plans*].

Similarly, in *Sherlock* Mycroft seems to have particular power over the flow of information in the government.

Too Much Information

What is interesting about these sources of information about Sherlock Holmes simultaneously acting as metaphors for the show itself is that they are also the cause of Holmes' downfall at the end of Series 2. In the original stories, Holmes' supposed death at the hands of Moriarty comes about simply because Holmes is close to proving Moriarty and his gang guilty and delivering them all into the hands of justice. Morarity therefore sets out to kill Holmes, first through a number of assassins and finally in a man-to-man fight. In *Sherlock*, however, it is the media's love for Sherlock and the dissemination of information about him that Moriarty uses to bring about Holmes' downfall through the ruining of his public reputation. Moriarty uses information about Sherlock, much of it gleaned from Mycroft during interrogations, to craft a new version of events: one in which Sherlock surreptitiously commits crimes, then makes a big show of "solving" them. Moriarty claims that he himself was an actor named Richard Brook who was hired by Sherlock to play the part of a criminal mastermind. The public, who had been so inundated with stories of Sherlock's brilliance, believe Moriarty's story and turn on Sherlock. Sherlock's downfall is a direct result of Mycroft/Mark Gatiss sharing too much information about him.

It is undoubtedly a bit of a stretch to claim that the show *Sherlock* is depicting itself as its own worst enemy. However, when combined with the showrunners' expressed fears about the damage that other versions of the Holmes stories may do to the "brand," the alteration in the story that firmly connects Sherlock's downfall with his reputation is suggestive.

John's and Sherlock's blogs, which act (John's in particular) as stand-ins for the television show itself, spread potentially damaging information about Sherlock and attract very dangerous "fans." This problem appears in the very first episode, "A Study in Pink." The villain of the week—a cabbie-turned-serial-killer—states, "Sherlock Holmes. Look at you! Here in the flesh. That website of yours: your fan told me about it."

SHERLOCK: My fan?
CABBIE: You are brilliant. You are. A proper genius. *The Science of Deduction* ["A Study in Pink"].

The "fan," who has been sponsoring the cabbie in his killing spree, turns out to be Sherlock's famous archenemy Moriarty. Information about Sherlock Holmes, presented on Sherlock's website, *The Science of Deduction*, is disseminated by a "fan" who is really Holmes' enemy. Information that Sherlock is sharing about himself online may be deadly to him. Metaphorically, information that the show creates and shares about the character of Sherlock may be misused by "fans" who are really his enemies—may be used to damage the reputation of the canonical Sherlock Holmes.

This anxiety about Sherlock's fans reappears in "The Reichenbach Fall," the episode that depicts Holmes' downfall. In a break during Moriarty's trial, Sherlock encounters reporter Kitty Riley, dressed as a Sherlock Holmes fan in a deerstalker and an "I (heart) Sherlock" pin.

KITTY: I'm a *big* fan.
SHERLOCK: Evidently.
KITTY: I read your cases; follow them all. Sign my shirt, would you? *(She pulls back her coat to reveal her cleavage.)*
SHERLOCK: *There are two types of fans.*
KITTY: Oh?
SHERLOCK: "Catch me before I kill again," Type A...
KITTY: Uh-huh. What's Type B?
SHERLOCK: "Your bedroom's just a taxi ride away."
KITTY: Guess which one I am.

Sherlock immediately deduces that Kitty is not a fan but a journalist, and she offers to help him tell his side of the story to the press, which he declines:

KITTY: Wow, I'm liking you!
SHERLOCK: You mean I'd make a great feature: "Sherlock Holmes: The Man beneath the Hat."
KITTY: ... There's all sorts of gossip in the press about you. Sooner or later you're gonna need someone on your side. Someone to set the record straight.
SHERLOCK: ... I look at you and I see someone who's still waiting for their first big scoop so that their editor will notice them.... I don't see smart, and I definitely don't see trustworthy, but I'll give you a quote if you like: three little words. *You repel me.*

Sherlock clearly has a problem with "fans," believing that all of them are either psychotic and violent or sex-crazed (a stereotype of fans which we have discussed already). However, Sherlock also declares that there is a third kind of person who passes herself off as a fan: the kind who wants to use Sherlock for her own advancement and fame by writing about him.

This seems to imply that the fans who are actually emotionally caught up in a story are either insane or too sexually attracted to the characters or actors (Benedict Cumberbatch, who plays Sherlock in the show, became particularly popular with female fans). It also implies that those who write about the characters—the creators of fanfiction—are using the characters' (and the show's) already existent fame as a way to selfishly gain recognition for themselves, not to defend the "truth" about those characters. In this metaphor, the distortions the news media introduces into the story to gain money are similar to the distortions that deviate from the canon to create fanfiction in order for the fans to capitalize—in terms of money or fame—on the story of another.

This does not sound much like *Sherlock* fans, the ones who would actually be basing their fanart or fanfiction off of *Sherlock*'s depiction of Holmes and Watson: after all, such fanworks cannot legally make any money, and the fame that might accrue to their creators is basically limited to those already in the fandom. It sounds much more like the show *Sherlock* itself, capitalizing off of Conan Doyle's stories—and of course, CBS, doing the same in potentially a similar fashion. It also sounds like Mark Gatiss himself, who used his pro-fic of *Doctor Who* to launch his career in television. Though the invective in this exchange appears to be directed at obsessed amateur fans, it is actually a better description of pro fans whose fanfiction adaptations have the potential to make or lose money for one another by "damaging the brand."

The show seems to recognize its own potential to hurt the reputation of the entire Sherlock Holmes franchise. Anxieties about the series' depiction of Sherlock and how it may negatively affect his reputation among viewers are indicated by Sherlock's hurt feelings about John's first case study blog post, "A Study in Pink"—referring to the first Conan Doyle Sherlock Holmes story, "A Study in Scarlet," and also the title of the first episode.

> SHERLOCK: I see you've written up the taxi driver case.
> JOHN: Uh, yes.
> SHERLOCK: "A Study in Pink." Nice.
> JOHN: Well, you know, pink lady, pink case, pink phone.... There was a lot of pink. Did you like it?
> SHERLOCK: Um, no.
> JOHN: Why not? I thought you'd be flattered.
> SHERLOCK: Flattered? "Sherlock sees through everything and everyone in seconds. What's incredible, though, is how spectacularly ignorant he is about some things."
> JOHN: Now hang on a minute. I didn't mean that in a—
> SHERLOCK: Oh, you meant "spectacularly ignorant" in a nice way! ["The Great Game"].

Sherlock is hurt that John is spreading information, not only about the good aspects of his character, but about the bad aspects as well. If the show is a televised version of the blog (with its first episode sharing the title "A Study in Pink"), then the show also has the potential to convey a negative impression of Holmes to viewers. As a matter of fact, this has been one of the more common criticisms of *Sherlock* as a Conan Doyle adaptation: Sherlock is considerably more abrasive in this version than in the canonical stories. David Stringer, a contributor to *Den of Geek*, pointed this out as the most obvious difference between this adaptation and the original:

> The Sherlock Holmes of the books is often detached and unemotional, but it's always clear that he cares about Watson. There is a certain tenderness in Holmes—a detached, Victorian tenderness—but it is there. The worst of his antisocial tendencies ... stem from caring more about getting his mind to work to its best, than he does about social conventions.
>
> However, Sherlock Holmes in Steven Moffat and Mark Gatiss' *Sherlock* at times feels genuinely nasty. Telling children that their grandfather is rotting in the ground, and being dismissively rude towards Russell Tovey's potential client, for instance. His telling Kitty Reilly, the journalist in The Reichenbach Fall, that "you repel me" was more than a little over the top.

The *Sherlock* writers seem aware that they are not only updating Conan Doyle's story to modern times, but also making Sherlock Holmes a considerably less likeable person—even John calls him "an annoying dick" ("The Reichenbach Fall"). The anxiety expressed here is not just about the fans distorting *Sherlock*, but about *Sherlock* distorting or somehow doing a disservice to the Sherlock Holmes image: that the show itself, as a fanfiction, may be helping to "damage the brand." This exaggeration of the negative side of Holmes' character could have a negative effect on viewers, potentially alienating them from Sherlock Holmes stories in general.

The show also expresses fears of competing representations of Sherlock Holmes, particularly through its depiction of the news media. There are increasing references throughout the second season, in the buildup to Sherlock's great downfall, to the detective's public persona as popularized by the news. In particular, repeated references are made to the deerstalker hat that Sherlock happens to grab backstage as he and John have to make their way through a crowd of reporters outside of a theater. The newspaper picture of Sherlock in the deerstalker is the most publicized image of him. Sherlock is annoyed by this attention to the hat. The deerstalker hat is, of course, one of the symbols of the character of Sherlock Holmes, popularized by the original illustrators of the Conan Doyle stories, Sydney Paget and Frederic Dorr Steele, despite the fact that the deerstalker hat is never directly referenced in the text ("Deerstalker" *Wikipedia*, "Deerstalker" *Baker Street*). In *Sherlock*, the deerstalker becomes part of Sherlock's official image, despite his objections that the hat is not his: fanon wins out over canon. John warns Sherlock not to tell the news media too much because "the press *will* turn, Sherlock. They always turn, and they'll turn on you." Not only could the show itself damage the reputation of the Holmes "brand," but other, competing profics and adaptations about Holmes could also cause the public to reject the brand entirely.

Though the metaphorical reading of various sources of information as different adaptations can be pressed too far, it is obvious that *Sherlock* expresses a great deal of anxiety about Holmes', and thus the "brand's," public reputation. This is far less of a concern to amateur, online fanfiction writers than it is to profic writers. Some fans try to distance themselves from other, more "obsessed" or less reputable fans, but in that case, they are worried about the reputation of the fandom, the community of fans to which they belong, rather than the reputation of the canon work itself. However, profic writers like the creators of *Sherlock* have to worry about anything that might harm their profits: a fandom with a poor reputation, fanfic or profic writers who violate copyright, profic writers whose work gets too far away from the canon or otherwise damages the brand, or the quality of their own profic and how it might be harming their ratings.

Frankenfanon

Ironically, while many canon and profic writers direct their concerns at online fanfiction, perhaps it is legal adaptations and profics they should be fearing more. Commercial fanfictions and adaptations like *Sherlock* that are "legitimated" by their secure legality under copyright law and their ability to make money can paradoxically cause greater harm to the reputation of the canon work than internet fanfictions, which have a considerably less secure legal position. Online fanfiction has only a limited audience, one which already knows how fanfiction works and that the fanfic is no substitute for—and is not even an accurate representation of—the canon. But film and television adaptations and profics reach a much wider and potentially less knowledgeable audience and have a strong and lasting impression on a work's reputation. Their ability to damage the reputation of the canon work is multiplied tenfold because of the size of their publicity and distribution beyond the fandom.

Such legally protected, for-profit fanfictions and adaptations have an extraordinary power to solidify fanon. Anyone who has taught a literature class in which they ask students to read a novel that has been adapted for film can attest that students frequently mistake the plot and other elements of the film for the plot of the novel. In the public consciousness, Frankenstein is a green, high-foreheaded monster with bolts in his neck; Sherlock Holmes wears a deerstalker cap; and Legolas is blond—even though none of these things were ever mentioned in the original books. Canon writers may fear "illegitimate," non-profit fanfictions and their ability to create fanon, but perhaps they should fear "legitimate," for-profit adaptations and fanfictions far more.

It is money that makes the difference. Internet fanfiction is considered illegitimate, immoral, and illegal because it defies the copyright laws that were meant protect the original author's monetary interests and eschews the standards of originality that have grown from those laws. But legal profics and adaptations have the power to do far more damage to the image and reputation of the original work because they can legally make money—and therefore spend more money in their efforts to get their version of events into the public consciousness. Authors might want to think twice about allowing their work to be adapted for the screen, but it seems they have little to fear in endorsing the creation of internet fanfiction.

8

Schrödinger's Legolas

Appropriation of someone else's characters is a universal form of transgression in fanfiction: the genre is based upon it. So far we have discussed appropriation—the use of someone else's characters in one's own work—from a legal standpoint, through the lens of the financially-motivated copyright law. However, financial concerns are not the only reasons authors may object to the appropriation of their characters. Authors often feel a deep emotional connection to their characters, and frequently figure fan appropriation as stealing their belongings or even kidnapping their children. This metaphorical view of fan appropriation is reproduced in some fanfictions, such as the PPC stories.

However, other fanfictions figure such appropriation in less transgressive terms, asserting the rights of loving fans to depict their favorite characters in more accurate ways than their original creators did, or depicting the multifarious nature of characters or a multiverse conception of fiction. These new conceptions of character appropriation and representation derive from the same absorbed reading that makes fanfiction possible in the first place. This chapter examines three fanfictions that figure appropriation in new ways: Angela Vaughan's "Salt in the Wound," Carrie Rivard's "Mary-Sue Mockfest," and Theresa Green's "Owner's Guides."

Theft and Kidnapping

The idea of intellectual property is strong in modern culture, and is one of the major reasons our culture looks askance at fanfiction. The wiki *Fanlore* has an article on "Professional Author Fanfic Policies," stating which authors have expressed approval of fanfictions made of their works and which ones have asked that fans not write it. While many have expressed their approbation of or indifference to fanfiction, plenty of authors feel very strongly that fanfiction is a violation of their intellectual property rights. Some of their objections are purely legal and commercial; others are far more emotional or moral. For instance, Lynn Flewelling, author of the Nightrunner series, has expressed both financial/legal worries and emotional/ethical ones, claiming, "No artist is flattered by their hard wrought creation being used by others without their express permission. Aside from the monetary considerations, it is rude. You wouldn't walk into someone's garage and take their lawnmower without asking, would you?... Fan fic amounts to the same thing" (qtd. in "Lyn Flewlling"). Similarly, science fiction author Stina Leicht writes, "To be honest, my feelings on fanfic run more in the territory of 'Keep your grubby paws off other people's shit. It's not yours. Buy or make your own.... Ask permission to borrow it first. You would if it were a car. If you don't ask permission that means you've stolen it.... See, if it were a car or a DVD player the police would pretty much agree with me on that front'" (Leicht). Both of these writers view the characters and other elements of their work—the material which the fanfiction writers remix—as singular objects which can be borrowed or stolen, like a lawnmower or a DVD player. According to this view, there is one Legolas (for instance), and any fanfic writer who "takes" and "uses" Legolas for their own purposes is guilty of stealing. Of course, this metaphor is not accurate in legal terms: clearly the police do *not* get involved when fan writers appropriate characters.

George R. R. Martin, the author of the *Song of Ice and Fire* series, has also been vocal about his negative emotional reactions to fanfiction, but he speaks of his characters as his children rather than his property:

> Many years ago, I won a Nebula for a story called "Portraits of His Children," which was all about a writer's relationship with the characters he creates.... My characters are my children, I have been heard to say. I don't want people making off with them, thank you....
>
> I have sometimes allowed other writers to play with my children. In Wild Cards, for instance, which is a shared world. Lohengrin, Hoodoo Mama, Popinjay, the Turtle, and all my other WC creations have been written by other writers, and I have written their characters. But I submit, this is NOT at all the same thing. A shared world is a tightly controlled environment. In the case of Wild Cards, it's controlled by me. I decide who gets to borrow my creations, and I review their stories, and approve or disapproval what is done with them. "No, Popinjay would say it this way," I say, or "Sorry, the Turtle would never do that," or, more importantly (this has never come up in Wild Cards, but it did in some other shared worlds), "No, absolutely not, your character may not rape my character, I don't give a fuck how powerful you think it would be."

And that's Wild Cards. A world and characters created to be shared. It's not at all the same with Ice & Fire. No one gets to abuse the people of Westeros but me ["Someone Is Angry"].

In this argument, the characters are not singular objects, like a DVD player, but singular people, who can be "controlled," either by the original author or by others: puppets on strings. Martin affectionately refers to them as his children, a common metaphor used by authors, who often feel they put something of themselves into their characters.

However, this metaphor clearly isn't a very exact one, either. As Martin points out, claiming his characters means that "no one gets to abuse" them but him. This is a tongue-in-cheek comment, as Martin is well known for doing terrible things to his characters in his narratives, including allowing them to be raped. But clearly, having children does not mean that the parents are the only ones allowed to "control" them or to "abuse" them. The strong emotional attachment Martin feels to his characters is doubtlessly there, but it is not the same as the relationship of a parent to their actual child. Nonetheless, the author expresses that he sees the character as a singular entity that is being illegitimately controlled by fan writers.

As a matter of fact, some fanfiction authors feel the same way about characters they have themselves created. Many fan writers agree that they are uncomfortable with someone else using their original characters, because such characters seem to them to be like real people—a view shared by Martin. Writers, pro and fan alike, seem to be engaged in absorbed writing as well as absorbed reading. However, most of these fanfiction writers realize that their feelings on this matter are a little hypocritical: if they want to argue that each reader has the right to interpret a character as they wish, they cannot object when their own readers reinterpret their original characters in ways they did not expect or approve ("Borrowing or Loan"). While emotional connection to one's own fictional creations, written absorbedly, is part of this deep feeling of possessiveness, that possessiveness also derives from the cultural norms that legally enforce writers' possession of their characters in the first place: copyright and intellectual property law. It is clear that the norms of intellectual property are very strong in our culture and can affect writers very deeply, fan- and non-fan writers alike.

George R. R. Martin's views from 2010 about his sole right to torture his characters may now seem hypocritical itself, since his *Song of Ice and Fire* series has been adapted by HBO as the television series *Game of Thrones*. This television series is known for being particularly graphic and brutal to Martin's characters, and has come under fire from a number of sources for the extra rape scenes it has included that did not appear in the book series. Martin disclaimed power over such scenes on his blog in June of 2015: "I cannot control what anyone else says or does, or make them stop saying or doing it, be it on the fannish or professional fronts. What I can control is what happens in my books, so I am going to return to that chapter I've been writing on *The Winds of Winter* now, thank you very much" (Martin, "Wars, Woes, Work"). Martin seems to indicate that he does not control who rapes his "children" on the television series he allowed to be written of his work, and either has decided he doesn't care anymore, or feels helpless to stop either party and has therefore ceased to try. It is impossible not to note the changes in his attitude since this televised fanfiction began to do for profit what his fans had been doing for years for fun alone.

It is also interesting how little affected Martin seems by the fact that *Game of Thrones* will apparently end long before he finishes writing and publishing the final book in the series. We've seen already how Martin has indicated on his blog that it is a bad idea for writers to read fanfiction of their work in case they are later sued by fan writers for copyright infringement if their later books seem to coincide with the fanfiction. Martin has promised repeatedly that his final book will be different from the final seasons of *Game of Thrones*, so that readers will have unspoiled plot twists to look forward to (and to pay money to read). He will have to be particularly careful that he does not merely copy what the television show does, or his profits will be in jeopardy. Likewise, while the television show will act as a kind of widespread advertising of his work, many members of the public will have their impressions of Martin's work forever shaped by the adaptation. Yet Martin, who is so adamant in his arguments against amateur fanfiction, does not seem to have any major complaints about this professional fanfiction adaptation.

There seems to be a perpetual power struggle surrounding the question of who is allowed to interpret or reinterpret fictional characters and their lives and who is not. One article by Laura Miller about the struggle between published authors and fan writers is tellingly titled "You Belong to Me." In it, Miller writes that, "in the last few years, writers, filmmakers, and other artists have seen fans seize control of their creations and reimagine them as fanfiction, or fic, as its aficionados like to call it." The

8. Schrödinger's Legolas 165

fans, in the phrase "seize control," are seen as usurping the author's position, changing the power balance. In the appropriative act of creating fanfiction, fans seize the power by becoming creators themselves and by criticizing and changing the source text. Miller observes, "Fans these days aren't satisfied to just sit back and consume. They want to participate. They want to create. And they don't want to wait for anyone else's permission to do it."

Tumblr user earlgreytea68 responds directly to this portion of the Miller article and its view of fan appropriation, particularly its assumption that professional authors have—and should have—more power than readers and fan writers over the meaning of a text and the behavior of characters:

> There is a lot of unpleasant judginess in the way people talk about fanfiction, as if they are offended entirely by the fact that it gives a voice to people who apparently aren't supposed to have one. Like, the reader. This is a little remarkable, because I think everyone who holds an English degree would agree with me that most of what we read is influenced by us as readers: We see so much that the writer never intended. A writer never has the ability to control readers' thoughts. We try, as much as we can, to get our point across, and then we have to mostly shut up. The quote from Annie Proulx at the beginning of the [Miller article] about how people not liking her ending and wanting to rewrite it "drives her wild" comes across a little bit like sour grapes. They didn't bow down to you as Supreme Creator and dared to question your vision? Shame on the peasants! [Earlgreytea68].

As Lev Grossman and other commenters have pointed out, fanfiction changes the power dynamics of writing. Fan writers do not merely appropriate other authors' characters; they appropriate the power over those characters and, to a certain extent, how people may perceive them, at least while reading that fanfiction. In return, authors often express the desire that fans would wait for permission from them to use their characters, which would allow the original authors to retain the power in this relationship.

When Characters Turn

The appropriation that fan writers engage in (and the authors' illusion that their characters are real people, similar to their children) has its roots in absorbed reading. As established earlier, absorbed readers frequently feel that the characters are in some sense real, and therefore have an existence separate from the text in which they appear: that this is only one slice of their lives, or one interpretation of their stories. This allows the fan writer space to create more stories for the character, to change or expand the existing canon.

This is not the only way that absorbed reading encourages the appropriation of characters. Absorbed reading, because it lends characters a seeming reality, can sometimes cause readers to feel that they understand the characters even better than their authors do. Sheenagh Pugh points out,

> It is possible for [a character's] creator, by understanding her imperfectly, to make her say or do something which goes against that reality, against the essence of herself.... Most of us have at some time thought "this doesn't ring true" even when reading the best authors.... A writer can create fictional characters who come alive so fully that readers feel they *know* them, can understand their motives, predict their actions, continue their stories and grieve when they "die." But once that has happened, they can no longer be solely "my characters" [17].

The seeming reality of characters who are viewed through absorbed reading makes fans feel free to appropriate these characters in ways that the authors clearly did not intend and would not appreciate.

This motive for appropriation is figured plainly in the fanfiction "Salt in the Wound" by the fan Angela Vaughan (screen name Ericiz Mine), from the Southern Vampire Mysteries/*True Blood* fandom. This story appropriates the characters and turns them against the original writer in a particularly aggressive way. Vaughan depicts how fictional characters, if they had an existence separate from the texts in which they appear, might turn against their own creators, just as a great deal of the Southern Vampire Mysteries fandom turned against the author of the books they loved when they felt that the quality of her writing had declined.

The story begins with the vampire Eric and the human Sookie having a fight. Sookie's anger seems over the top and inappropriate. This is somewhat similar to the canon, in that Eric and Sookie frequently do not get along, despite being in a relationship. Eric states, "I'd be thrilled if you simply told me what I've done to annoy you. I can't begin to apologize if I'm unsure of where to start." Sookie responds, "I don't know why I'm so angry. I don't know why you never do or say the right thing." The two decide to gather their friends together to figure out what the problem is.

When they meet with their friends, Sookie discovers that they have kidnapped a woman they address as "Charlaine" (Charlaine Harris, the author of the Southern Vampire Mysteries series on which the show *True Blood* is based). She is tied to a wheelchair, and the characters, disturbingly, take turns throwing darts at her: three darts apiece, each one representing a grievance.

The first character to take a turn is Sam:

> "Hey Charlaine, remember me?"
> "Of ... of course I do.... You're the conflicted, but supportive best friend archetype."
> Sam didn't hesitate. "Best friend" earned her a dart in her leg. "Best friend, huh? Did you really have to make me a damn dog? Seriously? NINE god damn books and I turn into a lion for like five minutes and then I need a nap!"
> He threw another one hitting her in the side. "*That* is for only hooking me up with that psycho Tonya and..."
> Another dart. "*That* one is for shooting my mom! I mean come on! You didn't mention that I even have a family until *You. Shot. My. Mom.*"

The second character, Arlene, complains, "'Alright then, *This* one is for having me married ump'teen damn times! No wonder I don't get a boyfriend worth a hoot for the other books! You coulda hooked me up with Sam as filler or something, but *noooo*! You're too hell bent on making us lonely losers!'" The third, Bill, simply throws the three darts straight at the center of the author's chest and returns to his seat. "Pam ran her teeth over her lips as she shook away her baffle [sic]. 'Bill, don't you want to tell her why?' He huffed, dramatically. 'She knows what she did'" (Vaughan).

Each character there takes a turn throwing darts at their creator, and at last it's Sookie's turn. But she doesn't get any darts. Eric hands her a drum of salt, explaining, "Because you get to do to her, what she's been doing to you ... rub salt in each wound." This is emblematic of Sookie's treatment by the series. She is attacked in some way in practically every book: beaten up, kidnapped, raped, etc.

The exercise of attacking Harris acts as catharsis for all the characters. In the end it is revealed that it was not Charlaine Harris at all that was captured and tortured, but the shapeshifter Preston in Harris' form. Preston is released—and then Eric announces that it is time to bring in the "guest of honor." "[Sookie] laughed slightly. 'Like the last one wasn't enough? Who could be better than Charlaine Harris?' He smiled and pulled her to him for a kiss. 'Alan Ball.'" Ball is the producer of the television series *True Blood*.

The initial horror of the characters physically attacking the author in such a sadistic manner is assuaged by the knowledge that this is not the author but a fellow character, and the torture of the producer is never shown. Nonetheless, Vaughan has appropriated the characters to allow them to violently criticize the way they are written by the canon author. Interestingly, these do not appear to necessarily be the criticisms of the reader projected onto the characters. Most of the grievances are about the way the characters are treated in the story, not about the writing itself (one exception being Pam's complaint that the "lemons"—erotic scenes—are poorly described).

The implication of all this is twofold. First, the fic implies that Vaughan knows the characters and how they feel better than their creator, Harris, does. She claims a special knowledge of their feelings about their own story that Harris does not seem to have access to. Second, "Salt in the Wound" implies that despite an author's strong possessive feelings for her characters, the characters themselves, if they were cognizant of their own fictional status, would not necessarily feel any particular loyalty to their creator. In this fic, they would most likely side with Vaughan, for giving them the opportunity for revenge, over Harris. When Vaughan calls herself Ericiz Mine, she indicates her position: she has not only appropriated Harris' characters, she has also alienated their loyalty from their original creator and possibly taken Harris' place in her characters' affections.

This fanfiction is symptomatic of the anger of some parts of the Southern Vampire Mysteries series fandom in general. Some fans were very upset with the way Harris ended the series in 2013. A copy of the text of the final novel was leaked two weeks before official publication, and there was an immediate uproar. Some of the fan dissatisfaction was with the fact that Sookie didn't end up with Eric at the end. Others felt the book was poorly written and inconsistent. An article in *The Guardian* states that Harris received "death threats, suicide threats and more prosaic threats to cancel book orders" once fans had read or heard about the leaked manuscript (Flood). Harris did later receive some apologies from fans (Stengle).

But the feelings of fan dissatisfaction had apparently been building for some time. Harris had originally had a contract to write ten books in the series for her publisher, but when the series was adapted for TV by HBO, she signed a contract for a further three books (Carone). Some fans began to feel that the book series didn't have the enthusiasm and quality it had once had. Fans complained that the final books featured a lot of discrepancies with the previous books and dropped story lines.

Many of them seemed to feel that Harris no longer cared about her work and was only doing it for the money, a theory that may have been strengthened by the fact that she had written so many books for the series and had allowed it to be adapted by HBO. One fan, who signs herself Kabuki Girl, writes,

> The fans are angry because she basically gave up on this series 2 books ago. She had a ocntract [sic] to fulfill and could have cared less about her characters anymore.... As if the Trueblood [sic] series not sticking to ANY of the plot lines in the books and going WAAAAAY crazy are not bad enough!!!!... Your fans put ALOT [sic] of time into reading 15 books Ms Harris and you made ALOT of $s off of them. Your fans and your characters desrved better ["*True Blood*: Author Charlaine Harris"].

Another fan (Iamsickofit) opined in the same comment section, "If you read the series you can see tthat [sic] the last book has [sic] just slapped together. Story line inconsistencies, etc, etc, etc. She sold out to HBO and let her literary fans down big time" ("*True Blood*: Author Charlaine Harris").

Harris herself has indicated to the press that she had begun to have problems remembering all the details of the complicated mythology she had established, and had lost her enthusiasm for the series. The *Wall Street Journal* notes,

> But after more than a decade, Ms. Harris, a cheerful 61-year-old grandmother, grew tired of the characters, even as her hyper-dedicated followers lusted for more. She ran out of fresh story lines about her bubbly blond protagonist, Sookie Stackhouse, a telepathic waitress who tangles with an ever-expanding supernatural cast of vampires, werewolves, shape-shifters, demons, goblins, elves, witches and fairies. She struggled to keep track of the convoluted mythology she'd invented. Things that used to excite her, like unveiling new supernatural creatures, started to feel stale [Alter].

The fans seem to have picked up on this loss of enthusiasm and dedication. After receiving the violent blowback from her fans for the final book, an understandably upset Harris attacked some of these fans in an interview:

> There are some people who evidently have no life what so ever, that are evidently going to pursue this until they drop dead of old age, and I don't know what to think about that. Are their lives so empty that they cannot get over a book series ending in a way they had not anticipated?...
> One reader said "You should turn over characters to someone who can write them they [sic] way we want them." I said "You know, you don't get it. It's not like going into a bakery and ordering a cake where you say 'I want butter cream filling and chocolate icing and I want a decoration of pink roses.' Writing a book is not like

that. You don't get to vote on how I write my books. They're mine, and they would have never have met any of those people if they hadn't come out of my head. They say "You sold out" and I say "To whom?" To whom did I sell out? [qtd. in Mel, italics mine].

While it is true that Harris has the right to write whatever she likes in her own books, her fans also have the right to feel upset when her series does not deliver the quality they had come to expect. (Of course, this did not give them the right to attack her. Don't like; don't read.)

The fans felt betrayed by Harris' agreement to write more books when she clearly had lost her enthusiasm for the series. They enjoyed the characters and plots that Harris had originally created, but didn't think that she was doing them justice by the end. The solution to this was for the characters to be turned over to "someone who can write them the way fans wanted": for fanfiction writers to step in and take over. Vaughan herself writes on the front page of her fansite, "Keep in mind that my use of canon ends with *Dead And Gone* [the ninth book out of thirteen].... Anything established in the more recent books doesn't exist in my little world" (Vaughan, "Index"). Vaughan appears to be among those fans that feel that Harris did not do her characters and her fictional world justice, particularly in her later writing, and so appropriates Harris' characters, depicting them as having turned against their original creator. Meanwhile, Harris refuses to see that her behavior in writing more books than she had enthusiasm for gave rise to fan indignation at the failing quality of the writing. Her attitude, while understandable, especially in someone who has been the recipient of such harsh blowback from her fans, is also rather dismissive and antagonistic toward the very people whose ardent enthusiasm for her earlier work made so much fame and profit for her.

Uses for Your Model

In "Salt in the Wound," Vaughan depicts the characters in much the same way many canon authors do in their comments about fanfiction: singular objects or people who can only be owned, used, or controlled by one person at a time. Vaughan's addition to this view is that the characters are aware of their fictionality and can object to the way they are depicted by the canon author. Fanfiction, informed by absorbed reading, frequently figures its own appropriation of characters very differently: not as stealing a singular character, but as adding potential variations to that character.

A number of metafictional fanfictions depict this manifold aspect of fictional characters. The "Owner's Guides" series by Theresa Green, for example, figures each fictional character as a model of mass-produced androids that can be purchased and manipulated (within limitations) by their new owners. These fics are written as instructions for owners of these fictional "Aragorn," "Legolas," and "Boromir" units. Each of these guides begins with a section of "technical specifications," including height, weight, and—ahem—"length." The "operating procedure" section offers a number of suggestions of uses for each unit, including doctor, children's party organizer, and bloodhound ("Aragorn"); snow plough, child-carrier, fencing instructor, and waiter ("Boromir"); and illumination, child-minding, horticulture, recitation, and winter chores ("Legolas"). The guides also include sections on compatibility with other models, programming, frequently asked questions, and troubleshooting, all of which are full of funny allusions to both the books and the films of *Lord of the Rings*.

In a metaphor for writing fanfiction, Green depicts Tolkien's characters, not as the intellectual property of their creator, but as androids that she and other fans can own and manipulate. Knowing the characters' "specifications," fan writers can acquire a Legolas or a Boromir and use them in their own writing to achieve their own ends. Each Guide begins with some variation indicating ownership of a mass-produced unit and the freedom of the new owner to manipulate said unit: "CONGRATULATIONS! You are now the proud owner of an ARAGORN! Please follow the procedures detailed in this manual in order to use your Heir of Isildur to his full potential" ("Aragorn").

This could be seen as a metaphor for fans' use of canon characters in fanfiction. The literal objectification of another author's characters may seem to support the metaphor of stealing. However, there is one major difference: the androids described by Green have been apparently mass-produced. If a fan uses her Legolas unit, she hasn't stolen it from Tolkien's garage: she has her own. There is more than one Legolas to go around. In this metaphor, characters are objects, but not singular objects. Therefore the fan writer's use of the character is not transgressive because the fan is not stealing.

Accepting the Role

A fanfiction that takes a very different view of appropriation—well, actually two different views—is "Mary-Sue Mockfest" by Carrie Rivard (screen name Noble Platypus). Like the PPC stories, the "Mockfest" depicts fanfiction writers as possessing and/or psychically controlling unwilling characters to create their fics. However, the final chapter offers a second explanation of how fanfictions can reuse canon characters and yet not commit an act of appropriation or psychic enslavement. This chapter depicts the characters as actors who (apparently voluntarily) act out the scenes created for them by fanfiction writers.

The first depiction of the nature of fictional characters follows offended authors' concept of fanfiction writers stealing and manipulating the singular character for their own purposes. The Mockfest begins when a college student named Randi is abducted by Celestina Windbreaker, Goddess of Mary Sues, and dumped in Middle-earth as a half-elf. There, Randi is forced to enact Celestina's fanfiction as a Mary Sue: Elrond's long-lost, third-cousin's niece. Very much against her will, she is sent with the Fellowship as a tenth walker. Rivard, like Boz4pm, is parodying the stereotypical characteristics of Mary Sues.

Randi tries everything she can to stop being a Mary Sue. She attempts to trip and fall in the mud, thus ruining her perfect appearance, but is caught by Legolas. She tries to get herself killed by orcs and thus go home, but the orcs impale themselves on her sword in hordes. Randi finally succeeds in at least tearing up the rules that Celestina has written regarding Mary Sues, only to find that without the rules she, like Penny Baker, has to deal with a realistic and slightly frightening Fellowship that doesn't even speak English. The rules of the Mary Sue story protect her from the dangers of more realistic fiction.

Once the rules are rewritten, Randi temporarily convinces Legolas that he is being controlled by an evil goddess. Unfortunately, Celestina thwarts her again, and Randi has to continue on her Mary-Sueish career, telepathically befriending a horse, Ed (who only wants to talk about dirt), and spontaneously and unwillingly bursting into Evanescence songs. At long last, Celestina's fanfiction warps the canon too much. When Randi accidentally saves Merry and Pippin from being captured by the Uruk-hai like they were supposed to be, Celestina's mother, the Goddess of Canon, appears and grounds her daughter, forcing Celestina to send Randi home once more and fix the Fellowship.

8. Schrödinger's Legolas

Celestina's relationship with Randi and the Fellowship could easily be taken as a representation of the relationship between a fanfiction writer and the canon characters, and a condemnation of Mary Sue writers who misrepresent the characters they appropriate. Celestina appropriates and takes control of the canon, distorting the personalities of the characters by only emphasizing certain traits. When Randi rips up Celestina's rules and returns the characters to their canonical form, Celestina explains,

> "My point ... is that in this particular Mary-Sue realm, Legolas is a sensitive archer who is madly, madly in love with you!... Those are the only aspects of his character that have even remotely been explored or developed! And these rules that you so thoughtfully ripped to shreds have KEPT him the polite, sensitive, one-dimensional puppy dog that he's been so far!... To put it simply, the Legolas you have been dealing with has been filtered and translated to suit the author's needs! And now that you've wrecked the rules, the filters have been removed!" [Chapter 8].

Celestina, as the symbol of a fanfiction writer, controls Legolas like a puppetmaster by only developing certain aspects of his canonical character in her story. She, like fan writers, thus becomes a goddess of the fanfiction world she is creating. In fact, Randi only barely manages to keep Celestina from telepathically controlling her every movement by arguing that if Celestina *forces* Randi to fall in love with Legolas, then it won't be true love. Celestina has a power over the characters that would be terrifying if those characters were real people. George R. R. Martin's metaphor of his characters as children that only he is allowed to control takes on an alarming meaning in this depiction of author as god or goddess of a fictional world.

In the end, Celestina is punished by the Goddess of Canon, who could be seen as standing for the author or the integrity of the original work. She tells Celestina, "I am SICK of your antics! You ought to be ASHAMED of yourself! I haven't been this disgusted since your sister [the goddess of slash] paired Frodo and Aragorn!" (Rivard Chapter 18). Celestina's Mary Sue story, like her sister's slash fanfiction, portrays a level of appropriation that the Goddess of Canon cannot bear. When Pippin does something out of character and Celestina makes the excuse that he's cuter this way, the Goddess of Canon exclaims, "HE ISN'T SUPPOSED TO BE CUTE, YOU TWIT, HE'S SUPPOSED TO BE HIMSELF!!!! HOW DARE YOU TURN THESE WONDERFUL CHARACTERS INTO THESE… THESE PATHETIC SHADOWS OF THEIR FORMER SELVES?!" (Chapter 18). The Goddess reacts violently to this appropriation and transformation of the characters, just as canon authors and protective fans do to fanfictions they find objectionable.

The characters themselves, when they are not under Celestina's sway, are also disgusted by the way she has controlled and changed them. When Legolas is temporarily himself again, he is clearly disturbed by what has happened and is determined to break Celestina's spell over the other characters. Unlike in "Salt in the Wound," it is the fanfiction author, represented by Celestina, who has skewed the depiction of her characters, to those characters' horror. Much like in PPC missions, Legolas and the other have been transformed and controlled against their will by the appropriating fanfiction author, who is duly punished for her transformation of canon. The main part of Rivard's fanfiction thus condemns fan writers who make large changes to the characterization and plot of the canon on much the same grounds as the original authors themselves often object to fanfiction: that fanfiction writers "steal" the singular canon characters like a DVD player or a lawnmower, and transform, control, and use them for their own ends.

While Rivard uses the objection of stealing and controlling a singular object in her criticism of Mary Sues, she utilizes a concept of manifold variations of those characters in her celebration of her own fanfiction. The epilogue of "Mockfest" consists of a series of interviews with the characters, based on the interviews with the cast of Peter Jackson's *Lord of the Rings* film trilogy that appear in the DVD special features. Unlike the vision of fanfiction Rivard presents in the main story, in which the fanfiction writer controls the characters against their wills, here the characters are actors who are offered and voluntarily accept the roles they play in the fanfiction:

> RANDI: Well, when Platy [Noble Platypus, the fic author] offered me the role, I said yes right away. I mean, it's rare that you get a chance to work with someone so ... you know... (waves hand vaguely)
> *(cut to Legolas, in a similar chair)*
> LEGOLAS: (looking kinda at the ground) I've done a lot of serious stuff, a lot of romances.... God, a lot of romances ... and I kind of wanted to break out of that, you know ... show my versatility. I didn't want to limit myself, if ... does that make any sense? (looks thoughtfully up at camera).

In this epilogue, characters are both singular people whose primary existence is in the canon, and actors who can appear in multiple fanfictions without altering their original personalities or the depiction of events presented in the canon version. Rivard points to this inviolate canon through an interview with a fictionalized version of herself who appears as the director of this fanfiction:

> PLATY: This project was really something special, I think. We got the entire Fellowship back together, which I know was fun for all of them.

This conception of characters from the canon as actors who can appear in fanfictions as if they were films both preserves the idea of an original version of the character, as presented in the canon by the original author, and simultaneously allows for innumerable variations on that character in innumerable fan versions of events.

Unlike the vision of fanfiction given in the story, in which the fanfiction writer controls the characters against their wills, here the characters are actors who are "offered" and accept the roles they play in the story. The Fellowship are a canonical group of friends from Tolkien's world, but they are also actors who can enjoy themselves by appearing together in people's fanfictions. Though Legolas appears to have gotten bored with being in so many romances, he doesn't seem angry or disgusted by it, and some of the other characters actually enjoy getting to play out of character:

> PIPPIN: Well, how can you *not* enjoy yourself?
> MERRY: We got to act like complete prats! (grins)
> ...
> FRODO: (frowns thoughtfully) We weren't in this much, were we?
> SAM: No, Mr. Frodo, we weren't.
> FRODO: (short pause) Kinda nice, wasn't it?
> SAM: (nods wordlessly).

The characters even seem to have the sort of friendly relationship that is part of the point of a Mary Sue story. The "actor" Randi becomes very good friends with the members of the Fellowship, especially Legolas. Throughout the interviews, Randi and Legolas tease and joke with one another. The interviews also indicate how well Randi has integrated with the rest of the fictional cast:

> PLATY: The last day of filming, we had a huge party.... On the one hand, it was a relief to be done, but on the other hand ... we'd all become such good friends. It was rough saying goodbye. (clip of cast members hugging and sobbing)

(cut to Legolas)

LEGOLAS: Well, the rest of us knew we'd be working together soon, so it wasn't really that sad. But it was hard saying goodbye to Platy, Randi, and Ed ... because who knew when or if we'd ever get to work with them again?

This seems to be precisely the kind of camaraderie enjoyed by Mary Sues when they are inserted into canon worlds. Here the fanfiction author herself gets to become friends with the canon characters who "act" in her fic.

Even the relationship between canon and fanfiction is different in this chapter. The Goddess of Canon often becomes annoyed with fanfictions, but it seems she doesn't actually put a stop to them:

GoC: I thought [the ending] was very... fitting, I guess. I mean, I can't tell you how many times I have wanted to... you know, just swoop in some story and set things right. It can be very frustrating. Oh, Celestina IS my daughter, by the way. (smiles a bit) I think some people have trouble believing that. But it's true.

(cut to Celestina)

CELESTINA: Yes, she is my mother... but she would never ground me in real life. I'm too powerful.

(cut to GoC)

GoC: She is NOT more powerful than me! I mean sure, she's a bit younger... in her prime, really... but I've got age and wisdom on my side. Not to mention the right, for crying out loud!

(cut to Celestina)

CELESTINA: She's just jealous. (smirks)

Though the Goddess of Canon has the "right" (and the age and wisdom) to put a stop to fanfictions and punish the writers, she doesn't actually do so, possibly because she doesn't have the power to do so. This parallels the canon writers' inability to stop fan writers (often younger than them) from creating their fanfictions and publicly sharing them.

Some of the objections that authors raise about fans appropriating their characters seem to arise from the feeling that characters are singular objects, like DVD players or lawnmowers that can be "stolen" by fanfiction writers. As in the metafictional universe of the PPC, these writers must telepathically control the unwitting or unwilling characters, transforming their personalities and keeping them under some kind of hypnotic sway to make them act out their fantasies. However, the epilogue of the Mockfest offers a different way of looking at these characters: as actors who willingly play the parts cast for them by fanfiction writers. They may get "typecast" in the same kind of role over and over again if a certain plotline becomes a cliché, but in general they seem to enjoy the acting experience and can become good friends with the writers, Mary Sues, and other original characters they "work with." This vision of fanfiction doesn't show a fan writer transforming characters and plots that are not hers, but rather creating a second layer of mediation, another story laid over top of the first.

A Multiverse of Fiction

Fanfiction reminds us that a character can never be a singular entity. Every reader's interpretation of the character will be slightly different. Fandom displays this concept most clearly in the term *headcanon*. As defined by *Fanlore*, "Headcanon (or *head canon, head-canon*) is a fan's personal, idiosyncratic interpretation of canon, such as the backstory of a character, or the nature of relationships between characters.... Headcanon may represent a teasing out of subtext present in the canon" ("Headcanon"). The less detailed the descriptions of characters, the more headcanons fans may create about them. For example, Tolkien spends little time describing the elf Legolas' backstory or his personal appearance: fans may therefore develop headcanons about Legolas' family, his childhood, his age, and even his hair color.

As all of these headcanons are permitted by the text, fans, as a community of absorbed readers, perceive them all as potential truths about the character. These various interpretations of the character exist side by side without canceling one another out. As in the famous thought experiment of Schrödinger's Cat, which could be considered both alive and dead simultaneously, fans see many contradictory versions of fictional characters and events as simultaneous potential truths. This concept of fiction expands to fit not only headcanons limited by the canon, but headcanons that may contradict the canon. *Fanlore* observes, "[Headcanon] can be affected both by professional tranformative works, such as art, movies and audiobooks, and by fanworks such as fanart, fanfiction, cosplay, manips, vids and podfic. Headcanon may ... directly contradict canon" ("Headcanon"). This makes canon only one more version of the characters or plots, simultaneously productive of and equal to any fanfictions based on it.

Furthermore, authoritative versions of the canon may contradict one another just as fanfiction may contradict the canon. Fandom uses special terms to signal which version of the canon a fanfiction is based on: *bookverse* and *movieverse*. As these terms indicate, officially authorized and/or legal film adaptations of books may contradict elements from the books they are adapting, so fanfiction writers sometimes find it helpful to indicate which canonical universe's version they are operating within. *Fanlore* explains,

> *Movieverse* as a term refers to the film adaptations of books, comics, TV series, etc.; the term is used by the fanfiction community to mark stories which are based explicitly and exclusively on the film adaptation.
> For example, in *The Lord of the Rings* fandom, fans of the book!verse see Faramir as a noble Gondorian who wouldn't take the Ring if it was lying before him in the road. In contrast, fans of the movie!verse see him as deeply tempted by the power of the Ring, but finally convinced to let the Hobbits go. Also, in the book!verse, Denethor doesn't take a flaming leap off of Minus Tirith ["Movieverse"].

Fans use these terms to specify which version of canon they are working from. In many of these cases, the film adaptations have large enough differences from the original books—such as the change in Faramir's character or Denethor's demise—that the film could be considered a fanfiction of the book.

Green alludes to this concept of multiple canonical versions of a character in her treatment of the "Legolas" unit. Because Legolas appears slightly differently in the Jackson films than he does in the books, Green separates "Legolas" units into "Mk I," the bookverse version from Tolkien's original text, and "Mk II," the movieverse version from Jackson's adaptation. Under "Colour" in the specifications section, Green notes, "Mk I LEGOLAS—Uncertain. Mk II LEGOLAS—Blond" ("Legolas"). This is because Legolas' hair color is never actually described in the books. That means that every reader of the text, if not unduly influenced by Jackson's film adaptation with its blond Legolas, could be imagining a Legolas of a different color. Every reader's absorbed experience of the text is different, and in fact two different canons can produce two very different kinds of "androids," which can then be manipulated by their new fan owners.

The terms "movieverse" and "bookverse" indicate that the two are conceptualized as separate but parallel universes, with different versions of the characters (movie!Faramir or book!Faramir). In this vision of fanfiction, the characters are not even singular actors enacting various versions of the stories, but actually, in a sense, separate versions of the characters, existing in parallel universes: sharing a general nature, but experiencing potentially vastly different events. A character, in this metaphor, cannot be stolen from the canon work because the character is not a singular person. Instead, each fanfiction creates a new, parallel version of characters and events. Just as every reader's conception of a character, even when reading the canon work, may be slightly different, so every writer's version of a character is slightly different. Fanfiction would then not be an act of stealing or illegitimate appropriation, but rather the result of inspiration and sub- or para-creation[1]: the making of a fictional universe parallel to that of the canon work.

These new ways of conceptualizing fanfictions and characters as having a multiple existence derive specifically from absorbed reading, which sees characters as being separate from the texts which originate them. The character of Legolas in Tolkien's books, in Peter Jackson's film adaptations, and in countless internet fanfictions are all in some sense the same Legolas, but all slightly different versions of him. Internet fanfiction acknowledges Tolkien's version as the originating one, but has no qualms about creating other versions in other fictions of the metafictional multiverse. Fans see Legolas as having an existence that is larger and more full of possibilities than Tolkien's original text.

As the terms *headcanon, bookverse,* and *movieverse* indicate, fictional characters have never been singular entities entirely controlled by one person at a time: reading (especially absorbed reading), legal adaptation, and fanfiction create innumerable variations of those characters, inspired partly by the canonical text and partly by the readers and interpreters of that text. As Edmund Wilson wrote in *The Triple Thinkers,* "In a sense, one can never read the book that the author originally wrote, and one can never read the same book twice" ("Edmund Wilson"). Fanfiction merely makes this aspect of writing—people's simultaneous shared and yet unique understanding of the text—more obvious.

While all fanfiction transgresses cultural values in that it appropriates' others intellectual creations, the appropriation that occurs in fanfiction is not as simple as it is described by many authors, as comparable to the case of a stolen DVD player or lawnmower. It can be conceptualized in multiple ways, some of them ethically dubious and others more acceptable. While stealing or telepathically controlling a character seems deeply transgressive, giving a character a new role to play or even creating a parallel version of a character are considerably less negatively emotionally charged acts. The conceptualization of how characters are appropriated in fanfiction deeply affects whether the act of appropriation is seen as acceptable or unacceptable, and while some fanfictions, like the PPC, condemn particular appropriations based on the "kidnapping/stealing/skewing" concept, other fanfictions like the epilogue to Rivard's "Mockfest" offer new visions of fanfiction's appropriations which do not necessitate the semi-hypocritical stance of the PPC or even the partially self-deprecating mockery displayed in the rest of the "Mockfest."

Furthermore, the existence of multiple versions of the characters means that fanfiction does no harm to the original version or the author's control of that version. While stealing a lawnmower means that the first owner can no longer use it, and kidnapping a child or hypnotizing and controlling a person can cause them emotional harm and take them away from the protective embrace of a parent, the new metaphors presented by fan writers indicate that the original writer controls the original, unharmed character, while the fan writer only controls an android copy, a parallel version, or the script that that character "enacts" in their fanfiction. The original version of the character remains embodied, unharmed, in the original text, and under the canon author's control.

Because fanfiction has its source in absorbed reading it often presents fictional characters not as singular objects that can be stolen and controlled by only one writer at a time, but as multitudinous variations of the same person, existing side-by-side in parallel versions of the story. Though fans may echo authors' copyright-inspired paradigms of characters as stolen objects or hypnotized children in their criticisms of one another's fanfiction, they may just as easily deploy the parallel variations paradigm in celebration of their own. An understanding of absorbed reading reminds us that characters are already multitudinous the moment they are read by multiple readers with their own imaginative interpretations of those characters. Fictional characters are always, to some extent, out of the author's control and in the hands of readers. Fan writers' fictional appropriation of these characters merely makes this truth more visible.

Conclusions

Here is the most basic message, and it is one that fans have said for a long time in responses to criticisms of their work: "Don't like, don't read." Tastes are socially constructed but also very subjective, and reading according to our tastes should not be a guilty pleasure. We should not have to defend our enjoyment of fanfiction, of science fiction, of romance novels, of superhero films, of children's cartoons. While it is important to examine the depictions of life in media that can affect the culture on a broad scale, we also need to remember that criticizing only the media consumption of certain groups and the media written to appeal to them is discriminatory and self-sabotaging. If media can change people's behavior, then it can change everyone's behavior, not just the behavior of women, or "middle-brow readers," or pop culture aficionados, or young people, or fans. None of these people should be mocked for their tastes in reading or writing. Such squelching of the pleasure in pleasure reading/watching is inhibiting for children, ridiculous for adults, and insulting and hurtful for all. Equally nonsensical is decrying a lack of originality in some literature when many classics are also derivative, complaining about women's *bovarysme* when such heroic self-reimagining has been a norm for men for thousands of years, valuing art's rational effects over its emotional effects when both can be inherently valuable, or reasoning that a genre's ability to earn a profit proves its superiority while also claiming that monetary considerations should be separate from aesthetic considerations.

Because of the long history of discrimination in our culture against absorbed readers and fans, particularly women, fans often show signs of internalized discrimination. This includes the guilt that some fans feel at their own participation in fandom and other "guilty pleasures"; the ways that fan writers may sabotage their own writings by attempting to avoid themes and tropes with low cultural prestige, such as self-indulgence, idiosyncratic pleasure, and self-insertion/*bovarysme*; and how members of fandom may try to police fanfiction and strongly criticize one another's work in an attempt to make fanfiction more palatable to the general culture.

There are a number of things that those within the fandom community can do to fight this kind of internalized discrimination. The first thing is to recognize that our culture does look down on absorbed reading, fandom, fanfiction, and women's media consumption. We need to learn to recognize the stereotypes and prejudices associated with this species of taste discrimination and misogyny and to combat them. As the *Community Tool Box* points out, "People simply can't fight effectively for themselves when they believe the problem is their own fault or that something is inherently wrong with them."

Community Tool Box makes a number of suggestions for dealing with all kinds of internalized discrimination, and many of these could be useful approaches for fans. The website suggests that members of groups that have been discriminated against "take pride and celebrate [their] culture": that members of the group "encourage each other to remember that they are good, worthy, capable, intelligent, beautiful, etc. and that others in their culture are good as well." Group members can also share stories about how they have been discriminated against and how it made them feel, helping them to remove "the illusion that the experience is somehow inherently their problem alone—and that they are the only source of their own difficulties, rather than problems in the society at large." Fans frequently engage in this behavior at conventions and online, through websites like *Tumblr*.

Community Tool Box also suggests that members of groups that have been discriminated against "take action against injustice and oppression" and speak up when they notice the operation of internalized discrimination within a group. In other words, when fans notice negative trends in fandom that reveal the operation of internalized discrimination, they can break free from negative patterns and model respectful, encouraging behavior. Since internalized discrimination is not the fault of the victims, fans should point out this problem without assigning blame. Instead of criticizing, shaming, or belittling fans who are displaying internalized discrimination, other fans should explain how they see that discrimination operating and kindly encourage more positive dialogue.

Fans can explain to others what internalized discrimination and misogyny are and how they are operating in the group. They can also fight internalized discrimination by being welcoming to new fans and fan writers rather than gatekeeping, policing ranks, or telling others that they are not "real" fans. *Community Tool Box* notes that groups "can tend to exclude new people much in the same way that their group has been excluded by the larger society." Instead of acting as gatekeepers and perpetuating the myth of the "fake geek girl" or boy, fans can welcome others warmly into the community.

Those who are not fans or absorbed readers, who are not part of the group that is being discriminated against, still have the responsibility, as they do with far more serious forms of discrimination and oppression, to speak up and confront negative stereotypes when they encounter them. All of us, fans or not, need to know what the stereotypes are, how they function, and what their effects are in order to counter them. Then we need to work kindly against discrimination, both within fan culture in the larger culture. This includes taking a very serious look at our copyright laws and how far they may be protecting authors' profits—or only squelching derivative creativity.

Discrimination against fans and those who engage in "guilty" pleasure reading and viewing is one manifestation of the larger issue of invisible misogyny in our culture, and combating it can make a more just and pleasant world for everyone. After all, as Julia Donaldson's poem reminds us, absorbed reading and fanfiction are not the end of the world: they are entrances to new ones.

Glossary

The following glossary may provide further background, not only as an explication of fandom vocabulary but as a primer in the ways fans conceptualize fanfiction and other fan products and activities.

General

BNF Big Name Fan. A fan who is well known in his or her fandom.

Bookverse/Movieverse The version of canon based on the book (Bookverse) or the film adaptation (Movieverse). Depending on how many liberties the adaptation takes, the two may present very different versions of events.

Canon The work or works on which a fanfiction is based; the authoritative version of events; of or pertaining to this version. What constitutes canon may be a matter of debate within a fandom.

Con Short for *convention*, as in a convention of science fiction fans, like ComicCon. Con can also be short for *consent* in fics with sexual content: *Non-Con* stands for *nonconsensual sex* and *Dub-Con* for *dubious consent*.

Fandom Fannish activities or the fan community in general. Can also refer to the communities surrounding particular texts, such as the *Star Trek* fandom or the Harry Potter fandom.

Fanfic A short form of *fanfiction*. Can also be called *fic*. Writing fanfic can be called *ficcing*.

Fannish Of or pertaining to fans.

Fanon A widespread trope or convention within a fandom—such as a common pairing or common depiction of a character—which may eventually be so widespread as to be confused with the canon.

Fanservice References in the canon that are meant as a nod or concession to the fans. An example would be characters on the television show *Lost* referring to the passengers from the tail section of the plane as *tailies*, a term that originated among the fans on *Lost* message boards, or the author of a series of books including more scenes with a character who is a fan favorite. Can also refer to things the canon does just to make the fans happy, such as an anime giving a female character large breasts in consideration of its male viewers.

Headcanon The version of an event or character that is accepted by an individual fan as his or her personal canon. For example, as Legolas's hair color is not described in Tolkien's *Lord of the Rings* books, some fans may have a headcanon that Legolas is a blond or a brunet.

Original Fiction Fiction that is not fanfiction.

Profic Professionally written and published fanfiction, such as tie-in novels for a film or television franchise, or professionally published novels based on texts like the Jane Austen novels that are in the public domain.

Kinds of Fanworks/Fannish Activity

Cosplay Costume Play: dressing up in costume as a character, usually for a role-play game or a convention.

Fanart Art by fans that illustrates events in the canon or other scenes with the characters.

Fanvid Fanmade videos.

Filk Also known as *Songfic*: musical fanfiction.

IRL In Real Life, as opposed to online.

Meta Short for *metaliterature*. Can also refer to a discussion of the canon, fandom, etc. *Metafic* is a fanfiction genre in which the fictional characters comment on the canon, fandom, etc.

RPG/RP Role-Playing Game/Role-Play. Can refer to written RPs in which fans communally write a story, each one controlling the actions of a single character; tabletop RPGs such as *Dungeons & Dragons* (DnD); or a LARP—Live-Action Role-Play—in which the players act out the actions of their chosen characters, often in costume.

Creating and Consuming Fanfiction

A/N Author's Notes.

Beta reader Also referred to as a Beta. A fan who acts as an editor for another fan's fics.

Concrit Constructive criticism.

Feels Intense feelings.
MST3K/MST *Mystery Science Theater 3000*. A piece that mocks someone else's fanfiction in the style of the television series of the same name, quoting the fanfiction and then adding cynical one-liners.
Pairing Two characters a fan wants to be in a relationship. Also called a *ship*.
Plotbunny An idea for a story.
OTP One True Pairing: the one pairing the fan is most devoted to.
Rec Recommendation: a recommended fanfiction.
To ship When a fan wants two characters—a pairing—to be in a relationship. Someone who ships a couple—pairs them together—is called a shipper.
To spork To make fun of someone else's fanfiction, sometimes line by line.
WIP Work In Progress.

Fanfiction Genres

Alternate Universe Also referred to as AU. A fanfiction that is based on an alternate version of events (a universe in which some event happened differently), or placed in a different setting, such as a different time period or country.
Badfic Fanfictions that are held to be especially badly written or that were intentionally badly written.
Crackfic Also called *crack*. A fanfiction with such strange events and crossovers that the reader may receive the impression that the writer was on crack cocaine. Can also refer to a fanfiction that is as addictive as crack.
Crossover A fanfiction that mixes together two or more fandoms—like Harry Potter joining the Fellowship of the Ring.
Drabble A short fanfiction of no more than 100 words.
Fix-it Fic A fanfiction that fixes things that the fan did not like about the canonical work.
Fluff Fanfiction that is light and pleasant.
Genderbend A fanfiction that changes the gender of one or more characters.
Het Fanfiction with a heterosexual pairing or pairings.
Hurt/Comfort Also known as H/C. A fanfiction in which a character is hurt, either physically or emotionally, in order to be comforted by

another character. The pairing involved can be in a romantic/sexual or platonic relationship. The hurting of a character may also be referred to as "Whump."

Mary Sue   An overly idealized female original character; can be shortened to Sue. Male Mary Sues may be called Marty Stus, Gary Stus, or Stus. The author of a Mary Sue story is called a Suethor. Mary Sues that appear in the canon rather than the fanfiction are called Canon Sues or Canon Stus.

One-shot   A short fanfiction that consists of no more than a single chapter.

OOC   Out of Character.

Original Character   Also referred to as an OC. A fanfiction character that was completely invented by the fan writer.

PWP   Stands for "Plot? What Plot?" Usually refers to a short fanfiction that focuses simply on an erotic encounter between characters with little surrounding plot. Can also mean "Porn Without Plot."

Racebend   A fanfiction that changes the race or ethnicity of one or more characters.

RPF   Real Person Fic. Fanfiction written about a real person, such as Johnny Depp fanfiction or fictional stories written about the band One Direction.

Slash   Homoromantic or homoerotic fanfiction. Usually refers to fics with male/male pairings, but can also refer to female/female pairings. Fanfic with female/female pairings can also be called femslash.

Reboot   The complete rewriting of a work. The new *Star Trek* films, which rewrite the old Original Series films, are a reboot.

Punctuation and Portmanteaus

Bang paths   *Fanlore* explains, "An exclamation mark (sometimes called a 'bang') between two words denotes a trait!character relationship between them, especially between a character and a trait of that character. For example, CAPSLOCK!Harry refers to Harry Potter shouting in capslock during much of The Order of the Phoenix, while Femme!Blair would refer to a characterization of Blair behaving in fanfiction in a way some might consider stereotypically effeminate" ("!"). Raincityruckus explains that this form of description probably developed from "bang paths" in old email systems: "If you wanted to write a mail to the Steve here in Engineering, you just wrote 'Steve' in the to: field and the computer sent it to the local account named Steve. But if it was Steve over in the physics department you wrote it to phys!Steve; the computer sent it to the 'phys' computer, which sent it in turn to the Steve account" (qtd. in "!").

Keysmash/keymash Usually some mix of the letters on the home row of a qwerty keyboard, such as *asldkf;j*. Meant to indicate an excitement so great as to cause the fan to become inarticulate.

Ship names Shippers frequently invent names for their favorite ships, usually expressed as a portmanteau of the two characters' names. For instance, Draco and Hermione from *Harry Potter* become *Dramione*. For details on how such ship names are constructed, see DiGirolamo.

Chapter Notes

Introduction

1. The original work on which a fanfiction is based. See the glossary of fanfiction terms in the appendix.

Chapter 2

1. Jeanne uses *settei* to refer to the basic premises and character designs of manga and anime.
2. Cherry Ames was a Nancy Drew–like nurse detective in a series of mystery novels written by Helen Wells and Julie Campbell Tatham between 1943 and 1968 ("Cherry Ames").
3. See "*Batman* (1989) Awards."

Chapter 3

1. Orlando Bloom, the actor who played Legolas in Peter Jackson's *Lord of the Rings* trilogy.

Chapter 4

1. What is particularly ironic about Pirhana's line is that the actress who plays Pirhana, Gugu Mbatha-Raw, later played the titular character in the 18th-century costume drama *Belle*, about a biracial upper-class woman of the period and the conflicts she encounters due to her race.

Chapter 5

1. The premise of these stories—agents bodily entering fiction in order to protect it from wrongdoing—is very similar to the premise of Jasper Fforde's Thursday Next series. The first Thursday Next book, *The Eyre Affair*, came out in July 2001, only about half a year before the PPC series began. However, I have seen no evidence that the PPC was based on Fforde's work. The popularity of the fanfiction trope of fans falling into the worlds of their favorite stories makes it likely that this was a coincidence.
2. As mentioned earlier, the PPC is run by giant sentient flowers.
3. Sometimes Camilla Sandman's screenname appears as "Miss Cam."
4. Balrogs are fiery, demonic creatures in *Lord of the Rings*.
5. Galadriel has the ability to read minds, and in "OFUM" she is occasionally disturbed by the sexual content of the students' thoughts.
6. Aragog is a giant spider in the Harry Potter series.
7. Ironically, Tungsten Monk seems to have misspelled this creature's name as "Ammet."

Chapter 6

1. This is one place where Seth Grahame-Smith's much-debated *Pride and Prejudice and Zombies* and related works from the same publisher (Quirk Books) are substantially different from internet fanfictions: *Pride and Prejudice and Zombies* contains quite a lot of text directly copied from *Pride and Prejudice*, which is not at all characteristic of internet fanfictions in general.
2. An odd statement, considering how many authors jealously guard their ideas as intellectual property.

Chapter 7

1. The 1995 film clearly took for part of its inspiration the Shirley Temple film of 1939, which also reunited Sara and her father, who in this version was reported to have died in the Siege of Mafeking.

Chapter 8

1. It would be interesting to compare the sub-creation of fanfiction to the sub-creation described by J. R. R. Tolkien in the act of mythopoeia: creating a fictional world in imitation of the real world created by God ("Sub-creation").

Works Cited

"!" *Fanlore*. Fanlore, 24 Aug. 2015. Web. 3 Sept. 2015. http://fanlore.org/wiki/!.

"About *The 100* and Its Controversy." *We Deserved Better*. We Deserved Better, n.d. Web. 19 July 2016. http://wedeservedbetter.com/background.

Aesi. "Mary Sue." *Urban Dictionary*. Urban Dictionary, LLC. 30 Jan. 2008. Web. 6 Jan. 2015. http://www.urbandictionary.com/define.php?term=Mary+Sue.

"Aesthetic Judgment." *Stanford Encyclopedia of Philosophy*. The Metaphysics Research Lab at Stanford University, 26 Aug. 2014. Web. 27 Dec. 2016. https://plato.stanford.edu/entries/aesthetic-judgment/.

Alanna. "Gender Roles in Fandom—The Fake Geek Girl Dilemma." *Black Girl Nerds*. Black Girl Nerds, 23 Oct. 2014. Web. 28 June 2016. http://blackgirlnerds.com/gender-roles-fandom-fake-geek-girl-dilemma/.

Alter, Alexandra. "How to Kill a Vampire (Series)." *Wall Street Journal*. Dow Jones & Co., 2 May 2013. Web. 5 Sept. 2015. http://www.wsj.com/articles/SB10001424127887324482504578453062428371352.

"Anne Rice." *Fanlore*. Fanlore, 20 Oct. 2015. Web. 2 July 2016. http://fanlore.org/wiki/Anne_Rice.

Anunexpectedhotdwarf. "Will It Ever Stop?" *Rage and Serenity*. Tumblr, 16 Aug. 2015. Web. 5 Nov. 2015. http://anunexpectedhotdwarf.tumblr.com/post/126831175264/will-it-ever-stop-will-i-ever-stop-falling-in.

Archive of Our Own. The Organization for Transformative Works, n.d. Web. 2 July 2016. https://archiveofourown.org/.

Atomos. *Atomos*. Tumblr, n.d. Web. 13 Feb. 2015. http://atomos.tumblr.com/post/11741071308.

Austen, Jane. "Letter 61." *The Republic of Pemberley*. The Republic of Pemberley, n.d. Web. 28 June 2016. http://www.pemberley.com/janeinfo/brablt11.html#letter61.

_____. *Northanger Abbey*. Project Gutenberg. Project Gutenberg, 24 Sept. 2013. Web. 3 Sept. 2015.

"Author." *PPC Wiki*. N.p., n.d. Web. 2 Sept. 2015. http://ppc.wikia.com/wiki/Author.

"Author-Requested Mission." *PPC Wiki*. N.p., n.d. Web. 2 Sept. 2015. http://ppc.wikia.com/wiki/Author-Requested_Mission.

Bacon-Smith, Camille. *Enterprising Women: Television Fandom and the Creation of Popular Myth*. Philadelphia: University of Pennsylvania Press, 1992. Print.

Baker-Whitelaw, Gavia, and Aja Romano. "A Guide to Fanfiction for People Who Can't Stop Getting It Wrong." *The Daily Dot*. Daily Dot LLC, 17 June 2014. Web. http://www.dailydot.com/geek/complete-guide-to-fanfiction/.

Baldick, Chris. *The Concise Oxford Dictionary of Literary Terms*. Oxford: Oxford University Press, 2001. Print.

Barner, Ashley. "Apparently There's…" *Fans Talking about Fandom*. Tumblr, 3 Feb. 2016. Web. 30 June 2016. http://fandomisreality.tumblr.com/post/138635231627.

_____. "Do You Ever Think…" *Fans Talking about Fandom*. Tumblr, 9 Oct. 2014. Web. 30 June 2016. http://fandomisreality.tumblr.com/post/99614367607/do-you-ever-think-youll-stop-drawing-fanart-no.

_____. "Found on *Facebook*." *Fans Talking about Fandom*. Tumblr, 24 Dec. 2015.

Web. 24 Dec. 2015. http://fandomis reality.tumblr.com/post/135849204177/found-on-facebook.

———. "New Faces." *Archive of Our Own*. The Organization for Transformative Works, 20 Oct. 2013. Web. 17 Nov. 2015. http://archiveofourown.org/works/724541/chapters/1344237.

"Barnes and Noble Interview, March 19, 1999." *Accio Quote!* N.p., n.d. Web. 5 Nov. 2015. http://www.accio-quote.org/articles/1999/0399-barnesandnoble.html.

Barney, Stephen A. "Introduction to *Troilus and Criseyde*." *The Riverside Chaucer*. 3rd ed. Ed. Larry D. Benson. Boston: Houghton, 1987. 471–72. Print.

"*Batman* (1989) Awards." *IMDB.com*. IMDB.com, Inc., n.d. Web. 4 Feb. 2016. http://www.imdb.com/title/tt0096895/awards.

Behindtheplottwist. "You Say They're Only Characters." *Behind the Plot Twist*. Tumblr, 8 May 2014. Web. 12 Nov. 2015. http://behindtheplottwist.tumblr.com/post/85172345334/theyre-more-than-fiction-they-were-there-for-me.

Bell, Alice. "A Brief History of Fan Fiction." *How We Get to Next*. Ed. Ian Steadman and Duncan Geere, n.d. Web. 16 Sept. 2015. https://howwegettonext.com/a-brief-history-of-fan-fiction-81c3a54ff5ad.

Berggren, Anne. "Reading Like a Woman." *Reading Sites: Social Difference and Reading Response*. Ed. Patrocinio P. Schweickart and Elizabeth A. Flynn. New York: MLA, 2004. 166–88. Print.

Bertelsen, Lance. "A Portrait of Mrs. Bingley." *Journal of the Jane Austen Society of North America* Persuasion 8 (1986): 37–38. Web. 28 June 2016. http://www.jasna.org/persuasions/printed/number8/bertelson.pdf.

Bonaparte, Lilian-Ann. "For Black Girls Who Considered Esmerelda Black When Cinderella Wasn't Enuf: The Importance of Race-Bending Fan-Art." *The Mary Sue*. The Mary Sue, 14 Sept. 2015. Web. 18 Nov. 2015. http://www.themarysue.com/the-importance-of-race-bending-fan-art/.

"Borrowing or Loan out of Original Characters." *FanFiction.net*. FanFiction.net, 5 May 2014. Web. 5 Sept. 2015. https://www.fanfiction.net/topic/2872/35435691/General-Borrowing-or-Loan-out-of-Original-Characters.

Bow, James. "Bite Me Stephanie [sic] Meyer!" *Bow. James Bow*. Bow, 15 Aug. 2008. Web. 30 June 2016. http://bowjamesbow.ca/2008/08/15/bite-me-stephan.shtml.

Boyle, James. "Here are 2 points." @thepublicdomain. Twitter, 8:47 AM, 7 Aug. 2009. Web. 21 Nov. 2016. https://twitter.com/thepublicdomain/statuses/3179288729/.

———. "No work created." @thepublicdomain. Twitter, 8:48 AM, 7 Aug. 2009. Web. 21 Nov. 2016. https://twitter.com/thepublicdomain/statuses/3179305900/.

Boz4pm. "Don't Panic!" *FanFiction.net*. Fanfiction.net, 27 March 2004. Web. 12 Feb. 2015. https://www.fanfiction.net/s/1690622/1/Don-t-Panic.

———. "Don't Panic!" *Stories of Arda*. Nilmandra, n.d. Web. 17 Nov. 2015. http://www.storiesofarda.com/chapterlistview.asp?SID=4250.

———. "Okay, NOW Panic!" *FanFiction.net*. Fanfiction.net, 13 Sept. 2008. Web. 25 July 2016. https://www.fanfiction.net/s/1812394/1/Okay-NOW-Panic.

Brewer, David A. *The Afterlife of Character, 1726–1825*. Philadelphia: University of Pennsylvania Press, 2005. Print.

Brotherson, Laura M. "The Twilight Obsession and Its Effect on Marriages." *Self-Growth.com*. SelfGrowth.com, n.d. Web. 6 Jan. 2015. http://www.selfgrowth.com/articles/the-twilight-obsession-and-its-effect-on-marriages.

Brunner, Jeryl. "Happy 60th birthday, Whoopi Goldberg!" *Huffington Post*. TheHuffingtonPost.com, Inc., 14 Nov. 2015. Web. 30 June 2016. http://www.huffingtonpost.com/jeryl-brunner/happy-60th-birthday-whoop_b_8565494.html.

Bryanthechosen1. "Wheatley damn it (Comment)." *Danny Phantom Mary Sues*. HermyStar, 19 April 2012. Web. 6 Jan. 2015. http://phantomsues.livejournal.com/67168.html.

Canavan, Gerry. "Adult Fantasy Author Lev Grossman on His Work, Harry Potter and Evelyn Waugh." *Indy Week*. Indy Week, 24 Aug. 2011. Web. 5 Sept. 2015. http://www.indyweek.com/indyweek/adult-fantasy-author-lev-grossman-on-his-work-harry-potter-and-evelyn-waugh/Content?oid=2640669.

Card, Orson Scott. "Questions for a Research Paper." *Hatrack River: The Official Web Site of Orson Scott Card.* Hatrack River Enterprises Inc., 1997. Web. 21 July 2016. http://www.hatrack.com/cgi-bin/print_friendly.cgi?page=/research/interviews/yoda-patta.shtml.

Caron, Nathalie. "Now That He's Seen It, What Does Steven Moffat Think of *Elementary*?" *Blastr.* Syfy, 17 Dec. 2012. Web. 3 Sept. 2015. http://www.blastr.com/2012/05/now_that_hes_seen_it_what.php.

Carone, Angela. "*True Blood* Panel: Alan Ball, Charlaine Harris, Sookie and More." *KPBS.org.* KPBS Publishing, 26 July 2009. Web. 5 Sept. 2015. http://www.kpbs.org/news/2009/jul/26/true-blood-panel/.

Cartwright, Mark. "Greek Tragedy." *Ancient History Encyclopedia.* Ancient History Encyclopedia Ltd., 16 March 2013. Web. 16 Sept. 2015. http://www.ancient.eu/Greek_Tragedy/.

Centrumlumina. "Age." *The Slow Dance of the Infinite Stars.* Tumblr, 1 Oct. 2013. Web. 13 Nov. 2015. http://centrumlumina.tumblr.com/post/62805734754/age.

_____. "Fandom's Race Problem and the AO3 Ship Stats. *The Slow Dance of the Infinite Stars.* Tumblr, 13 Aug. 2016. Web. 1 Sept. 2016. http://centrumlumina.tumblr.com/post/148893785870/fandoms-race-problem-and-the-ao3-ship-stats.

_____. "Gender." *The Slow Dance of the Infinite Stars.* Tumblr, 1 Oct. 2013. Web. 15 Feb. 2015. http://centrumlumina.tumblr.com/post/62816996032/gender.

_____. "M/M Fans: Sexuality and Gender." *The Slow Dance of the Infinite Stars.* Tumblr, 7 Oct. 2013. Web. 1 Sept. 2016. http://centrumlumina.tumblr.com/post/63373124511/mm-fans-sexuality-and-gender.

_____. "Popular Fandoms." *The Slow Dance of the Infinite Stars.* Tumblr, 3 Oct. 2013. Web. 13 Nov. 2015. http://centrumlumina.tumblr.com/post/63005760587/popular-fandoms.

Chapman, Brian. "10 Reasons Why *Elementary* Is Better than *Sherlock*." *What Culture.* N.p., n.d. Web. 3 Sept. 2015. http://whatculture.com/tv/10-reasons-elementary-better-sherlock.php.

"Chapter 27, Section 3: Healing from the Effects of Internalized Oppression." *Cultural Competence and Spirituality in Community Building.* Community Tool Box, n.d. Web. 28 June 2016. http://ctb.ku.edu/en/table-of-contents/culture/cultural-competence/healing-from-interalized-oppression/main.

Char. "Does Anyone Else Ever…" *Multishipperpirateking.Tumblr.com.* Tumblr, Aug. 2014. Web. 15 May 2015. http://multishipperpirateking.tumblr.com/post/92539871205/does-anyone-else-ever-think-about-how-traditional.

"Cherry Ames." *Wikipedia.* Wikimedia, 1 March 2015. Web. 28 March 2015. http://en.wikipedia.org/wiki/Cherry_Ames.

"Clarke/Lexa." *Fanlore.* Organization for Transformative Works, 16 April 2016. Web. 19 July 2016. http://fanlore.org/wiki/Clarke/Lexa.

Coker, Catherine. "The Contraband Incident: The strange case of Marion Zimmer Bradley." *Transformative Works and Cultures* 6 (2001): n. pag. Web. 21 July 2016. http://journal.transformativeworks.org/index.php/twc/article/view/236/191.

Colman, George (the Elder). *Polly Honeycombe. Georgian Theatre and Novel: Rivals for the Repertory.* The Georgian Theatre and the Novel project, 2013. Web. 23 Sept. 2016. https://georgiantheatrenovel.wordpress.com/performances/polly-honeycombe-performance/polly-honeycombe-script/.

"A Comprehensive Guide to Austenesque Novels." *Austenesque Reviews.* Austenesque Reviews, n.d. Web. 1 July 2016. http://austenesquereviews.com/a-comprehensive-guide-to-austenesque-novels.

Cox, Christopher. "Annie Proulx." *The Paris Review.* The Paris Review, n.d. Web. 17 Nov. 2015. http://www.theparisreview.org/interviews/5901/the-art-of-fiction-no-199-annie-proulx.

Curtin, Mary Ellen. "Statistics." *Alternate Universes: Fanfiction Studies.* Curtin, 17 March 2003. Web. 30 Dec. 2013. http://www.alternateuniverses.com/stats.html.

"Deerstalker." *Baker Street.* N.p., n.d. Web. 3 Sept. 2015. http://bakerstreet.wikia.com/wiki/Deerstalker.

"Deerstalker." *Wikipedia.* Wikimedia Foundation, Inc., 2 Sept. 2015. Web. 3 Sept. 2015. http://en.wikipedia.org/wiki/Deerstalker.

"Department of Author Correspondence." *PPC Wiki*. N.p., n.d. Web. 2 Sept. 2015. http://ppc.wikia.com/wiki/Department_of_Author_Correspondence.

Destinationtoast. "AO3 Relationships." *Destination: Toast!* Tumblr, 5 June 2013. Web. 1 Sept. 2016. http://destinationtoast.tumblr.com/post/52261319793/next-up-in-my-ongoing-series-on-ao3-stats-a.

———. "F/F Stats: Femslash February 2016." *Destination: Toast!* Tumblr, 15 Feb. 2016. Web. 1 Sept. 2016. http://destinationtoast.tumblr.com/post/139410106784/toastystats-ff-stats-femslash-february-2016.

DiGirolamo, Cara M. "The Fandom Pairing Name: Blends and the Phonology-Orthography Interface." *Names: A Journal of Onomastics* 60.4 (2012): 231–43. Print.

Donaldson, Julia. "About Me." *Julia Donaldson*. Donaldson, n.d. Web. 13 Feb. 2015. http://www.juliadonaldson.co.uk/about.htm.

Doody, Margaret Anne. *The True Story of the Novel*. New Brunswick: Rutgers University Press, 1996. Print.

Doyle, Arthur Conan. *The Adventure of the Bruce-Partington Plans*. Project Gutenberg. Project Gutenberg, 23 Oct. 2008. Web. 22 July 2016. http://www.gutenberg.org/files/2346/2346-h/2346-h.htm.

———. *The Sign of Four*. Project Gutenberg. Project Gutenberg, 19 Nov. 2008. Web. 22 July 2016. https://www.gutenberg.org/files/2097/2097-h/2097-h.htm.

———. "A Scandal in Bohemia." *The Adventures of Sherlock Holmes*. Project Gutenberg. Project Gutenberg, 18 April 2011. Web. 22 July 2016. http://www.gutenberg.org/files/1661/1661-h/1661-h.htm.

Doyle, Sady. "The 'Feminized Society' Myth." *In These Times*. In These Times and the Institute for Public Affairs, 22 Jan. 2014. Web. 18 Jan. 2016. http://inthesetimes.com/article/16157/our_feminized_society.

Earlgreytea68. "If You Want to Talk about Something Weird, Let's Talk about Geoducks, Not Fanfiction." *Possibly, I'm Insane*. Tumblr, 13 March 2015. Web. 29 April 2015. http://earlgreytea68.tumblr.com/post/113486132836/if-you-want-to-talk-about-something-weird-lets.

Eddy, Cheryl. "A Brief History of 'Satanic Panic' in the 1980s." *Io9*. Gawker Media, 20 Jan. 2015. Web. 2 July 2016. http://io9.gizmodo.com/a-brief-history-of-satanic-panic-in-the-1980s-1679476373.

"Edmund Wilson." *Wikiquote*. Wikimedia Foundation, Inc., 13 Nov. 2016. Web. 26 Dec. 2016. https://en.wikiquote.org/wiki/Edmund_Wilson.

Elementary. CBS. 2012–2016. Television.

Eliot, George. "Silly Novels by Silly Lady Novelists." *The Essays of George Eliot*. Ed. Nathan Shepherd. *Project Gutenberg*. Project Gutenberg, 9 March 2009. Web. 3 Sept. 2015. http://www.gutenberg.org/files/28289/28289-h/28289-h.htm#page178.

Ellis, Lindsay. "Stop Asking 'Is This Feminist?'" *The Mary Sue*. The Mary Sue, LLC, 12 June 2015. Web. 5 Sept. 2016. http://www.themarysue.com/stop-asking-is-this-feminist/.

Emily (The Slut). "Abusive Is the New Sexy: Why Books Like Twilight Are Dangerous." *Feministing Community*. Feministing, 6 April 2011. Web. 6 Jan 2015. http://feministing.com/2011/04/06/abusive-is-the-new-sexy-why-books-like-twilight-are-dangerous/.

"Fan Fic: The Subspace Emissary's Worlds Conquest." *TV Tropes*. TV Tropes, n.d. Web. 3 July 2015. http://tvtropes.org/pmwiki/pmwiki.php/FanFic/TheSubspaceEmissarysWorldsConquest.

"Fanfic Recs *The Lord of the Rings* Discussion." *TV Tropes*. TV Tropes Foundation, LLC, 18 April 2014. Web. 3 Sept. 2015. http://tvtropes.org/pmwiki/remarks.php?trope=FanficRecs.TheLordOfTheRings.

"Fanfiction." *Fanlore*. Organization for Transformative Works, 7 Sept. 2015. Web. 16 Sept. 2015. http://fanlore.org/wiki/Fanfiction.

"FanFiction.Net." *Wikipedia*. Wikimedia Foundation, Inc., n.d. Web. 13 Nov. 2015. https://en.wikipedia.org/wiki/FanFiction.Net.

"Fanon" *Urban Dictionary*. Urban Dictionary, LLC, n.d. Web. 3 Sept. 2015. http://www.urbandictionary.com/define.php?term=fanon.

FFN Research. "Fan Fiction Demographics in 2010: Age, Sex, Country." *Fan Fiction Statistics*. FFN Research, 18 March 2011. Web. 13 Nov. 2015. http://ffnresearch.blogspot.com/2011/03/fan-fiction-demographics-in-2010-age.html.

___. "*FanFiction.net* Story Totals." *Fan Fiction Statistics*. FFN Research, 6 July 2010. Web. 5 Nov. 2015. http://ffnresearch.blogspot.com/2010/07/fanfictionnet-story-totals.html.

Fforde, Jasper. "Frequently Asked Questions." *JasperFforde.com*. Jasper Fforde, n.d. Web. 21 July 2016. http://www.jasperfforde.com/faq.html#u.

Fielding, Henry. *An Apology for the Life of Mrs. Shamela Andrews*. Gutenberg.org. Project Gutenberg, 14 Jan. 2010. Web. 12 Nov. 2015. http://www.gutenberg.org/files/30962/30962-h/30962-h.htm.

"*Fifty Shades of Grey*." *Wikipedia*. Wikimedia Foundation, Inc., 2 Sept. 2015. Web. 3 Sept. 2015. http://en.wikipedia.org/wiki/Fifty_Shades_of_Grey.

"Filing off the Serial Numbers." *Fanlore*. Fanlore, 14 Feb. 2015. Web. 3 Sept. 2015. http://fanlore.org/wiki/Filing_Off_The_Serial_Numbers.

Flint, Kate. *The Woman Reader, 1837–1914*. Oxford: Clarendon, 1993. Print.

Flood, Alison. "Charlaine Harris Threatened by Fans Over Final Sookie Stackhouse Novel." *The Guardian*. Guardian News, 10 May 2013. Web. 5 Sept. 2015. http://www.theguardian.com/books/2013/may/10/charlaine-harris-sookie-stackhouse-true-blood.

Flourish Kink. "Five Tropes Fanfic Readers Love (And One They Hate)." *Fansplaining*. Medium.com, 27 Oct. 2016. Web. https://medium.com/fansplaining/five-tropes-fanfic-readers-love-and-one-they-hate-73843372408c#.ik01w8f1d.

Fogisbeautiful. "Changing Histories: Choices." *Archive of Our Own*. Organization for Transformative Works, 20 April 2015. Web. 25 July 2016. http://archiveofourown.org/works/2299565/chapters/5058149.

Forablueeyedmiracle. "Fandom Is Knowing." *Baby, Babyluv*. Tumblr, 25 April 2012. Web. http://forablueeyedmiracle.tumblr.com/post/21773440202/fandom-is-knowing-that-across-the-globe-hundreds.

Fozmeadows. "Fandom Thoughts." *What Happens Next: A Gallimaufry*. Tumblr, 22 June 2014. Web. 27 June 2015. http://fozmeadows.tumblr.com/post/89576778116/fandom-thoughts.

Gallagher, Catherine. *Nobody's Story: The Vanishing Acts of Women Writers in the Marketplace, 1670–1820*. Berkeley: University of California Press, 1994. Print.

Gomez, Tim. "Do The Math: 8 Reasons *Harry Potter* Is Greater Than *Twilight*." *CinemaBlend*. Cinema Blend, LLC, 16 July 2009. Web. 5 Nov. 2015. http://www.cinemablend.com/new/Do-The-Math-8-Reasons-Harry-Potter-Is-Greater-Than-Twilight-13981.html.

Green, Theresa. "Aragorn: The Owner's Guide and Maintenance Manual." *The Council of Elrond*. Council of Elrond, n.d. Web. 5 Sept. 2015. http://www.councilofelrond.com/fanfiction/aragorn-the-owners-guide-and-maintenance-manual/.

___. "Boromir: The Owner's Guide and Maintenance Manual." *The Council of Elrond*. Council of Elrond, n.d. Web. 5 Sept. 2015. http://www.councilofelrond.com/fanfiction/boromir-the-owners-guide-and-maintenance-manual/.

___. "Legolas: The Owner's Guide and Maintenance Manual." *The Council of Elrond*. Council of Elrond, n.d. Web. 5 Sept. 2015. http://www.councilofelrond.com/fanfiction/legolasthe-owners-manual-and-maintenance-guide/.

Greenberger, Robert. "Nichelle Nichols: An Officer and a Heroine." *The Science Fiction Universe* 100, n. p. "Starlog Magazine Issue 100." *Internet Archive*. Internet Archive, n.d. Web. 3 June 2016. https://archive.org/stream/starlog_magazine-100/100_djvu.txt.

"Guide to the PPC." *PPC Wiki*. N.p., n.d. Web. 20 July 2016. http://ppc.wikia.com/wiki/Guide_to_the_PPC.

Haberman, Clyde. "When Dungeons & Dragons Set Off a 'Moral Panic.'" *The New York Times*. The New York Times Company, 17 April 2016. Web. 2 July 2016. http://www.nytimes.com/2016/04/18/us/when-dungeons-dragons-set-off-a-moral-panic.html.

Hamilton, Ashley. "17 Secrets Only Book Lovers Are in On." *BookBub Blog*. Book-Bub, 23 June 2015. Web. 5 Nov. 2015. https://media.bookbub.com/blog/2015/06/23/secrets-booklovers-are-in-on/.

Hellekson, Karen. "A Fannish Field of Value: Online Fan Gift Culture." *Cinema Journal* 48.4 (2009): 113–18. *ProjectMuse*.

Web. 25 July 2016. http://dx.doi.org/10.1353/cj.0.0140.

"Headcanon." *Fanlore*. Fanlore, 15 Aug. 2015. Web. 21 Nov. 2015. http://fanlore.org/wiki/Headcanon.

Hickey, Walt. "The Dollar-And-Cents Case Against Hollywood's Exclusion of Women." *FiveThirtyEightLife*. ESPN Internet Ventures, 1 April 2014. Web. 15 Nov. 2015. http://fivethirtyeight.com/features/the-dollar-and-cents-case-against-hollywoods-exclusion-of-women/.

"History of the PPC, Part One." *PPC Wiki*. N.p., n.d. Web. 1 April 2015. http://ppc.wikia.com/wiki/History_of_the_PPC,_Part_One.

Hodgson Burnett, Frances. "Sara Crewe; or, What Happened at Miss Minchin's." *St. Nicholas: An Illustrated Magazine for Young Folks* 15 (Nov. 1887–April 1888): 97–105. Print.

Horn, Paul. "Fanboy." *Urban Dictionary*. Urban Dictionary, LLC. 22 Aug. 2003. Web. 11 July 2016. http://www.urbandictionary.com/define.php?term=fanboy.

Hussein, Sana. "Literary or Not: The Reality of Escapist Fiction." *The Missing Slate*. Low Key/Slate Publications, Summer 2014. Web. 13 Nov. 2015. http://themissingslate.com/article/literary-or-not/.

"If Fanfiction Is Legitimate, Doesn't That Mean Publishers or Studios Can Produce Derivative Works without Compensating Original Authors?" *Organization for Transformative Works*. OTW, n.d. Web. 3 Sept. 2015. http://transformativeworks.org/if-fanfiction-legitimate-doesnt-mean-publishers-or-studios-can-produce-derivative-works-without.

Ilovecatz44. *Just Call Me Satan*. Tumblr, 9 August 2015. Web. 28 June 2016. http://ilovecatz44.tumblr.com/post/126261749105/does-anyone-else-just-lay-in-bed-for-an-hour-or-so.

Imorca. "To an Extent." *Fans Talking about Fandom*. Tumblr, n.d. Web. 17 Nov. 2015. http://fandomisreality.tumblr.com/post/120439253392/to-an-extent-its-a-problem-with-fandom-the-fact.

Jay and Acacia. "Jay and Acacia: The Original Series." *PPC: The Lost Tales*. Neshomeh et al., n.d. Web. 2 Sept. 2015. http://plotprotectors.tripod.com/TOS/.

Jeanne. "Shameless Setteis." *Aestheticism.net Archive*. N.p., 1999–2000. Web. 13 April 2015. http://web.archive.org/web/20010610043559/http://www.aestheticism.net/visitors/editor/jeanne/shameless/index.htm.

Jenkins, Henry. "Digital Land Grab." *MIT Technology Review*. MIT Technology Review, 1 March 2000. Web. 9 July 2016. https://www.technologyreview.com/s/400696/digital-land-grab/.

———. *Textual Poachers: Television Fans and Participatory Culture*. Updated Twentieth Anniversary Edition. New York: Routledge, 2013. Print.

Jones, Cleolinda. "Twilight." *Cleoland*. PBworks, n.d. Web. http://cleoland.pbworks.com/w/page/10373763/Twilight#Lolfan.

Jones, Ross. "*Sherlock* Facts: 21 Things You Didn't Know." *The Telegraph*. Telegraph Media Group Ltd., 25 April 2015. Web. 3 Sept. 2015. http://www.telegraph.co.uk/culture/tvandradio/10537064/Sherlock-facts-21-things-you-didnt-know.html.

Julyflame. "Mission: Swim." *Julyflame.LiveJournal.com*. Livejournal, 9 May 2008. Web. 11 April 2015. http://julyflame.livejournal.com/18401.html.

Jusino, Teresa. "Time Warner's Jeff Bewkes Should Probably Realize That Women Have Always Loved Genre." *The Mary Sue*. The Mary Sue, 8 Dec. 2015. Web. 18 Jan. 2016. http://www.themarysue.com/women-love-genre-jeff-bewkes/.

Klimchynskaya, Anastasia. "Sherlock Holmes: The Original Fandom." *Den of Geek*. DoGTech LLC, 30 Jan. 2014. Web. 1 July 2016. http://www.denofgeek.com/tv/sherlock/29056/sherlock-holmes-the-original-fandom.

Konkoa. "This Has Been a PSA." *Blog Titles Are Hard*. Tumblr, 9 Feb. 2013. Web. 24 Jan. 2016. http://konkoa.tumblr.com/post/42720198220/this-has-been-a-psa.

Lachenal, Jessica. "A List of All the Asians in *The Force Awakens*, and Why Representation Matters." *The Mary Sue*. The Mary Sue, 23 Dec. 2015. Web. 23 Jan. 2016. http://www.themarysue.com/asians-in-tfa-and-representation/.

Lackey, Mercedes. "#246." *Making Light*. Teresa Nielsen Hayden et al., 26 April 2006. Web. 3 Sept. 2015. http://nielsenhayden.com/makinglight/archives/007464.html#122173.

Ladyloveandjustice. "Mary Sue, what are you? or why the concept of Sue is sexist." *Adventuresofcomicbookgirl with a new codename.* Tumblr, 8 Dec. 2011. Web. 7 Jan. 2015. http://ladyloveandjustice.tumblr.com/post/13913540194/mary-sue-what-are-you-or-why-the-concept-of-sue.

Lamb, Jean. "Re: The Infamous Marion Zimmer Bradley Case." *Google Groups: rec.arts.sf.written.* Google, 19 March 2001. Web. 3 Sept. 2015. https://groups.google.com/forum/#!original/rec.arts.sf.written/JkmjWyZBdbg/-cE1Xj7bwYAJ.

Leicht, Stina. "Fan Fiction, Ethics, and Authors." *Have Online Dictionary Will Travel.* LiveJournal, 5 May 2010. Web. 21 Nov. 2015. http://stina-leicht.livejournal.com/221884.html.

Letamendi, Andrea. "The Psychology of the Fake Geek Girl: Why We're Threatened by Falsified Fandom." *The Mary Sue.* The Mary Sue, LLC, 21 Dec. 2012. Web. 28 June 2016. http://www.themarysue.com/psychology-of-the-fake-geek-girl/.

Lettherebedoodles. "Racebent Disney." *Let There Be Doodles.* Tumblr, n.d. Web. 17 Nov. 2015. http://lettherebedoodles.tumblr.com/tagged/racebent-disney.

Lig Na Baste. "Fanboy." *Urban Dictionary.* Urban Dictionary, LLC. 10 July 2008. Web. 11 July 2016. http://www.urbandictionary.com/define.php?term=fanboy.

"List of Longest Novels." *Wikipedia.* Wikimedia Foundation, Inc., 22 July 2016. Web. 25 July 2016. https://en.wikipedia.org/wiki/List_of_longest_novels.

"List of *Star Trek* Novels." *Wikipedia.* Wikimedia Foundation, Inc., 11 Aug. 2015. Web. 3 Sept. 2015. http://en.wikipedia.org/wiki/List_of_Star_Trek_novels.

"List of *Star Wars* Books." *Wikipedia.* Wikimedia Foundation, Inc., 2 Sept. 2015. Web. 3 Sept. 2015. http://en.wikipedia.org/wiki/List_of_Star_Wars_books.

A Little Princess. Dir. Alfonso Cuarón. Perf. Liesel Matthews, Eleanor Bron, Liam Cunningham, and Vanessa Lee Chester. Warner Bros., 1995. Film.

A Little Princess. Dir. Carol Wiseman. Perf. Amelia Shankley, Maureen Lipman, and Nigel Havers. LWT, 1986. Television miniseries.

Lord, Emma. "13 Things Fan Fiction Writers Are Very Tired of Explaining." *Bustle.* Bustle, 23 March 2015. Web. 18 Nov. 2015. http://www.bustle.com/articles/71438-13-things-fan-fiction-writers-are-very-tired-of-explaining.

Lost in Austen. Dir. Dan Zeff. Perf. Jemima Rooper, Elliot Cowan. Mammoth Screen: 2009. DVD.

"*Lost in Austen*: Behind the Scenes." *Lost in Austen.* Dir. Dan Zeff. Perf. Jemima Rooper, Elliot Cowan. Mammoth Screen: 2009. DVD.

Lukipela. "People that Should Have to Register as Sex Offenders." *Cheezburger.com.* Cheezburger, Inc., n.d. Web. 12 Nov. 2015. http://cheezburger.com/3031252224.

Lylestyles. "Twilight Fans' Vampire Addiction Affecting Relationships." *Where the Sideblog Ends.* Lylestyles, 30 June 2010. Web. 6 Jan. 2015. http://lylestyles.wordpress.com/2010/06/30/twilight-fans-vampire-addiction-affecting-relationships/.

"Lyn Flewelling." *Fanlore.* Organization for Transformative Works, 7 Aug. 2014. Web. 5 Sept. 2015. http://fanlore.org/wiki/Lynn_Flewelling.

Madison, Charles. "*Wicked* Movie Finally Seems To Be on Course, Set for 2016 Release." *FilmDivider.com.* Film Divider, 1 Dec. 2014. Web. 16 Sept. 2015. http://www.filmdivider.com/7062/wicked-movie-finally-seems-to-be-on-course-set-for-2016-release/.

Mae. "Last Night after Ghostbusters." *The Girl with Three Faces.* Tumblr, 17 July 2016. Web. 6 Aug. 2016. http://the-girl-with-three-faces.tumblr.com/post/147545639382/last-night-after-ghostbusters-i-stopped-to-talk.

Mandalorianed. "Hey Dora." *"Be Strong," Saith My Heart.* Tumblr, n.d. Web. 5 Nov. 2015. http://mandalorianed.tumblr.com/post/122224331256.

"Mark Gatiss." *Sherlockology.* Hartswood Films Ltd., n.d. Web. 3 Sept. 2015. http://www.sherlockology.com/crew/mark-gatiss.

"Mark Gatiss." *Wikipedia.* Wikimedia, 5 July 2016. Web. 22 July 2016. https://en.wikipedia.org/wiki/Mark_Gatiss.

Martin, George R. R. "Someone Is Angry on the Internet." *Grrm.LiveJournal.com.* Livejournal, 7 May 2010. Web. 3 Sept. 2015. http://grrm.livejournal.com/151914.html.

———. "Wars, Woes, Work." *Grrm.Live Journal.com*. Livejournal, 10 June 2015. Web. 3 Sept. 2015. http://grrm.livejournal.com/151914.html>

"Mary Sue." *Fanlore*. Fanlore, 13 Dec. 2014. Web. 6 Jan. 2015. http://fanlore.org/wiki/Mary_Sue.

Mel. "Charlaine Harris Talks about Fan Reactions to *Dead Ever After*." *True-Blood.net*. Nice Girls Media LLC, 14 June 2013. Web. 5 Sept. 2015. http://trueblood.net/2013/06/14/charlaine-harris-talks-about-fan-reactions-to-dead-ever-after/.

Metrowebukmetro. "How Fan Fiction Is Conquering the Internet and Shooting up Book Charts." *Metro*. DMG Media, 11 Nov. 2012. Web. 3 Sept. 2015. http://metro.co.uk/2012/11/11/how-fan-fiction-is-conquering-the-internet-and-shooting-up-book-charts-617396/.

Mildmanneredmuse. "The Importance of Writing Carefree Blackness™." *The Pensieve of L*. Tumblr, 24 Dec. 2015. Web. 23 Sept. 2016. http://mildmanneredmuse.tumblr.com/post/135878093715/the-importance-of-writing-carefree-blackness.

Miller, Laura. "You Belong to Me." *Vulture*. New York Media LLC, 11 March 2015. Web. 29 April 2015. http://www.vulture.com/2015/03/fanfiction-guide.html.

Miss Cam. "Reviews for 'The Official Fanfiction University of Middle-earth.'" *Fanfiction.net*. Fanfiction.net, 8 March 2002. Web. 11 May 2015. https://www.fanfiction.net/r/644826/.

"Mission Writing Guide." *PPC Wiki*. N.p., n.d. Web. 2 Sept. 2015. http://ppc.wikia.com/wiki/Mission_Writing_Guide.

Mlawki, Shana. "Why I'm Not Going to Read Your Fanfic." *Overthinking It*. Overthinking It, 22 Sept. 2008. Web. 25 Nov. 2014. http://www.overthinkingit.com/2008/09/22/why-im-not-going-to-read-your-fanfic/.

Monicam. *Monmon Is the Name*. Tumblr, 22 July 2015. 28 June 2016. http://monicam.tumblr.com/post/124777576330/whistles-lowly-pulls-out-magnifying-glass-are.

Monkey. "Fangirl." *Urban Dictionary*. Urban Dictionary, LLC. 6 Dec. 2004. Web. 11 July 2016. http://www.urbandictionary.com/define.php?term=fangirl.

Monkmunk. "Mary Sue." *Urban Dictionary*. Urban Dictionary, LLC. 11 April 2015. Web. 25 July 2016. http://www.urbandictionary.com/define.php?term=Mary+Sue.

Moore, Trent. "Not So Elementary: BBC *Sherlock* Creators May Sue over CBS' Holmes." *Blastr*. Syfy, 16 Dec. 2012. Web. 3 Sept. 2015. http://www.blastr.com/2012/01/not_so_elementary_bbc_she.php.

Moore, Wendy. "Love and Marriage in 18th-Century Britain." *Historically Speaking* 10.3 (19 June 2009): 8–10. Print.

Morrison, Ewan. "In the Beginning, There Was Fan Fiction: From the Four Gospels to *Fifty Shades*." *The Guardian*. Guardian News and Media Ltd., 13 Aug. 2012. Web. 10 Jan. 2016. http://www.theguardian.com/books/2012/aug/13/fan-fiction-fifty-shades-grey.

Moss, Laura. "Why Must We Hate the Things Teen Girls Love?" *Mother Nature Network*. Narrative Content Group, 9 Oct. 2015. Web. 28 June 2016. http://www.mnn.com/lifestyle/arts-culture/stories/why-do-we-hate-things-teen-girls-love.

"Most Fanfic Writers Are Girls." *TV Tropes*. TV Tropes Foundation, LLC, n.d. Web. 12 Feb. 2015. http://tvtropes.org/pmwiki/pmwiki.php/Main/MostFanficWritersAreGirls.

"Movieverse." *Fanlore*. Organization for Transformative Works, 29 Jan. 2012. Web. 4 May 2015. http://fanlore.org/wiki/Movieverse.

Musashden. "Walking Dead—copy and paste when it comes to sues." *Bastion of Questionable Sanity*. The Mary Sue Society, 31 Aug. 2013. Web. 6 Jan. 2015. http://marysues.livejournal.com/2945485.html.

Naomideplume. *Naomi de Plume*. Tumblr, 21 Feb. 2016. Web. 28 June 2016. http://naomideplume.tumblr.com/post/139742883350/ilovecatz44-does-anyone-else-just-lay-in-bed.

"Narrative and Dramatic Sources of all Shakespeare's Works." *The Bard of Avon: Shakespeare in Stratford-upon-Avon*. N.p., n.d. Web. 16 Sept. 2015. http://www.shakespeare-w.com/english/shakespeare/source.html.

Nell, Victor. "The Psychology of Reading for Pleasure: Needs and Gratifications." *Reading Research Quarterly* 23.1 (1988): 6–50. Print.

Nepveu, Kate. "Diana Gabaldon & Fanfic Followup." *Kate-nepveu.LiveJournalcom*. Live journal, 10 May 2010. Web. 3 Sept. 2015. http://kate-nepveu.livejournal.com/483239.html.

"Nichelle Nichols." *National Space Society*. National Space Society, n.d. Web. 30 June 2016. http://www.nss.org/about/bios/nichols.html.

"1994 Baker Street: Sherlock Holmes Returns." *Wikipedia*. Wikimedia Foundation, Inc., 26 April 2015. Web. 3 Sept. 2015. http://en.wikipedia.org/wiki/1994_Baker_Street:_Sherlock_Holmes_Returns.

Nscangal. "Mary Sue." *Urban Dictionary*. Urban Dictionary, LLC. 29 July 2005. Web. 6 Jan. 2015. http://www.urbandictionary.com/define.php?term=Mary+Sue.

O'Keefe, Moira. "Uhura's Legacy: Media Images and Diversity in STEM Careers." *Visual Inquiry*. Annenberg School for Communication, 3 Aug. 2010. Web. http://www.visualinquiry.org/blog/?p=145.

Ozhawkauthor. "The Three Laws of Fandom." *Livin' on the MCU*. Tumblr, 1 Jan. 2016. Web. 1 July 2016. http://ozhawkauthor.tumblr.com/post/136380833197/the-three-laws-of-fandom.

Pearson, Jacqueline. *Women's Reading in Britain, 1750–1835: A Dangerous Recreation*. Cambridge: Cambridge University Press, 1999. Print.

"Permission." *PPC Wiki*. N.p., n.d. Web. 2 Sept. 2015. http://ppc.wikia.com/wiki/Permission.

Phelan, Stephen. "Renaissance Man." *The Sunday Herald* 7 Nov. 2004: n.p. *HighBeam Research*. Cengage Learning. Web. 3 Sept. 2015. http://www.highbeam.com/doc/1P2-10005417.html.

Pinkowitz, Jacqueline M. "'The rabid fans that take [Twilight] much too seriously': The Construction and Rejection of Excess in Twilight Antifandom." *Transformative Works and Cultures* 7 (2011): n. pag. Web. 7 Jan. 2015. http://journal.transformativeworks.org/index.php/twc/article/view/247/253.

PPC Wiki. N.p., n.d. Web. 2 Sept. 2015. http://ppc.wikia.com/wiki/PPC_Wiki.

Princessamericachavez. "On Star Wars, Representation and Straight White Males." *Princess America Chavez*. Tumblr, April 2016. Web. 18 Aug. 2016. http://princessamericachavez.tumblr.com/post/142481569623/way-back-on-the-seventies-even-before-the-first.

"Professional Author Fanfic Policies." *Fanlore*. Fanlore, 19 Nov. 2015. Web. 22 Nov. 2015. http://fanlore.org/wiki/Professional_Author_Fanfic_Policies.

"Profile." *Bastion of Questionable Sanity*. The Mary Sue Society, 23 Oct 2014. Web. 6 Jan. 2015. http://marysues.livejournal.com/profile.

Pugh, Sheenagh. *The Democratic Genre: Fan Fiction in a Literary Context*. Bridgend, UK: Seren, 2005. Print.

Radway, Janice. *A Feeling for Books: The Book-of-the-Month Club, Literary Taste, and Middle-Class Desire*. Chapel Hill: University of North Carolina Press, 1997. Print.

"The Return of Sherlock Holmes (1987 Film)." *Wikipedia*. Wikimedia Foundation, Inc., 13 Aug. 2015. Web. 3 Sept. 2015. http://en.wikipedia.org/wiki/The_Return_of_Sherlock_Holmes_(1987_film).

Riese. "All 160 Lesbian and Bisexual Characters On TV, And How They Died." *Autostraddle*. The Excitant Group, LLC, 11 March 2016. Web. 19 July 2016. http://www.autostraddle.com/all-65-dead-lesbian-and-bisexual-characters-on-tv-and-how-they-died-312315/.

Rivard, Carrie (Noble Platypus). "Mary-Sue Mockfest." *Nobleplatypus*. LiveJournal, 23 Jan. 2005. Web. 21 Nov. 2015. http://nobleplatypus.dreamwidth.org/tag/marysue+mockfest.

———. "A Very Mary Sequel." *Fanfiction.net*. Fanfiction.net, 7 April 2005. Web. https://www.fanfiction.net/s/1680337/1/A-Very-Mary-Sequel.

Roberts, Jeff. "Amazon's Fan-Fiction Portal Kindle Worlds Is a Bust for Fans, and for Writers Too." *Gigaom*. Knowingly, Inc., 17 Aug. 2014. Web. 7 July 2016. https://gigaom.com/2014/08/17/amazons-fan-fiction-portal-kindle-worlds-is-a-bust-for-fans-and-for-writers-too/.

Rogers, John. "Ephemera 2009 (7)." *Kung Fu Monkey*. Blogger, 19 March 2009. Web. 13 Nov. 2015. http://kfmonkey.blogspot.com/2009/03/ephemera-2009-7.html.

Romano, Aja. "I'm Done Explaining Why Fanfic Is Okay." *Let's Get the Seven Lines*. LiveJournal, 3 May 2010. Web. 1 July 2016. http://bookshop.livejournal.com/1044495.html.

Rosenerg, Adam. "Remember When Tom Hanks Starred in a Cautionary Tale about 'Dungeons & Dragons'?" *Mashable*. Mashable, Inc., 28 Oct. 2015. Web. 2 July 2016. http://mashable.com/2015/10/28/tom-hanks-dungeons-dragons/#mp_etoq9aZqq.

Sandman, Camilla. "The Official Fanfiction University of Middle-earth." *Lord of the Rings Fanfiction*. N.p. n.d. Web. 2 Sept. 2015. http://www.lotrfanfiction.com/viewstory.php?sid=463.

———. "Once More into the Urple Depths of OFUM." *Lord of the Rings Fanfiction*. N.p. n.d. Web. 2 Sept. 2015. http://www.lotrfanfiction.com/viewstory.php?sid=1693.

Sashayed. "Here's the Thing about *Jupiter Ascending*." *But Alas! The Creature Grows Degenerate*. Tumblr, 8 Feb. 2015. Web. 18 Jan. 2016. http://sashayed.tumblr.com/post/110444647320/heres-the-thing-about-jupiter-ascending.

"A Scandal in Belgravia." *Baker Street*. Wikia, n.d. Web. 22 July 2016. http://bakerstreet.wikia.com/wiki/A_Scandal_in_Belgravia.

Schlackman, Steve. "How Mickey Mouse Keeps Changing Copyright Law." *Art Law Journal*. Artrepreneur, 15 Feb. 2014. Web. 21 Nov. 2016. http://artlawjournal.com/mickey-mouse-keeps-changing-copyright-law/.

Schwabach, Aaron. *Fanfiction and Copyright: Outsider Works and Intellectual Property Protection*. Farnham, Surrey: Ashgate, 2011. Print.

Sega Slayer. "Fanboy." *Urban Dictionary*. Urban Dictionary, LLC. 26 June 2003. Web. 11 July 2016. http://www.urbandictionary.com/define.php?term=fanboy.

Sendlor, Charles. "Fan Fiction Demographics in 2010: Age, Sex, Country." *Fan Fiction Statistics*. FFN Research, 18 March 2011. Web. 12 Feb. 2015. http://ffnresearch.blogspot.com/2011/03/fan-fiction-demographics-in-2010-age.html.

Sherlock. BBC. 2010–2016. Television.

"Sherlock Holmes (1939 Film Series)." *Wikipedia*. Wikimedia Foundation, Inc., 16 July 2015. Web. 3 Sept. 2015. http://en.wikipedia.org/wiki/Sherlock_Holmes_(1939_film_series).

Sherwin, Adam. "Legal Thriller Looms as Sherlock Takes His Caseload to New York." *The Independent*. Independent Digital News & Media, 20 Jan. 2012. Web. 25 July 2016. http://www.independent.co.uk/arts-entertainment/tv/news/legal-thriller-looms-as-sherlock-takes-his-caseload-to-new-york-6292682.html.

Silver, Anna. "Twilight Is Not Good for Maidens: Gender, Sexuality, and the Family in Stephenie Meyer's *Twilight* Series." *Studies in the Novel* 42.1 (Spring-Summer 2010): 121–38. Print.

Skywalkers. "Edgelord." *You Have Bewitched Me, Body and Soul*. Tumblr, 18 July 2016. Web. 15 Nov. 2016. http://skywalkers.tk/post/147596109211/edgelord-the-worst-way-to-end-something-is.

"So You Want To: Avoid Writing a Mary Sue." *Fanlore*. Fanlore, n.d. Web. 14 Nov. 2015. http://fanlore.org/wiki/Mary_Sue.

Stengle, Jamie. "Charlaine Harris Looks to New Series after Sookie." *Huffington Post*. TheHuffingtonPost.com, 1 Nov. 2013. Web. 5 Sept. 2015. http://www.huffingtonpost.com/2013/11/01/charlaine-harris-ner-series-_n_4190073.html.

Stephemu. "Fangirl." *Urban Dictionary*. Urban Dictionary, LLC. 24 April 2006. Web. 11 July 2016. http://www.urbandictionary.com/define.php?term=fangirl.

Stone, Lawrence. *Family, Sex and Marriage in England, 1500–1800*. New York: Harper, 1977. Print.

Stringer, David. "Sherlock Holmes vs. Sherlock." *Den of Geek*. DoGTech LLC, 22 Jan. 2012. Web. 22 July 2016. http://www.denofgeek.com/tv/sherlock/21056/sherlock-holmes-vs-sherlock.

Tatum, Erin. "What Kristen Stewart Taught Me About Internalized Misogyny." *Everyday Feminism*. Everyday Feminism, 2 Feb. 2015. Web. 4 July 2016. http://everydayfeminism.com/2015/02/kristen-stewart-internalized-misogyny/.

"Thirty Years Hence." *The Twisted Skein.* Huinesoron's Webplex, n.d. Web. 2 Sept. 2015. http://twistedskein.webs.com/End Hence.htm.

"So You Want To: Avoid Writing a Mary Sue." *Fanlore.* Fanlore, n.d. Web. 14 Nov. 2015. http://fanlore.org/wiki/Mary_Sue.

"The Three Laws of Fandom." *Fanlore.* Fanlore, 2 Sept. 2016. Web. 5 Sept. 2016. http://fanlore.org/wiki/The_Three_Laws_of_Fandom.

Tolkien, J. R. R. "On Fairy Stories." *The Pathology Guy.* Pathguy.com, n.d. Web. 1 July 2016. http://www.pathguy.com/ofs.htm.

Treehouseman. "Pit of Voles." *Urban Dictionary.* Urban Dictionary, LLC, 5 June 2005. Web. 13 Nov. 2015. http://www.urbandictionary.com/define.php?term=pit+of+voles.

"*True Blood*: Author Charlaine Harris THREATENED by Fans over Story Ending!!" *PerezHilton.com.* PerezHilton.com, 8 May 2015. Web. 5 Sept. 2015. http://perezhilton.com/2013–05-08-trueblood-author-charlaine-harris-threatened-over-series-ending#.VU4P9yFViko.

Tungsten Monk. "Suicide, Diocletian, and Ithalond: RC 2771a." *PPC: The Lost Tales.* Neshomeh et al., n.d. Web. 2 Sept. 2015. http://plotprotectors.tripod.com/sudiolond/.

Twimomsdiaf. "Twimom." *Urban Dictionary.* Urban Dictionary, LLC, 21 June 2008. Web. 6 Jan. 2015. http://www.urbandictionary.com/define.php?term=Twimom.

Undie Girl. "Why Is It So Hard To Talk about Fanfiction?" *The Geekiary.* The Geekiary, 23 March 2015. Web. 2 Sept. 2015. http://thegeekiary.com/why-is-it-so-hard-to-talk-about-fanfiction/22673.

Urmamason. "Mary Sue." *Urban Dictionary.* Urban Dictionary, LLC. 20 May 2013. Web. 6 Jan. 2015. http://www.urbandictionary.com/define.php?term=Mary+Sue.

Valis2. "Avoiding Mistakes in Fanfiction Writing: A Beginner's Guide." *Sycophant Hex.* Sycophant Hex, n.d. Web. 9 Nov. 2015. http://www.sycophanthex.com/index.php?option=com_content&task=view&id=45&Itemid=41.

Vaughan, Angela. "Index." Ericizmine.com. Angela Vaughan, n.d. Web. 30 April 2015. http://ericizmine.com/index/one-shots/sitw/.

———. "Salt in the Wound." Ericizmine.com. Angela Vaughan, n.d. Web. 30 April 2015. http://ericizmine.com/index/one-shots/sitw.

Verba, Joan Marie. *Boldly Writing: A Trekker Fan and Zine History, 1967–1987.* 2nd ed. Minnetonka, MN: FTL Publications, 2003. Web. 16 Sept. 2015. http://www.ftlpublications.com/bwebook.pdf.

Walker, Cynthia W. "A Conversation with Paula Smith." *Transformative Works and Cultures* 6 (2011): n. pag. Web. 6 Jan. 2015. http://journal.transformativeworks.org/index.php/twc/article/view/243/205.

Walton, Jo. "Fantasy, Reading, and Escapism." *Tor.com.* Macmillan, 5 April 2013. Web. 13 Nov. 2015. http://www.tor.com/2013/04/05/fantasy-reading-and-escapism/.

Weiss, Suzannah. "7 Sneaky Ways Internalized Misogyny Manifests In Our Everyday Lives." *Bustle.* Bustle.com, 18 Dec. 2015. Web. 4 July 2016. http://www.bustle.com/articles/130737-7-sneaky-ways-internalized-misogyny-manifests-in-our-everyday-lives.

Wellhalesbells. "Fanfiction Isn't Written." *Halla.* Tumblr, 20 June 2016. Web. 26 Dec. 2016. http://wellhalesbells.tumblr.com/post/146214158829/fanfiction-isnt-written-for-you-its-shared.

Wendig, Chuck. "Pointing the Cannons at Canon." *Terribleminds.com.* Wendig, n.d. Web. 24 Jan. 2016. http://terribleminds.com/ramble/2015/09/29/pointing-the-cannons-at-canon/.

"What Exactly Is Fair Use?" *Organization for Transformative Works.* OTW, n.d. Web. 3 Sept. 2015. http://transformativeworks.org/what-exactly-fair-use.

"What We Believe." *Organization for Transformative Works.* OTW, n.d. Web. 21 Nov. 2015. http://transformativeworks.org/about/believe.

"Where Has Anne Rice Fanfiction Gone?" *Croatoan Fanfic.* N.p., n.d. Web. 2 July 2016. http://www.angelfire.com/rant/croatoan/.

"Why Does Everyone Hate Wesley Crusher?" *Quora.* Quora, n.d. Web. 28 June 2016. https://www.quora.com/Why-does-everyone-hate-Wesley-Crusher.

Wibbleformebibble. "Fangirl." *Urban Dictionary*. Urban Dictionary, LLC. 22 May 2007. Web. 11 July 2016. http://www.urbandictionary.com/define.php?term=fangirl.

Wollstonecraft, Mary. *A Vindication of the Rights of Woman, with Strictures on Political and Moral Subjects*. Project Gutenberg. Project Gutenberg, n.d. Web. 11 July 2016. http://www.gutenberg.org/cache/epub/3420/pg3420-images.html.

"Word World." *PPC Wiki*. N.p., n.d. Web. 2 Sept. 2015. http://ppc.wikia.com/wiki/Word_World.

Wrede, Patricia C. "Originality, Fanfiction, and a Few Other Things." *Six Impossible Things*. Patricia C. Wrede, 30 March 2014. Web. 9 Feb. 2016. http://www.pcwrede.com/originality-fanfiction-and-a-few-other-things/.

Young, Cathy. "Lee Goldberg's War on Fanfic." *The Y-Files*. Cathy Young, 7 Feb. 2007. Web. 21 Nov. 2015. http://cathyyoung.blogspot.com/2007/02/lee-goldbergs-war-on-fanfic_07.html.

Index

adaptation 5, 136, 145–146, 159–160, 163–164, 177–179
advertising 5, 87, 138–139, 142–144, 164
Aesi (*Urban Dictionary*) 44
The Afterlife of Character, 1726–1825 see Brewer, David A.
age *see* young readers/viewers
Alanna (*Black Girl Nerds*) 71
Alter, Alexandra 142
anime *see* manga
Anunexpectedhotdwarf (*Tumblr*) 33
AO3 *see* Archive Of Our Own
appropriation 5–6, 131, 161, 165–166, 168, 170–174, 176, 179–180
Archive of Our Own 31–32, 88, 94–95 103, 127, 136–137, 148
Atomos (*Tumblr*) 13
Austen, Jane 18–19, 43, 73, 75–76, 79–80, 99, 121, 126; *Northanger Abbey* 18–19, 43, 99, 121; *Pride and Prejudice* 73–78, 80–81, 84, 133–134, 191ch6n1
Autostraddle 93

Bacon-Smith, Camille 50; *Enterprising Women* 38–39, 48
Baker-Whitelaw, Gavia 134
Baldick, Chris 43
bang path 178, 188
Barney, Stephen A. 124
Batman 49–50
BBC 5, 145, 149–150, 153
Bechdel, Allison 52–53
Beekveld, Erwin 137
Behindtheplottwist (*Tumblr*) 13
Bell, Alice 126
Berggren, Anne G. 8, 9, 14 20
Black Girl Nerds 71
Bonaparte, Lilian-Ann 90
Bonneville, Hugh 75
bookverse 178–179, 185
bovarysme 2–3, 43–45, 47–51, 55–57, 77, 79, 81, 86, 90–92, 94, 99, 116, 181–182
Bow, James 102
Boyle, James 130

Boz4pm 60–61, 73; *Don't Panic!* 3, 58–65, 68–69, 80, 84, 97, 99, 103, 148, 172; *Okay, NOW Panic!* 59, 65–70
Bradley, Marion Zimmer 139–141
Brewer, David A. 125
Brokeback Mountain see Proulx, Annie
Brotherson, Laura M. 21
Brunner, Jeryl 88
Bryanthechosen1 (*LiveJournal*) 42
bullying 4, 103–107, 117, 121

Canavan, Gerry 87
Card, Orson Scott 141–142
Caron, Nathalie 151
Carone, Angela 168
Cartwright, Mark 124
CBS 5, 149, 157
Centrumlumina (*Tumblr*) 31–32, 94–95, 113
"Changing History" *see* Fogisbeautiful (*FanFiction.net*)
Chapman, Brian 151–152
Char (*Tumblr*) 62
children 25, 26, 28, 33, 46, 56–57
children's fiction *see* children
The Chronicles of Narnia 120
classism *see* social class
Coker, Catherine 139
Collins, Suzanne 13
Colman, George (the Elder) 16–17
Community Tool Box (website) 98–99, 121–122, 182–183
Conan Doyle, Arthur 125, 126, 147, 149–151, 153–154, 157–158, 160
copyright law 4–5, 123, 127–133, 135–136, 138–139, 141–142, 146, 159–161, 163–164, 180, 183; *see also* intellectual property
Cowan, Eliot 75
Cox, Chris 91
Curtin, Mary Ellen 141

The Democratic Genre see Pugh, Sheenagh
derivative literature 4, 124–127, 129, 131–133, 135–137, 181, 183
Destinationtoast (*Tumblr*) 95

DiGirolamo, Cara M. 189
disability 90
disclaimers 148
Disney 90, 129–130
Doctor Who 126, 153–154, 157
Don Quixote 43
Donaldson, Julia 11–13, 26, 40–41, 65, 183
Doody, Margaret Anne 23, 28, 44, 48, 116–117
Doyle, Sady 53
Dungeons & Dragons 22–23, 141, 186

Earlgreytea68 (*Tumblr*) 165
Eddy, Cheryl 23
Elementary 5, 150
Eliot, George 51–53, 55, 100
Ellis, Lindsay 113
Emily (The Slut) (*Feministing Community*) 20
Ericizmine *see* Vaughan, Angela
escapism 3, 12–13, 28, 58–59, 65–69, 73–76, 79–81, 84, 93, 100
ethics 14, 18, 22, 27–29, 66, 73, 86, 91, 109, 111–113, 116–117, 124, 131, 141, 160, 162, 179–180

fair use 135–139, 148
"fake geek girl" 71, 183
fanart 90
Fanfiction and Copyright: Outsider Works and Intellectual Property Protection see Schwabach, Aaron
Fanfiction.net 31–33, 103, 127, 134, 141, 143, 148
Fanlore 36, 38, 43, 93, 131, 133, 136–137, 161, 177–178
fanon 72–73, 147, 159–160, 185
Fansplaining 67
fantasy (genre) 22–23, 25–26, 28–29, 33–34, 62, 65, 94, 140, 117
fanzine 32–33, 36–37, 117, 126, 139
A Feeling for Books see Radway, Janice
feminism 20
femslash 95, 188
FFN Research 141
Fforde, Jasper 8, 104, 142–143, 191*ch5n*1; *Thursday Next* 8, 104
Fielding, Henry 14–17
Fifty Shades of Grey see James, E.L.
fix-it-fic 87–88, 187
Flewelling, Lynn 162
Flint, Kate 14, 17, 20
Flood, Alison 168
Flourish Kink (*Fansplaining*) 67
Fogisbeautiful (*FanFiction.net*) 39–41
Forablueeyedmiracle (*Tumblr*) 33
Fozmeadows (*Tumblr*) 71
Funke, Cornelia 8

Gabaldon, Diana 147
Gallagher, Catherine 127–128
Gatiss, Mark 5, 151, 153, 155, 157–158

Ghostbusters (2016 film) 53
Goldberg, Lee 131
Goldberg, Whoopi 88
Gomez, Tim 101
gothic novels 18–19, 26, 29, 99
Green, Theresa 6; *Owner's Manuals* 6, 161, 171, 178
Greenberger, Robert 88–89
Grossman, Lev 87–88, 165

Haberman, Clyde 22–23
Hake, Edward 14
Hamilton, Ashley 11–12
Harris, Charlaine 148, 166–170
Harry Potter 73, 101–102, 119–120, 138–139, 191*ch5n*6
Hartswood Films 149–151
headcanon 177, 179, 186
Hellekson, Karen 135
Hickey, Walt 52–53
Hodgson Burnett, Frances 146; *A Little Princess* 56–57, 146, 192*ch7n*1; "Sara Crewe or What Happened at Miss Minchin's" 56–57
Horn, Paul 30
Hussein, Sana 28

Iamsickofit (PerezHiltonwww) 169
Ilovecatz44 (*Tumblr*) 45
Imorca (*Tumblr*) 96
Inkheart see Funke, Cornelia
The Institute for Gender in Media 53–54
intellectual property 4–5, 123, 127, 131, 135, 146, 149, 162–163, 171, 191*ch6n*2; *see also* copyright law
internalized discrimination 3–4, 6, 98, 100–101, 121, 181–183

James, E. L. 133
Japanese culture 46
Jay and Acacia 104, 106
Jeanne (*Aestheticism.net*) 45–47, 111
Jemison, Mae 89
Jenkins, Henry 9–10, 27, 32, 86–87; "Digital Land Grab" 129; *Textual Poachers* 9–10, 27, 32, 86–87, 98–99
Jones, Cleolinda 102
Jones, Ross 153
Julyflame (*LiveJournal*) 108–109
Jupiter Ascending 55
Jusino, Teresa 55

Kabuki Girl (PerezHiltonwww) 169
Kindle Worlds 134–135
Kingston, Alex 75
Klimchynskaya, Anastasia 125
Konkoa (*Tumblr*) 86

Lachenal, Jessica 89
Lackey, Mercedes 140–141

Ladyloveandjustice (*Tumblr*) 49
Lamb, Jean 139–140
Lance Bertelsen 19
Leicht, Stina 162
Letamendi, Andrea 71–72
Lettherebedoodles (*Tumblr*) 90
LGBTQ issues 3, 54, 87, 89–95, 135, 151–152, 173
Lig Na Baste (*Urban Dictionary*) 30
literary academy 8–9, 32, 65–66, 86–87, 101, 114
LiveJournal 35, 42, 127
lolfan 101–102
Lord, Emma 65, 98
Lord of the Rings 3–4, 28, 39–41, 59, 61–66, 69–70, 72–73, 104, 106, 109–110, 115–116, 120, 160, 171–172, 174–175, 178–179, 191*ch*5*n*4
Lost in Austen 3, 58, 73–84, 90, 191*ch*4*n*1
Lukipela (Cheezburgerwww) 21
Lylestyles (*Wordpress*) 21

Madame Bovary 43
Madison, Charles 126
Mae (*Tumblr*) 53
Mandalorianed (*Tumblr*) 33
manga/anime 33, 46, 94, 186, 191*ch*2*n*1
Martin, George R.R. 139–140, 162–164, 173
The Mary Sue (website) 35, 55
"Mary-Sue Mockfest" *see* Rivard, Carrie
masochism 47, 66, 73
Mazes and Monsters 22–23
Mbatha-Raw, Gugu 191*ch*4*n*1
Mel (*TrueBlood.net*) 170
mental health 2, 7, 10, 13, 19, 22, 25, 27, 44, 55–56, 74, 77, 92–94, 109, 113–114, 156, 182
meta 86–87, 112, 186
Metrowebukmetro (*Metro*) 133, 143
Meyer, Stephenie 20–22; *Twilight* 20–22, 24–26, 50, 101–102, 133
Mildmanneredmuse (*Tumblr*) 92
Miller, Laura 164–165
misogyny *see* sexism
Miss Cam *see* Sandman, Camilla
Mlawki, Shanon 1
Moffat, Steven 151, 153, 158
Monicam (*Tumblr*) 72
Monkey (*Urban Dictionary*) 29
Monkmunk (*Urban Dictionary*) 36
Moore, Trent 150
Moore, Wendy 78
morality *see* ethics
Morrison, Ewan 1
Moss, Laura 24–25
movieverse 178–179
Musashden (*LiveJournal*) 42

Naomideplume (*Tumblr*) 45
Nell, Victor 113–114
Nepveu, Kate 147

Nichols, Nichelle 88–89
1994 Baker Street: Sherlock Holmes Returns 150
Noble Platypus *see* Rivard, Carrie
Nobody's Story: The Vanishing Acts of Women Writers in the Marketplace, 1670–1820 see Gallagher, Catherine
Northanger Abbey see Austen, Jane
Nscangal (*Urban Dictionary*) 36, 47

Official Fanfiction University of Middle-earth 4, 103, 109–110, 114–117, 120, 191*ch*5*n*3–7;
Once More into the Urple Depths of OFUM 110–111
OFUM *see Official Fanfiction University of Middle-earth*
O'Keefe, Moira 89
The 100 93–94
Organization for Transformative Works 136, 148
originality 123, 125, 127–129, 131–132, 146, 149, 160, 181
OTW *see* Organization for Transformative Works
Ozhawkauthor (*Tumblr*) 111–113

Pamela see Richardson, Samuel
parody 16, 36, 37, 60, 67, 69, 135–136, 172
Pearson, Jacqueline 15
Phelan, Stephen 154
Pinkowitz, Jacqueline M. 101
Polly Honeycombe see Colman, George (the Elder)
PPC *see* Protectors of the Plot Continuum
Pride and Prejudice see Austen, Jane
Pride and Prejudice and Zombies 191*ch*6*n*1
Princessamericachavez (*Tumblr*) 54
profic 131–133, 145–146, 149, 157, 159–160, 164, 177–178, 186; *see also* tie-in novel
profits 4–5, 131–135, 137–139, 142–146, 149, 152, 157, 159–160, 162, 164, 169–170, 181, 183
Protectors of the Plot Continuum 4, 103–109, 117–121, 142, 172, 174, 176, 180, 191*ch*5*n*1–2
Proulx, Annie 91, 165; "Brokeback Mountain" 91–92
public domain 129–130, 186
Pugh, Sheenagh 10, 45–46, 87, 125, 166

race 3, 54, 88–95, 113, 146, 151, 188
Radway, Janice 9
Raincityruckus (*Fanlore*) 188–189
Rathbone, Basil 150
"Reading Like a Woman" *see* Berggren, Anne G.
realism 3, 28, 58–59, 61–64, 66–69, 73, 84, 116–117, 121, 123, 172
The Return of Sherlock Holmes 150
Rice, Anne 143

Richardson, Samuel 14–16
Riese (*Autostraddle*) 93
Rivard, Carrie 6, 148; "Mary-Sue Mockfest" 6, 161, 172–176
Roberts, Jeff 134–135
Rogers, John 28
role-playing game 22, 186
romance literature/film 3, 10, 17, 20–21, 23–28, 56–57, 75–83, 100, 181
Romano, Aja 125–127; *see also* Baker-Whitelaw, Gavia
Rosenberg, Adam 22
Rosenberg, Melissa 25
Rowling, J. K. 12
RPG *see* role-playing game

Sandman, Camilla 109–110, 115–117, 148, 191ch5n3
Sashayed (*Tumblr*) 56
Schlackman, Steve 129
Schmich, Mary 11–12
Schwabach, Aaron 135, 137–139, 141, 148
science fiction 10, 28–29, 32–34, 36–37, 117, 126, 141, 181
Sega Slayer (*Urban Dictionary*) 30
Sendlor, Charles 31
sentimental literature 20, 26, 46–47, 56–57, 62, 100
sexism 6, 13–14, 23–26, 30, 34–35, 47–52, 54, 57, 71–72, 95, 99–101, 121, 182–183
"Shamela" *see* Fielding, Henry
Sherlock (television series) 5, 145, 149–159
Sherwin, Adam 149–150
shipping 90, 93–95, 112–113, 187, 189
Silver, Anna 24
Skywalkers (*Tumblr*) 92
slash 95, 173, 188
Smith, Paula 36–37, 50
social class 6, 9, 28, 56–57, 101, 116–117
spelling 1, 101, 110, 116, 118, 120, 191ch5n7
sports 30–31, 72
Star Trek 31–32, 36–37, 46, 48–50, 87–89, 117, 126, 131
Star Wars 50, 54–55, 72, 89, 92, 131
Statute of Anne 127–128
Stengle, Jamie 168
Stephemu (*Urban Dictionary*) 29
Stone, Lawrence 79
Stringer, David 158
"The Subspace Emissary's Worlds Conquest" 86

taste 3, 9, 19, 27–28, 32, 51, 56, 73, 75, 97–98, 101, 103, 109–118, 181–182
Tatum, Erin 100
Textual Poachers see Jenkins, Henry

"They're Taking the Hobbits to Isengard" *see* Beekveld, Erwin
tie-in novel 131–132, 153, 186; *see also* profic
Tolkien, J. R. R. 128, 148; *see also* Lord of the Rings
transformative literature 129, 135–137, 139
Transformative Works and Cultures 36–37, 136–137
transgender issues 151
Treehouseman (*Urban Dictionary*) 32
The Trevor Project 93
The True Story of the Novel see Doody, Margaret Anne
Trueblood see Harris, Charlaine
Tumblr 12, 30–31, 33–34, 45, 49, 53–54, 56, 71–72, 86, 88, 92–96, 111–113, 127, 165, 182
Tungsten Monk 104, 106, 119–120, 191ch5n7
TV Tropes 31, 35–36, 43, 48, 68, 86
Twilight see Meyer, Stephenie
Twimomsdiaf (*Urban Dictionary*) 21

Undie Girl (*The Geekiary*) 114
Urban Dictionary 21, 29–30, 32, 36, 44–45, 47, 51
Urmamason (*Urban Dictionary*) 51

Valis2 (*Sycophant Hex*) 45, 52
Vaughan, Angela 5, 148, 168, 170; "Salt in the Wound" 5–6, 161, 166–168, 170, 174
Verba, Joan Marie 32, 126
Vertue, Sue 149–150
video games 22–23, 30, 32, 86
A Vindication of the Rights of Woman see Wollstonecraft, Mary

Walker, Cynthia 36–37
Walton, Jo 28
Warner Brothers 138–139
Wattpad 133
Weiss, Suzannah 99–100
Wellhalesbells (*Tumblr*) 112
Wendig, Chuck 70
Wibbleformebibble (*Urban Dictionary*) 29
Wilson, Edmund 179
Wollstonecraft, Mary 20, 100, 102; *A Vindication of the Rights of Woman* 20
The Woman Reader: 1837–1914 see Flint, Kate
Women's Reading in Britain: 1750–1835 see Pearson, Jacqueline
Wrede, Patricia C. 123

Young, Cathy 148
young adult fiction 25, 26, 28, 33, 46, 56–57
young readers/viewers 7, 10, 13–15, 17–18, 22–24, 26, 29, 31–32, 34, 49, 56–57, 181